THE
MONEY
MAKERS

THE
MONEY
MAKERS

How Extraordinary Managers Win

in a World Turned Upside Down

ANNE-MARIE FINK

CROWN
BUSINESS
NEW YORK

All rights reserved.
Published in the United States by Crown Business, an imprint of the
Crown Publishing Group, a division of Random House, Inc., New York.
www.crownpublishing.com

CROWN BUSINESS is a trademark and CROWN and the Rising Sun colophon
are registered trademarks of Random House, Inc.

Library of Congress Cataloging-in-Publication Data

Fink, Anne-Marie.
The moneymakers: how extraordinary managers win in a world turned
upside down/Anne-Marie Fink.
p.   cm.
Includes index.
1. Industrial management.   2. Strategic planning.   3. Corporations—Growth.
4. Corporations—Valuation.   5. Customer relations.   I. Title.
HD31.F5227 2009
658.4'012—dc22   2008029834

ISBN 978-0-307-39630-3

Printed in the United States of America

Design by Lauren Dong

10   9   8   7   6   5   4   3   2   1

First Edition

To all the investors and company managers
who taught me about success in business, and
to Brian, Brianna, and Aidan,
who brought me success in life

Contents

Chapter 6

ECONOMICS TRUMPS MANAGEMENT *149*

Chapter 7

THE BEST COMPANIES TO INVEST IN ARE THE WORST
TO WORK FOR *169*

Chapter 8

GOOD PERFORMANCE REQUIRES INEFFICIENCY
AND DUPLICATION *197*

Chapter 9

MEGATRENDS START AS RIPPLES *219*

Chapter 10

WE'RE ALL DEAD IN THE LONG RUN *243*

Chapter 11

SHRINK TO GROW AND OTHER BACKWARD
STEPS FORWARD *269*

Conclusion

WHAT INVESTORS WANT: GOOD NUMBERS
THAT LAST *289*

THE CHASM AND HOW

TO BRIDGE IT

TODAY'S BUSINESS WORLD IS FILLED WITH BANKRUPT-cies and bailouts, ousted CEOs and massive layoffs, organizations spinning off expensive acquisitions made only a few years earlier, companies struggling to grow, and entire industries chasing the same strategies like lemmings to the sea. As if this weren't enough, the U.S. federal government, as I put the finishing touches on this book, is engaged in an unprecedented intervention in the workings of the marketplace to save the financial system from its self-inflicted wounds.

Alternative ideas for running a business are clearly and increasingly necessary.

As a manager, you face a gap—actually, it's more like a canyon—between the results expected of you and the tools you have for delivering that performance, productivity, and profitability. This gap is only getting wider as aggressive rivals from unexpected places, increasing costs, and an uncertain economy are eroding differentiation and profitability across all industries. At the same time, shareholders and other owners are demanding ever more of the executives who run companies. Yet the methods you have at your disposal, the traditional management tenets you have been taught, rarely deliver strong operating and financial results, and often exacerbate problems. For instance, the financial industry crises of 2008—the bankruptcy of Lehman Brothers, the shotgun mergers for Merrill Lynch and Bear Stearns, and the government takeovers of Fannie Mae, Freddie Mac, and American International Group (AIC)—were the result of executives at these firms listening to their customers, driving out all inefficiencies, and believing all growth was good. This management orthodoxy led them to overextended customers, nonexistent checks and balances, untenable debt levels, and their days of reckoning.

For more than a decade I have confronted the conventional myths about performance, productivity, and profit as a buy-side* equity analyst—and thus an investor in and owner of companies—for J.P. Morgan Asset Management. Unlike consultants and academics who opine about management, I have real money at stake; literally billions of dollars rest on my assessment of companies and their managements. Since I win only when the companies whose stock I own win, I work obsessively to determine which company leaders are long-term winners—moneymakers—and which aren't.

When I get together with fellow investors on bus trips to visit companies or at "idea dinners,"‡ the talk naturally turns to whether company executives are moneymakers or value de-

---

*The Wall Street investment community is split between the sell side—research analysts who study companies and write reports to support their firms' brokerage (and, in the past, investment banking) business—and the buy side. Mutual funds, hedge funds, and investment advisers like J.P. Morgan Asset Management invest funds on behalf of our pension fund, endowment, and individual clients.

‡Idea dinners are conversations, generally over dinner, where professional investors pitch one another their ideas on which companies are good investments and why. The group then debates the thesis underlying the investment case.

stroyers. True moneymakers are that rare breed who perform consistently; they are the managers we invest with regardless of the business and economic environment. Though their companies' stock prices can drop in the short term due to market factors, their companies receive a premium valuation because they are there creating value. A leader who is a moneymaker is very profitable all around—for shareholders as well as the company and its employees. Since I benefit from companies with strong leaders and I've repeatedly seen widely touted "best practices" lead managers astray, I wrote this book to share what my investing colleagues and I have learned—and never before divulged—about how to bridge the chasm and achieve results.

I've seen firsthand what it takes to be a moneymaker. My role as an owner affords me tremendous access to a wide swath of firms. Day in and day out I meet with CEOs, CFOs, and division heads, and peer into the guts of their businesses. I ask pointed, sometimes uncomfortable, questions and seek answers that get to the heart of the matter: Is this organization going to win or lose? Should my firm invest serious money in this company?

Moreover, I don't rely just on what senior managers are saying. I use my owner's access to a company's competitors, its suppliers, and its customers to gather more information. I've chased down employees, combed through the fine print of regulatory filings, visited far-flung operations, hired industry experts, and done whatever was necessary to understand why a company gets the results—both good and bad—that it does.

Professional investors like me—with our exhaustive information gathering and outsider's perspective—are often the first to grasp what's impacting operations, frequently before the executives running a company do.

- When Lehman Brothers announced in September 2008 that it was only beginning to explore asset sales to shore up its overly leveraged balance sheet, investors knew the company would not make it.

- When Motorola declared in October 2006 that a temporary delay in telecom customers' investments had caused a minor shortfall in mobile handset sales, savvy investors knew the problem was deeper. The firm had been propping up its aging RAZR franchise with price cuts, but had not developed a successful new handset in years. Soon the mobile division was losing money, and it has struggled ever since.
- When mortgage lender Countrywide Financial announced higher default rates on its home equity prime loans in summer 2007, we saw that its business model was broken. (It only avoided likely bankruptcy by selling itself to Bank of America six months later.)
- While Ford Motor Company's management spent most of the 2000s waiting for a stronger economy to lift profitability, we recognized that the real problem was overcapacity in the auto industry, and the only solution was to reduce production. Ford managers arrived at this conclusion only years and billions of dollars in losses later.
- When AOL was gearing up to offer innovative new features for its online service, we knew that competitor Yahoo! had rolled out the same features months earlier.

We don't just see the bad news before everyone else; sometimes we see, before the rest of the world notices, leaders launching strategies or implementing policies that will result in sustained, sometimes spectacular growth. When Mark Hurd focused on the details of Hewlett-Packard's operations, we knew the company would, after years of trying, finally compete successfully with Dell in personal computers. As oil prices rose, we realized the long-standing investment in intermodal operations of Burlington Northern Santa Fe Railroad would finally pay off, since the truck-competitive service was more fuel efficient. When Genentech didn't agonize over trade secrets and openly shared its research with the academic community, we grasped that the biotech firm was creating a symbiotic relationship that would fuel its growth for years.

In short, professional investors possess insights about business that others lack. We see the big picture, have extraordinary access to executives and information, and are unbiased. We can spot significant trends early and identify strategic strengths and flaws with great clarity. This wisdom, though developed for making investment decisions, has much broader use for managing businesses, both short and long term.

OVER THE YEARS, as I've dug deeply into organizations and compared notes with colleagues, I realized that I was formulating a set of "rules" significantly different from the so-called best practices of management strategy and leadership. Even though these principles often run counter to conventional approaches—or perhaps because they do—they have regularly proved to be excellent guidelines for business decision making. Time and again, the experiences of the thousands of companies my colleagues and I have followed and the dozens of real moneymakers we've observed in action have borne out the wisdom of these rules.

The eleven management rules found in the following pages are designed to improve the performance, productivity, and profitability of your business and career. They apply equally to CEOs and people just entering the management ranks. I've backed them up with real, insider stories about brilliant and blockheaded organizational moves, leaders who have embraced flexibility to position themselves for the future and others who have charged straight into strategic walls; companies where leaders "get it" and those where executives are clueless.

These "investors' rules" differ significantly from the lessons taught in business schools and the standard operating procedures in most companies. Derived from the actions of moneymakers who have overcome challenges and delivered results, they provide fresh, proven approaches to achieve business success. They're not contrary for contrary's sake, but because real-world results dictate that they be so. The eleven rules are:

1. *Think like an investor to establish your edge.* Though your business has a million details, investors focus on economic profit to distill businesses down to the most important factors. Don't rely on vague ideas such as "my people" or "my brand" to steer your business. By focusing on economic profit, you can hone in on the crucial elements that create an edge for sustainable success.

2. *With information "roach motels," problems won't check out.* Problems in a business are often like cockroaches—there's never just one. To catch problems before they infest your business, follow the money to open vital information pathways and to prevent bad news from getting caught in roach motels where it doesn't reach you.

3. *Avoid the trap of profitless growth.* Additional profit is an illusion if it consumes too much capital; only products that earn a strong return for the investment they require are worth pursuing. While others follow conventional wisdom and target growth, you can find the most durable breakthroughs by lowering investment, leveraging other people's money, and capitalizing on knowledge, the highest return asset.

4. *Don't be a customer fanatic.* Conventional wisdom about listening to customers above all else fails to recognize that they

have different economic incentives than you do. They want lower prices and tailored products, while you want higher profits and streamlined processes. Moneymakers succeed by knowing when to ignore their customers. Learn to trust what your knowledge and experience, rather than what your customers, tell you.

5. *Get more reward for the risk you take.* Business forecasts are less accurate than weather predictions; executives who rely too heavily on their crystal balls raise their risk and lower their rewards. Positioning yourself for the future, rather than actively chasing it, produces greater rewards for the risk taken and tilts the risk-reward balance in your favor.

6. *Economics trumps management.* While your business can temporarily defy economic law, these forces will always bring you back to earth. Ignoring bedrock economic laws—such as supply and demand—is akin to ordering the tides to stay in place; it never works.

7. *The best companies to invest in are the worst to work for.* Traditional thinking has it backward; happy employees don't make for high-performance workplaces. Rather, high-performance workplaces make for happy employees. Conventional systems to encourage cooperation and teamwork don't work and paying people collectively decouples reward from performance. Synergies have to be hand-crafted, and employee goals must reflect owners' needs.

8. *Good performance requires inefficiency and duplication.* Achieving maximum efficiency and rooting out all duplication produces suboptimal results, because it stifles innovation and

lucky accidents. Use "wasteful" training and duplicative efforts to make your own luck.

9. *Megatrends start as ripples.* Position your business early so you can ride long-term waves, not be swamped by them. Be ready to hop off the trend currently driving your business before it peters out.

10. *We're all dead in the long run; use small steps to achieve big results.* While conventional wisdom often calls for bold transformations that promise results in some mythic future, moneymakers don't delay performance gratification but act incrementally to achieve their goals.

11. *Shrink to grow and take other backward steps forward.* Growing in areas that don't earn their cost of capital is like running on a treadmill—you're working hard but not getting anywhere. Instead bite the bullet, shrink down to a profitable core, and set yourself up for long-term prosperity.

These principles, distilled by investors who bring an insider's knowledge and an outsider's fresh perspective, offer an effective alternative to today's usual practices. I've seen countless instances where top executives would have benefited greatly from following these rules. For example, Michael Eisner, the former CEO of the Walt Disney Company, became so insulated from problems that they festered like cockroaches until in 2004 two dissident former board members initiated a proxy fight to oust him. An investor in Disney at the time, I (and other professional investors) were wooed by Eisner and his team as well as the dissidents, each side trying hard to convince us they were the best stewards for the company. Eisner, while brilliantly successful during the earlier years of his CEO tenure at Disney, had become too removed from the business, as information roach motels were keeping him from addressing the company's problems. The proxy contest came perilously close to succeeding, and Eisner and a number of his top reports "retired" a few months after the fight. If he had followed investors' second rule, a steady flow of information and ideas could have prevented the mess in which he became entangled.

Effectively implementing all eleven rules will deliver not only the revenue and profit results demanded of every manager but also a sustainable edge for your business and your career.

CHAPTER I

THINK LIKE AN INVESTOR TO ESTABLISH YOUR EDGE

M ANAGING YOUR BUSINESS CAN SEEM COMPLI-cated; there are so many details to attend to that you can easily lose the forest for the trees. As an investor, I have to understand not only one business, but many businesses and across multiple industries. To survive, I've learned how to distill companies down to their essence—economic profits; that is, the sustainable value they generate over and above the cost of the resources they use. To ensure those profits are sustainable, I've looked at the impact of competitors and external factors, and I've made sure I'm brutally honest about the businesses I own. (Despite popular belief, making money by strip-mining a company of its assets is not a strategy that investors reward over the long term.)

Moneymakers think like investors and simplify their businesses by focusing on economic profits and the essentials to make that value last. Knowing what levers to pull to deliver results, these exceptional leaders consistently generate economic profits and earn high returns on their investments.

I'm going to share with you the insights of investors on the best ways to create economic profits consistently and how some of the world's best managers implement this knowledge. I'll give you techniques to maximize your business in a way your competitors don't.

WHAT'S YOUR EDGE?

Economic profit comes from establishing a "value edge"* that enables you to offer customers something different and better than their next best alternative. Some point to "global presence" or their "brand" as an edge, but those are unlikely differentiators as they are too common. Executives at many companies have told me that their people are their edge. However, only Expeditors International of Washington, an international freight-forwarding firm with $5.4 billion in annual revenues, ever convinced me that this was really the case. The CFO explained that its employees had all sacrificed to become part of Expeditors. They had taken steps backward in their careers, either starting at more junior levels or having responsibility for smaller purviews than in their previous positions. Because of these sacrifices, Expeditors' employees were unusually motivated and qualified to grow the business in order to build back to their prior levels of responsibility. Expeditors' earnings certainly have borne out the CFO's contention. In the five years through the end of 2007, the company increased sales by 128 percent and earnings per share by 175 percent, and its stock price more than doubled.

Try this experiment to see if you have an edge:†

---

* Michael Cline, the managing partner of the private equity firm Accretive, which created thriving enterprises such as the Fandango online movie ticket service and Accretive Health, a payment processor for hospitals, coined the term.
† Jes Staley of J.P. Morgan Asset Management first introduced me to this strategy.

1. Write three to five bullet points that describe what most distinguishes the offering of your business or department. These features can be anything from "hard" traits, such as having the largest-size operation in your industry, to "soft" traits, such as a track record of developing more innovative products and services than your competitors'. Make each point as specific as possible. You can mention your industry, but not your company's name.

2. Give the list to an adviser, banker, lawyer, or other business-savvy friend. Have the friend show it to associates and other business friends anonymously, and see if they can identify your company. Alternately, post your bullets on www.moneymakersbook.com/valueedge, and see if the investing community can identify your company.

3. If people outside your company can make this identification, ask if they agree with the points listed or if they find one or more to be "generic" or inaccurate. If they can identify the company and agree with your bullet points, you have probably found your value edge. If they can't, you need to rework your business's value proposition.

For instance, if a high-tech company wrote the following bullet points:

- Consistently innovative consumer electronics products
- Distinctively designed and easy-to-use products
- Cool, iconoclastic image

most people would immediately recognize it as Apple. On the other hand, if a Wall Street firm wrote:

- Full-service broker-dealer offering a comprehensive range of products from investment banking through asset management
- Staffed with aggressive, smart, highly compensated individuals
- Strong sales culture

it could be Merrill Lynch, Morgan Stanley, or any number of other firms. However, add either one of two additional points, and the list of possible firms would narrow down to one, Goldman Sachs:

- Ingrained culture of internal cooperation and expectation of excellence
- Effectively leverages information from external client interactions to trade for own account, where it makes the vast majority of its profits

Now see if you can identify this company from the following bullet points:

- Specialist in auto insurance
- Low-cost provider, particularly for those with unconventional histories
- Makes profits from underwriting (premiums less claims) rather than from investing premiums
- Culture of experimentation and data mining

Anyone familiar with the insurance business would instantly recognize Progressive Corporation.

Progressive's value edge powered its rapid rise from the thirty-eighth largest property and casualty company to the third largest in ten years from 1990 to 2000 (a position it retains even as competitors adopt its practices). Under the leadership of then-CEO Peter Lewis, the company took share from much larger competitors because Lewis and his team so clearly understood their edge.

Property and casualty (P&C) businesses earn profits through pricing risk (underwriting), investing premiums, and managing operations. Most P&C insurers concentrate on investing premiums. They price risk as a loss leader, that is, they take in less in premiums than they pay out in claims. Their profits come from the returns they earn by investing the premiums before they have to pay out claims.

Lewis and his team, however, focused on the two areas, pricing risk and managing operations, that competitors were neglecting (Progressive minimized its attention to the investing side of the business by pursuing a conservative, low-risk/low-return investing policy). Progressive mined loss-experience data and developed highly sophisticated algorithms to determine policy costs, and thus priced risk more effectively than others. It determined that nonstandard drivers who lacked a long policy history, had a blemish or two on their record, or didn't speak English were not as risky as then-prevailing industry models assumed. What Progressive discovered was that income level was a better indication of a driver's riskiness than his or her policy history. With this better understanding of the risk of an individual client, Progressive was able to price its policies below those of its competitors while still generating more in premiums than it paid out in claims. By focusing intently on accurately pricing the likelihood and cost of accidents, Progressive has, with the exception of one aberrant year (2000), consistently made money on underwriting.

This strong understanding of its value edge kept Progressive from falling into the all-too-common trap of believing that one's value edge can be extended beyond its natural boundaries. For years, outsiders advised the company to expand into home owner's insurance, believing it could easily cross-sell home owners' policies to its current customers. Open to experimentation, Progressive launched a test in a few selected markets. It didn't work, and in early 2002 Progressive pulled the plug. The firm did not have the underwriting edge in home policies it had in auto insurance. More recently, it found a way to reenter the home owner's insurance business in a way more consistent with its value edge. Progressive now offers other firms' home owner's policies, which takes advantage of its customer relationships without requiring the edge in home owner's underwriting that it lacks.

Progressive also has been successful in aggressively managing the costs of operating its business. It was an early adopter of the Internet as a sales tool that lowered customer acquisition costs. The new sales channel allowed it to reach customers outside its traditional independent agent middlemen, cost-effectively extending its underwriting expertise to more customers and keeping the agent channel focused on adding its own value. It also developed a "concierge service," contracting directly with local auto body shops. When a customer has an accident, he can take his car directly to one of these shops, which will assess the damage, make the repair, and handle all the paperwork. Because Progressive works directly with the shops, paperwork is minimized and Progressive can negotiate better rates for the volume of repair work. The offering costs less for the company *and* provides convenience for customers. Streamlining the auto insurance process has allowed Progressive to extend its value edge effectively.

As with anything in business, no value edge remains sharp forever. Progressive's edge dulled between 2006 and 2008, when insurers industrywide improved their pricing models, accident rates fell, and many companies generated profits from underwriting. Progressive responded aggressively as it saw its value proposition becoming less distinctive.

Since its underwriting margins were double the industry average and three times its longtime 4 percent profit target, the leadership team recalibrated the balance between profitability and growth. They selectively lowered premiums, primarily for existing customers, to improve retention. What they didn't do was try to pursue new businesses in areas where the company didn't have an edge. Diversification, or "de-worse-ification," is frequently how corporate executives respond to more robust competition, but it usually creates more headaches than it cures.

Progressive knew that diversification didn't work in home owner's insurance and was unlikely to work elsewhere. Rather than let the cash on its balance sheet burn a hole in its pocket, in 2007 the board returned $3 billion in capital to shareholders through a $2.00 special dividend and a 100-million-share repurchase plan. While the stock declined as capital moved from the company to investors, management's actions—because they stayed true to their value edge—served shareholders and the company well. The multiple of earnings that investors pay for Progressive's stock is almost 50 percent more than its competitors', because investors have faith that Progressive will continue to outperform its peers.

To keep your value edge honed, you need to reassess it constantly. By habitually soliciting feedback on your strategic points of differentiation, you can determine the value of your edge and whether it needs to be rethought.

The semiconductor manufacturer Intel suffered when it neglected to recalibrate its value edge. It had enjoyed success for many years because it turned out new chips with faster clock (i.e., processing) speeds than anyone else. Indeed, Moore's Law—which accurately predicted an exponential pace of improvement in semiconductor speeds—originated with Intel cofounder Gordon Moore. However, by the early 2000s, improvements in clock speed were becoming less noticeable to the majority of consumers, resulting in less incentive to upgrade to computers with Intel's latest and most expensive chips.

Thinking like an investor also means recognizing when your edge has become perilously dull. Here is a sure sign a value edge has become ineffective:

You bring out "exciting" new products or services, and the market yawns.

If this happens, it's time to rethink your value proposition. Because Intel didn't realize that clock speed had become non-differentiating and commoditized, it did not change its strategy to adapt to the new realities. As a result, throughout the 2000s, the stock was stagnant, earnings bounced around without improving, and in 2006–07 the company had to lay off 10 percent of its workforce.

Inside Information

- Look for your value edge in the inherent characteristics of your business today rather than the business you want to be. Strong returns can be made in any type of business, as long as you treat it as what it is.

- Knowing your value edge offers a priceless road map for making decisions. Consult the key characteristics of your edge to have the foundation and fortitude to make tough choices.

REALITY, NOT BELIEFS

A value edge doesn't have to be based on superior technology or algorithms. Many companies establish their edge through an in-depth understanding of their business and how they organize themselves to meet a specific need. The differentiation is built up through the fine-tuning of numerous details. Though these kinds of edges are less obvious, they are often more durable. Walmart outcompeted Sears and Kmart to become the nation's largest retailer through better logistics that moved goods to stores more cheaply.

Your value edge can't just be a *belief* about what will confer value or what has worked for others. Don't make the mistake of trying to impose an edge that is artificial or at odds with your culture, core business, and traditions. Your value edge needs to be true to the underlying characteristics of your business.

Dow Chemical succeeds because it has no pretensions about the commodity half of its business. While spending money on advertising or building more plants would be more ego-gratifying, Dow knows that the only way to operate profitably in a commodity business is to have the lowest costs and control supply. In 2006, CEO Andy Liveris and his team closed three underperforming plants, even though the company was profitable. They didn't wait for their competitors to reduce capacity, but did what they could to improve the supply-and-demand balance in the face of higher prices for raw materials. Dow also pursued joint ventures with companies such as Saudi Arabia's Aramco to gain access to cheaper supplies of petroleum feedstocks and to lower costs through building larger-scale plants. Elsewhere Dow remains vigilant on expenses by stringently standardizing work processes to maximize efficiency.

Its uncompromising cost discipline also means that Dow knows when it has to raise prices and gives it the fortitude to do so—it raised prices by as much as 20 percent in 2008 in the face of relentless increases in input costs. Investors have rewarded the company for staying true to its value edge by bidding up its stock price by 30 percent from 2003 to 2007.

KNOW WHAT YOU'RE NOT

Knowing what your value edge is not is as important as knowing what it is. After a brief experiment, Progressive determined that its underwriting edge didn't extend to home owner's insurance and killed the new product. Even if you're very good at something, if all your competitors are similarly accomplished, you don't have an edge and won't earn economic profits.

Progressive could easily have devoted more effort to the investing portion of the insurance business, but its competitors had all focused there. The space was very crowded, making it unlikely that Progressive could differentiate itself. However, by concentrating on the largely ignored underwriting part of the business, Progressive found an edge where no one else was looking.

Organizations that are able to view their negative space—the areas where they can't compete or lack the skills and knowledge to be successful—can often work backward to find their edge based on their shortcomings.

That was the case with Advanced Micro Devices (AMD), a much smaller competitor of Intel in manufacturing CPUs. AMD recognized that it would never be able to beat the eight-hundred-pound gorilla at its own game of improving clock speed. So AMD tackled a different bottleneck that slowed computers' response time. For most operations, the CPU accesses items in a computer's memory. Intel put this memory controller on a separate chip, which connected to the CPU. AMD built an integrated memory controller that shortened the connection time and allowed AMD's chips to return results more quickly without increasing clock speed. When AMD rolled out its "Hammer" chips (later branded the Athlon 64 and Opteron chips) in 2002, it offered semiconductors it could sell on features other than price for the first time in years. With a true value edge, AMD was able to achieve operating profitability in 2004 and 2005, and its stock price soared by more than 300 percent over a three-year period starting in late 2002. (When it got too complacent about the durability of its edge and stopped innovating, AMD's advantage quickly evaporated as Intel copied its approach and regained market share from 2005 to 2008.)

AVOIDING YOUR NEGATIVE space, the areas where your competitors are strong, is a powerful tool that's not limited to small competitors or new entrants. The video game powerhouse Nintendo created a breakthrough product by recognizing its limits relative to its competitors. An early entrant in video games, Nintendo's NES (Nintendo Entertainment System) resurrected the nascent business in 1983–84. Later, by actively courting outside developers, Nintendo pioneered the current video game ecosystems of console makers and independent game-publishing studios working symbiotically. Nintendo remained quite successful through subsequent product cycles until 2000–01, when it and its competitors introduced the sixth generation of video game consoles. That's when Microsoft entered the industry with its Xbox console. Sony, another leader in video gaming, poured resources into defending its turf and rolled out PlayStation 2 with impressively realistic graphics. Sony won this product cycle, garnering a 51 percent market share, but Xbox, with a 34 percent share, established a respectable presence. Nintendo was essentially squeezed out, with its GameCube obtaining only a 15 percent share.

As the competitors geared up for the next product cycle, Nintendo's prospects looked grim. Microsoft, one of the world's richest companies, had set its sights on building a presence in the home. It had identified the video game console as the best way to achieve its goal, and it was willing to invest whatever it took to become a force in any sector it targeted.

Meanwhile, Sony needed to maintain its dominance in video games; its traditional consumer electronics businesses (television sets, video recorders, etc.) were struggling with low-cost competition from Korea, Taiwan, and China. Its entertainment properties were volatile (movies), disadvantaged (TV series production—as a non-U.S. company, it cannot own U.S. television stations), or declining (music). Sony planned to use its strength in video game consoles as a Trojan horse to reestablish a dominant position in consumer electronics; the PS3 included a high-definition Blu-ray player, Sony's entry in the next iteration of digital video disk (DVD) players. By using PS3s to get Blu-ray players into consumer households, Sony expected to establish its technology as the standard for next-generation DVD players. Though it wasn't certain who was going to win, this console battle would unquestionably be epic, and the two corporate behemoths would spend liberally to build the most powerful consoles possible.

Nintendo quickly recognized that it couldn't establish a value edge going head-to-head with these two determined and resource-rich behemoths, so it looked elsewhere to find its competitive differentiation. As its lead game designer, Shigeru Miyamoto, put it, "[Our] consensus was that power isn't everything for a console. Too many powerful consoles can't coexist. It's like having only ferocious dinosaurs. They might fight and hasten their own extinction."

Rather than tangle with Microsoft and Sony, Nintendo's development team began experimenting with a different approach: while the others targeted power, they worked on the controller. They built a motion-sensing technology that allowed players to play games such as tennis by swinging the controller like a racket. After five years of development, Nintendo introduced the Wii in 2006 in the midst of the battle between the next-generation Xbox 360 and Sony PS3. It's unlikely that anyone at Microsoft or Sony paid much attention to the Wii. The graphics were amateurish. The best independents had not developed games for the platform. What games there were lacked the complexity that appealed to hard-core gamers. Nonetheless, when the three consoles hit the market and customers spoke, Nintendo garnered the largest market share by appealing to both ends of the market. The simplicity of its games attracted casual gamers. The novelty of the motion-sensing controller appealed to hard-core and casual gamers alike.

Both AMD and Nintendo succeeded because they zigged when the competition zagged. Instead of engaging in a head-to-head battle, they recognized where they were weak and found strength by avoiding those areas.

Like Nintendo, AMD, and Progressive, more and more companies are gaining their value edges by avoiding the areas that most competitors are focused on. In a world of rapid change, both technological and social, consumers respond to products and services that take novel approaches. They get tired of the same old, same old faster than in the past, and they appreciate when a company reinvents a product or meets an emerging need. So stop playing to your competitors' strengths and start developing your own.

Inside Information

- Create a list of the things your competitors do almost as well as or even better than you. Eliminate them as the source of your value edge.

- Consider the space outside your competitors' areas of advantage. Examine why some customer segments are underserved or some parts of the business ignored. Pursue unconventional reformulations and tweak your offerings to meet a need that has yet to emerge.

- Be different. Many value edges come from merely focusing on different things than your competitors and conceding to them superiority in areas where they are ahead of you. Pursue more than one area of difference, since some differences will have no value. Have faith that room exists in big markets for unconventional approaches, especially in volatile times.

KNOW YOUR COMPETITORS

When considering an investment I meet with as many competing companies as I can, because it provides the best insights into an industry. By knowing your competitors you can gain this same depth and breadth of invaluable knowledge. If you understand what drives them, you'll be able to use that knowledge to your advantage. Many executives have only a casual understanding of their competition. They know various data related to their competitors' products and services, market position, and so on, but they fail to grasp the economic and cultural imperatives that drive their rivals.

There is often the assumption that competitors face the same pressures that you do, such as similar ROI requirements. In reality, competing companies can operate with vastly different financial imperatives. Costs of capital vary in different parts of the world. Changes in currency exchange rates may allow foreign competitors to grow their profits even when pricing aggressively. Moreover, the beauty of returns is in the eye of the beholder. For a business earning a 6 percent return or whose value proposition is becoming obsolete, entering a business with 8 percent returns is compelling. Incumbents earning 10 percent might think the new entrant is acting irrationally. If they wait for the incumbent to act more logically, they will sit by as their market share evaporates. Failing to recognize the imperatives that drive your competitors can prevent you from responding effectively.

For Whirlpool, the iconic American large-appliance manufacturer, understanding its competitors' economic realities has helped it maintain and strengthen its market position. The Korean chaebol (conglomerates) are Whirlpool's fiercest potential competitors. LG, Daewoo, and others do not export appliances to the United States because the shipping costs are prohibitive— washing machines and dryers take up a lot of container space relative to their value. It would be easy for CEO Jeff Fettig and his team to dismiss the potential risk from these competitors. However, Fettig is a much savvier manager than that. He recognizes that the chaebol will eventually figure out how to enter the U.S. market cost-effectively. When they do, their margin goals will be much lower than Whirlpool's. Fettig says, "We have to be seven percent better than they are," recognizing that their cost of capital and return goals are 7 percent lower than what his U.S. investors demand.

As an investor, I love leaders like this. Understanding the gestalt of competitors who only have to break even has prepared

Whirlpool for the imminent threat to its business. Even before the Koreans have shown up, Whirlpool has improved its cost position by moving its manufacturing operations to Mexico and accelerated its product cycles to use innovation to stay ahead of its competitors. As an added benefit, Whirlpool's preparations to compete have deterred the importers from entering the U.S. market. The stronger Whirlpool's value edge, the more difficult it is for new competitors to gain a foothold.

It's tough enough to understand the economics of your own business, so understanding your competitors' as well may seem like too much work. But it's worth it. By understanding the opportunities and threats your competitors face, you can anticipate their moves, shore up your weaknesses, and capitalize on theirs.

The U.S. cable operators Comcast and Time Warner misunderstood the likelihood of competition from telecom companies, because they believed that AT&T, Verizon, and Qwest would require the same returns on capital expenditures as they did. They dismissed the threat of the telcos entering their pay-TV business, arguing that the new entrants would never earn a return on their investment of tens of billions of dollars. The telcos would be the fourth competitor (two satellite providers also offer pay TV) in a mature market.

Yet in 2004, Verizon and AT&T announced that they were going to dig up the streets to upgrade their hundred-year-old copper wire to state-of-the-art fiber-optic cables so they could offer Internet connections faster than cable's and enter the pay-TV market. The cable executives failed to appreciate that the telcos' core business was dying. Mobile phones, Internet-based telephony, and the cable companies' telephone offerings were eroding residential landline phone connections by 5 to 10 percent a year. Without an improved offering, the traditional phone companies were doomed. As one equity analyst and former telecom business development executive put it, "When your base case is going out of business, strategic planning can justify a lot of investments."

Because they didn't understand the fear of extinction that drove their competitors, many cable operators were slow to roll out their own telephony offerings, create more responsive customer service organizations (as opposed to the quasi-monopolistic service they had traditionally offered), and offer more competitive pricing. Only twenty-four months after its introduction, Verizon's FiOS service had already achieved 15 percent penetration where it was available and the cable companies were unable to grow their subscriber bases (or their stock prices).

Inside Information

- Don't assume that your competitors have the same financial requirements as you do. Respond to the reality of their competitive moves, not to what they "should" do or what is fair.

- Anticipate your competitors' moves based on their economic imperatives; prepare competitive responses, even if the competitors may not move for months or years.

- Look for ways to expand the moat around your business—your protective value edge. Make it more difficult for your competitors to enter into your business and potentially even dissuade them from trying because the effort required (even if they have lower financial requirements) would be too great.

EXOGENOUS GENIUS

Creating a sustainable value edge requires not only being aware of your competitors' motivations, but also of any exogenous factors that can make or break your business. By definition, these factors—for instance, interest rates, currency exchange rates, regulations, commodity prices, and customer changes—are out of your control. But that does not mean you can forget about them. An "out of sight, out of mind" approach is a big mistake. Failing to prepare for the day when a favorable exogenous trend goes into reverse (most exogenous trends are cyclical) can be fatal. The mortgage company crisis of 2007 and the loss of thousands of jobs owed much to executives' failure to understand how unsustainably low interest rates had contributed to their business. Lenders were able to charge low interest rates, at least on a teaser basis, because they themselves could borrow at low short-term rates. Strong home price appreciation, due to the increasing number of buyers who could afford the teaser-rate payments, made loans less risky and encouraged borrowers to refinance repeatedly. You didn't have to be particularly astute to see that this cycle wouldn't last. Short-term interest rates fluctuate; they don't stay low forever. Indeed, the Federal Reserve had already started raising them a few years before the crisis unfolded. However, because so many mortgage brokers didn't appreciate the interest-rate risk they were taking, they were caught completely off guard when home values began to fall and mortgage defaults rise. Many had to downsize their operations dramatically, and were unable to borrow new capital. For a company such as New Century Financial Corporation, the inattention to exogenous factors proved deadly. It filed for bankruptcy in 2007 when it could no longer resell the mortgages it had originated.

Understanding your business's exogenous factors and how they can shift will keep you out of big trouble. Though you may not be able to predict when the cycles will change, you can be prepared for reversals in a trend.

Commodity producers suffer more than most from exogenous factors. They are "price takers" because their products are indistinguishable from those of competitors. As a result, they have virtually no influence over what they can charge. When business is good and prices are high, "the rising tide lifts all boats." Many executives look savvy, when mostly they've been lucky. The problems start when prices go down, which they always do in cyclical industries. Businesses are often unprepared and, like Bethlehem Steel in the 2001 downturn, can end up in bankruptcy. Savvy managers in these industries, such as Liveris's team at Dow Chemical, work assiduously to reduce the impact of prices on their business. They keep a tight lid on costs so they can control their destiny. Moreover, they remain prepared for periods of weakness and are never lulled into a false sense of security.

Assiduously understanding industry structure, another largely exogenous factor, has enabled Johnson Controls, a major supplier to the auto manufacturers, to enjoy double-digit growth in earnings throughout most of the 1990s and 2000s, despite operating in an industry littered with the carcasses of bankrupt companies. Johnson Controls succeeded where others failed because its management had no illusions about the structure of the industry. Unlike the Big Three carmakers and many of their suppliers, Johnson's management didn't "drink the Kool-Aid." They didn't believe the industry's difficulties were temporary or that the pressure to constantly reduce prices would abate once the economy improved. They understood that auto manufacturing was a bad (low-ROI) business suffering from overcapacity.

By appreciating the external industry backdrop and the issues facing its customers better than even its customers did, Johnson Controls created a thriving business. First, management targeted the most prosperous customers, Toyota and Honda, and became their suppliers. Because the profits of these manufacturers were not as thin as those of the Big Three, these firms did not require price cuts every year. Certainly with any new model (every four to five years), these manufacturers demanded 20 percent price cuts, but the longer lead times gave Johnson Controls the ability to engineer around the cuts and still maintain its profit margins. Moreover, Honda and Toyota, confident in their ability to sell their cars on their own merits, didn't insist on exclusivity for any of Johnson Controls' innovations, making devoting resources to new concepts more profitable.

Johnson Controls also appealed to its customers' customers. It understood that it would have more leverage with the auto companies if its products helped sell cars to the end consumers. So management homed in first on auto interiors, the part of cars that consumers see daily. It pioneered easily removable seats for minivans, a feature that carmakers highlighted in their ads and that "moved the metal" (sold cars). Next, it focused on batteries, which are important to distributors, another of its customers' key constituencies. In both these specialties, CEO Steve Roell and his team understood that they needed to innovate constantly; with new products the company would have pricing leverage since the carmakers didn't have a starting point from which to demand annual 5 percent cost reductions. By understanding the external factors that impacted the business and not being lulled into a false hope that difficulties would eventually fade away, Johnson Controls was able to control its destiny. It devised a strategy to counteract the negatives and produced admirable earnings growth, while its competitors slid into bankruptcy waiting for the day when conditions would improve.

Inside Information

- Take time to understand the external factors that impact your business; what you can't control can hurt you.

- Assess whether those factors are cyclical (will change) or secular (will continue for the foreseeable future). Devise your response accordingly.

- Focus on self-help—improve the factors that you can control. Limit the impact of those you cannot control. Be willing to sacrifice some profits in boom times to protect yourself in downturns. The upside of a downturn is that it will cull competitors from your industry.

DON'T IGNORE THE ELEPHANT IN THE ROOM

Investors spend a lot of time being wrong. At best, we get investments right about 60 percent of the time. That means that even the best of us are wrong 40 percent of the time. When I buy a stock and it goes down, the stock market decisively tells me that I've goofed. Honestly assessing these errors and making sure they don't cost too much is a painful yet crucial part of my job, as it should be for you. Most executives I've observed are reluctant to communicate honestly about business opportunities and challenges with all their constituencies: shareholders, employees, suppliers, and customers. They sweep mistakes, snafus, and weaknesses under the carpet rather than acknowledge them. I recall numerous uncomfortable meetings where the chief executive ignored the elephant in the room for fear of scaring investors or employees, or because he believed his own spin.

While optimism is generally a positive and the ability to spin can confer short-term benefits, the unwillingness to address problems can prevent you from improving the economics of your business. Here's an ironic truth:

Savvy partners—investors, employees, and others—know your operation's shortcomings; refusing to recognize them only makes you look weaker.

On numerous occasions, even as an outsider, I have created more accurate forecasts of a company's future revenues, earnings, and required capital spending than top management has. I simply saw the environment more clearly. Whenever this happens or when senior executives fail to acknowledge problems, I spend unproductive time trying to assess whether they are even aware of the challenges they face. And so do savvy employees, customers, and other partners. If problems are acknowledged, that's the first step to fixing them. But if you aren't seeing your challenges, they will only grow and fester.

More important, acknowledging threats to your business is the first step in counteracting them. Honesty can benefit you in unexpected ways. One smart hedge fund investor I know doubled his position in a company when the CEO said, "We really suck" during a conversation. My colleague had no idea how the CEO was planning to improve the business, but he did know that recognition of the firm's historically lackluster performance meant the leadership team was on its way to better results.

Similarly, have you ever wondered why a company's stock price rose when it announced bad news such as layoffs or write-downs? Investors bid the stock up because we saw that management was finally addressing problems, such as overstaffing or obsolete business models, that we had already pinpointed.

The stock price already reflected the problems, so signs that management was taking steps to correct the situation were an upside surprise. We pay more to own a business when its managers take steps to deal with their business's shortcomings, whether by shutting down uneconomic endeavors, increasing spending to address quality issues, or responding aggressively to competitors' market share gains.

Soon after Bob Iger succeeded Michael Eisner as CEO of the Walt Disney Company in 2005, he agreed to sell the company's ABC television shows through Apple's iTunes. Disney's stock price rallied 10 percent in the subsequent month. At first blush the $200 million increase in Disney's market capitalization may seem like irrational exuberance; it far outweighed the value Disney would generate from the deal. But investors were rewarding Iger's team for more than the deal; finally Disney was developing an answer to the Internet threat. Unauthorized versions of ABC's television shows were already showing up online, and investors worried that television would go the way of the music industry. Record label executives had ignored the challenge of Internet distribution until unpaid sharing of music files destroyed the industry's profitability. By doing a deal with iTunes, Iger showed that Disney would not meet the same fate. Offering legitimate versions of its programming online ensured that it would generate profits from the Internet.

A lack of honesty about its economics almost plunged Xerox into bankruptcy. An innovative high-tech company in the 1970s, Xerox rested far too long on the laurels of having invented and commercialized the photocopier. In the 1980s, it still created breakthrough products—developing the mouse and many other technologies that power today's computers—but had lost the ability to bring them to market effectively. At the same time, its core photocopier business became commoditized; customers no longer required the new features or high-touch service Xerox offered, so competitors' cheaper machines took a significant share of the market.

Though all technologies become commoditized over time, Xerox's biggest failing was its inability to acknowledge its situation; it continued to operate as though it were offering innovative, must-have products. Rather than face up to its changed reality, Xerox's top executives used accounting sleights of hand (mostly accelerated revenue recognition) to create the illusion of continued success. They funded this mirage with ever-increasing debt. These measures bought the company time but exacerbated the problem by raising revenue expectations. By the late 1990s, Xerox could no longer keep up the pretense, and things turned ugly. The Securities and Exchange Commission (SEC) launched an investigation into the company's accounting policies, and financial institutions would no longer lend it money. With $17 billion in debt and a liquidity crisis, Xerox's lack of honesty about its economic reality almost killed it.

Complete and brutal honesty saved Xerox and enabled it to avoid bankruptcy. In 2000, after the accounting problems were well known, Xerox's board cleaned house and unexpectedly appointed Anne Mulcahy as the company's COO (followed by a promotion to CEO in 2001). The biggest asset Mulcahy, who had been with Xerox for twenty-four years, brought to the role was her unvarnished honesty. Rather than try to spin the situation, she spoke frankly about Xerox's problems with everyone: employees, customers, lenders, and investors. At first investors and others reacted negatively—the stock price dropped by 26 percent after one particularly candid remark questioning the viability of Xerox's business model. However, over time investors appreciated and rewarded her honesty. Even better, Xerox's employees began fixing the challenges they faced as soon as the leadership started talking forthrightly about them.

Awakened by Mulcahy's candor, Xerox addressed its most fundamental weakness: its high-end product strategy had created an umbrella under which competitors could easily pick off market share. Employees developed a line of simpler, less expensive machines. Since they now recognized that their products didn't offer differentiation that customers would pay for, they knew they had to lower costs to survive. Since hyperefficient production was not one of Xerox's strengths, Mulcahy and her team outsourced production to a contract manufacturer.

They also outsourced their financing operations to GE Capital in the United States and to others around the globe. This move solved the liquidity problem and ensured that products were sold on economically profitable terms. Under the previous regime, many salespeople had sold Xerox's expensive products below cost in an effort to maintain market share. The company hoped to make up the lost profitability through financing charges on leased machines, but the strategy, requiring ever-increasing debt, was a house of cards that eventually collapsed and led to the liquidity crisis. As is often the case, the spin doctoring around Xerox's leading market share impacted the reality of operations.

Finally, because photocopiers were no longer a newfangled innovation and most customers did not need extensive hand-holding, Xerox began offering its products through reseller and wholesale channels, expanding its customer base beyond the large organizations reached by its own salespeople. The direct-sales team was transformed into more of a consulting operation, moving beyond hawking equipment to providing document management services, and outsourced corporate copy centers.

What Mulcahy and her team didn't do was eliminate the firm's considerable research and development operation. R&D did shrink to reflect the reality of Xerox's smaller business, but it remained between 5 percent and 6 percent of revenues. Though the products were more commoditized than in the past, opportunities for improvement and differentiation still existed. Maintaining the research budget ensured that Xerox was able to deliver increasing value for its owners in the years after the liquidity crisis dissipated.

Mulcahy and her team saved Xerox by using "shock honesty" to reorient it to the realities of its current situation. Though the company's revenues remain static—with scanning and e-mail the world is less paper dependent—it has dramatically improved its profitability and prospects. From a low of $3.75 in December 2000, the stock price quadrupled over the next three years as Xerox thought like an investor. Since 2003, Mulcahy's candor has continued to serve Xerox well. Realistic about the declines in the core business, Xerox has managed the decline while introducing color printers, driving into emerging markets, and expanding its service business, thus reestablishing its value edge.

Inside Information

- Be brutally honest with yourself, your employees, and the people to whom you report (especially investors) about where your business stands and its prospects for the future.

- Fight internal complacency by refusing to spin bosses, investors, and outsiders. Communicate the same messages both internally and externally.

- Address shortfalls and potential threats consistently if you want to keep your value edge. Don't shy away from admitting that something is wrong, as that's the first step toward fixing the problem.

•   •   •

How to Think like an Investor

By deeply understanding your business, what drives it, what value you bring to customers, and what your competitors are going to do, you buy yourself an insurance policy against the cyclical trends and negative events that can hit any organization. It's not that you know more than your competitors; you know the value-critical factors that your competitors may not appreciate. This knowledge helps defensively, and it can also enable you to find opportunities that others might miss. To think like an investor, ask yourself the following questions:

- What are the three to five factors that will drive your organization's results over the next twelve to twenty-four months? Though there are a million details that impact your business, you can distill them down to a handful of factors that really matter. Knowing your key factors is the first step in shifting them to your advantage.

- What are your market share trends? What was the response to your latest new-product introductions? Has any competitor gained more than a point of share over the last year? Even if this competitor still has a tiny share, pay attention to the trend. Your competitor may have built a better mousetrap, or your value edge may be slipping.

- What is your value edge? When was the last time you discussed it with customers and employees? Have you encouraged your people to push back, to continually challenge how valuable your edge really is? Have you looked online to see what customers, bloggers, and others are saying about your business? Have you done a reality check to make sure your perception of your company's value edge is consistent with that of independent observers?

- Have you thought about how long your edge is likely to last and what you can do to bolster it? If it's based on product innovation, you can be sure that competitors will catch up faster than in the past.

- What are your customers' alternatives to your business's offering? Did you consider nothing as one of their alternatives? Nothing is certainly the easiest option for your customers. How can you build your value edge to overcome the inertia of doing nothing or continuing on the same path?

- Are your competitors stronger in particular features? If so, have you considered reorienting your value proposition to a different customer group? Is there a customer group that's currently neglected because everyone "knows" it's not profitable? Or have you considered segmenting your customers more finely and offering more tailored products to the smaller segments? What is a feature of your product offering that people take for granted? Is there an opportunity to redevelop or rethink that feature? Often the most fruitful opportunities exist in negative space; explore that space.

- Have you put yourself in your competitors' shoes? Have you thought about the three to five factors that influence their business? How would you proceed if you were in their place *and faced the same pressures that they face*?

- Who else (customers, suppliers, regulators, financiers) meaningfully influences the success of your business? Have you considered the pressures they are facing? Have you contemplated the demands of their customers? (This doesn't require big, fancy consultant studies, just a willingness to be curious about the world, ask people in the know, and read as much as possible.) Have you considered the possibility that your customers and/or suppliers may have unrealistic expectations about their prospects and how that might affect you?

CHAPTER 2

WITH INFORMATION "ROACH MOTELS," PROBLEMS WON'T CHECK OUT

INVESTORS HAVE A MAXIM WE CALL THE "COCKROACH theory"; it recommends selling a company's stock at the first sign of trouble, because problems at a company are like cockroaches—there's never just one. If you see one (in your bathroom at night or in a quarterly earnings statement), there are likely many more. The advice works well because problems have generally festered a long time before top executives admit to them.

It's difficult as a manager to obtain an accurate and unvarnished view of your business, particularly any problems or weaknesses. Your employees and advisers rarely want to be the bearers of bad news; it's not typically in their economic interest. At the same time, you can rarely profit from bad news, unless it concerns your competitors. It's hard to tell your boss, board, customers, or analysts that a new initiative isn't living up to expectations. Therefore, it may become second nature to view all news in the rosiest possible light. Given this optimistic bias, it's not surprising how often I've heard executives

- Extolling "breakthrough" innovations that their competitors launched months before

- Describing sales as being delayed when customers had actually moved to new suppliers
- Insisting that their new products were well received when customers were telling me the exact opposite

Often all the competitors in an industry are similarly optimistic. On many occasions I've totaled companies' self-reported market shares and come up with an industrywide share of more than 150 percent.

To avoid an infestation of cockroaches, you can't let problems trapped in an information "roach motel" that prevents bad news or uncomfortable ideas from reaching you.

Information roach motels trap bad news and keep it from reaching business executives for many reasons: ego, incentives, image, and time pressures. Leaders may believe they are open to unconventional ideas and tell their people they want to hear the bad news first. But they don't realize how hard they have to work to make people, employees in particular, feel safe enough to be the bearers of bad news. Sharing negative information is economically risky and often unwise for an individual employee, even though the company as a whole benefits when challenges are acknowledged. In addition, many executives don't devote the time to dig for the information behind the numbers they receive, seek fresh comparative (and more objective) perspectives on their business, or take other steps to broaden and deepen the flow of knowledge.

Though keeping problems from festering in roach motels is difficult, it is also crucial. Moneymakers consistently find ways to do so; let's look at how.

Counteract the Impulse to
Withhold Bad News

Information roach motels form in environments without incentives to offset the natural reticence to deliver bad news. The sorry history of Enron illustrates this phenomenon well. Sherron Watkins became renowned as the whistle-blower who tried to warn CEO Ken Lay about the fraudulent transactions that CFO Andy Fastow was arranging. But she was only the most famous in a long line of Enron employees who warned Ken Lay (chief operating officer and, for a time, CEO) and Jeffrey Skilling about questionable practices and aggressive accounting. Lay and Skilling did not want to hear about problems and discouraged those who brought them negative information. Eventually, so many problems accumulated that the roach motel exploded, all the company's shortfalls were laid bare, and it couldn't survive.

Even in situations not involving fraud, senior managers' resistance to bad news can undermine performance. When top executives assume they're infallible, they discourage their people from telling them anything that suggests they may indeed be fallible. Just as worrisome, this autocratic demeanor prevents them from processing bad news, even when someone is brave enough to tell them. Michael Eisner allowed an information roach motel to form during his latter years as Walt Disney's CEO. He avoided investors, appearing less frequently at investor conferences as the questions from the audience became tougher. He refused to settle a lawsuit with his ousted studio chief, Jeffrey Katzenberg, even when internal experts told him how expensive not settling would be. When bidding to buy the cable network Fox Family Channel, Eisner had information that was so poor that Disney offered a billion dollars more than the next highest bid. The repeated missteps ultimately led to a shareholder revolt and Eisner's resignation.

Getting negative information to flow freely to top executives is difficult, and unfortunately, business leaders often need a crisis to motivate them. In 1998 the defense contractor Raytheon Company was drowning in $9 billion of debt, which had been taken on to fund an acquisition spree. At the same time, it was leaking cash; a number of its multiyear projects were costing more than the government had agreed to pay. An unwillingness to confront the overruns earlier meant they came at the worst possible time.

Under pressure to right the ship and prevent future cockroach infestations, CEO Dan Burnham added a special feature to Raytheon's process improvement and project management systems. Program managers were given a grace period to identify profit problems. If they identified potential shortfalls in projects' early stages, they didn't suffer any career repercussions. However, if they failed to identify them during the grace period, their careers suffered. With this new plan and other clear-eyed changes, Raytheon generated $1 billion in cash two years after its massive losses. Within six years it had worked its debt down to less than $6 billion, causing its stock price to rise from a low of $17.50 in 2000 to a high of $40.21 by 2005.

Inside Information

- Avoid both the reality and the perception of discouraging bad news. Try this technique to stimulate honest exchanges: plant a couple of employees in your audience at open-forum meetings. Give them express instructions to ask tough questions, and watch how these questions stimulate more meaningful questions and honest dialogue from your entire group.

- Develop a thick skin. Protect direct reports delivering bad news not only from your own negative reactions but also from those of others who may discourage them.

- Create specific incentives for your people to identify, communicate, and solve problems early on, providing a powerful counterweight against the tendency to hide problems. Institute an early grace period during which employees can raise alarms without fear of any negative repercussions.

The Numbers Tell the Story

Offer incentives that encourage your people to share even the most vexing problem or news, but don't expect this to result in your hearing all the news all the time. Information roach motels are resilient and need to be attacked on a number of fronts. You must build a robust feedback system that ensures that you have an accurate view of your business. Start with the numbers.

When first studying a company, I often ask business leaders: What metrics should I and other investors use to judge your success? I ask not only to know which operational numbers I should be watching but also to understand how the managers run their businesses. The vague answers I usually receive are disappointing, because deciding which operational metrics to focus on is one of the most important decisions leaders make. The right numbers provide the information that you need to guide your operations and identify issues before they become full-blown problems.

Moneymakers have one to three metrics that they watch daily, know by heart, and use to run their businesses. Because these metrics are operational in nature and every business is different, there are no standard formulas. However, the best leaders use the following approach.

1. Select one to three crucial metrics out of the hundreds your business produces. You will need to make a judgment call on what is crucial and what is secondary. Consider the three to five factors of your value edge to help make that call.

2. Choose numbers that summarize big portions of the business, knowing you can delve into the underlying details should a given metric show signs of deterioration.

3. Make sure your selected metrics encapsulate the trade-offs inherent in your business and reflect both revenue and cost factors. For instance, targeting only revenue growth can lead to bad decisions if the cost of achieving growth is not built in. For asset-intensive businesses, reflecting the cost of capital to buy those assets is important. Generally the most successful metrics are ratios: revenue or cost per operational unit. The operational unit selected should represent the company's most limiting or fixed factor, one that cannot be adjusted quickly.

Focusing on the right productivity measures can transform a business, while focusing on the wrong ones can lead to substantial mistakes. The newspaper publisher Knight Ridder suffered disastrous consequences when managers selected circulation growth as a key metric to determine executive bonuses in 2002. Management felt that stopping the slow, persistent decline in the number of copies sold was crucial to maintaining high advertising rates. High penetration rates—local newspapers often reached half the adults in their area—allowed Knight Ridder to charge handsomely for the ads that provide 70 to 80 percent of its revenue. Though Knight Ridder's logic was sound, the key metric chosen—growth in copies sold—did not incorporate the cost or revenues gained from additional circulation. To meet the target, market managers discounted subscription prices heavily. The tactic worked; the number of copies sold didn't fall for the first time in years. But it didn't help the bottom line; circulation revenue dropped by 5 percent, and ad sales did not increase. At the same time, Tribune Company, another major newspaper publisher, saw its circulation revenues increase 1 percent with flat ad sales despite modest declines in its number of copies sold. Knight Ridder continued its course for a couple of years with little impact beyond drops in circulation revenue. Ultimately, investors forced the company to sell itself to another newspaper chain.

The right productivity metrics, however, can transform a company, as Yahoo! discovered in 2001–02 as it sought to recover from the dot-com bust. During the Internet boom, the well-known portal was everyone's darling. CEO Tim Koogle appeared regularly on CNBC to tout the new era. He and his top executives participated fully in the Internet land grab, placing stakes in as many "spaces" of the Internet as possible. Yahoo! acquired dozens of companies and started units in everything from auctions to stores to video business news. Then the dot-com bubble burst in 2001; with start-ups no longer raising marketing funds from venture capitalists and traditional companies no longer reacting defensively, Internet advertising dried up. Yahoo!'s revenues, which relied almost exclusively on advertising, dropped 35 percent in 2001. To make matters worse, staff expenses rose despite layoffs. Employees now demanded cash compensation in lieu of stock options (at that time income statements were not required to record any expense for stock option compensation). The company lost $92.8 million in 2001, and in September of that year the stock price dropped under $5.00.

Against this backdrop Terry Semel joined as CEO in April 2001. With another newcomer, CFO Sue Decker, the two began paring back the sprawling land grab to a profitable and manageable core. They identified two key productivity metrics: revenue per user and revenue per employee. These metrics worked because they balanced both revenues and costs. The revenue/user measure reflected Yahoo!'s most valuable and fixed resource, users. Due to its size as one of the world's largest sites and the viral nature of building audiences online, increasing users was difficult. Yahoo! managers had to derive the most revenue from the users the company had. Similarly, on the cost side, the largest expense was employees. Driving revenue per employee was Yahoo!'s best measure of productivity.

Semel and Decker used these metrics to guide their simplification strategy. FinanceVision and several international operations were cut. The auction site was transformed from a free site into a paid site, effectively admitting defeat in Yahoo!'s attempt to challenge eBay. Though feathers were ruffled and employees departed, Semel and Decker returned the portal to profitability within a year. With a less expansive but profitable business, Yahoo! was able to begin growing again.

Inside Information

- Fashion one to three broad-brush productivity metrics unique to your business.

- Track the trends in these measures weekly. When you observe changes, both positive and negative, dig into the details to understand what's producing the change and how you can reinforce or reverse it.

- As your fortunes change, make sure to maintain a disciplined focus on the metrics.

UNDERSTAND WHAT DRIVES YOUR NUMBERS

Beyond actively encouraging bad news and tracking their key metrics, the next step moneymakers take to prevent information roach motels is to dig into the forces that drive their numbers. Broad-stroke numbers, particularly when they are strong, can create the illusion that you're on top of your business, even when the foundation is being eroded by competitors or imminent cost increases. Top-performing managers consistently ask themselves whether the numbers make sense. Answer the following questions to ascertain the reality underlying your numbers.

- Does it make sense that you have as much market share as the numbers imply?
- Is that share sustainable? Why?
- How much of your growth comes from long-term trends and how much is from cyclical variation that can quickly reverse?
- What produces your profits?
- How much of your results come from financial decisions, onetime mergers, and other factors that behave differently than the underlying business does?

Enron, WorldCom, and HealthSouth offer extreme examples of what happens when managers don't pay attention to the forces behind their numbers. But, even without fraud, failure to grasp the underlying drivers can prove disastrous, a lesson Delta Air Lines learned as it slid into bankruptcy.

In 1999, Delta CFO Warren Jenson and his team presciently hedged the company's considerable oil exposure. Jet fuel generally consumes around 10 to 20 percent of a full-service airline's revenues; with operating margins of only 8 percent in the best of years, fluctuations in oil costs can make the difference between profit and loss for airlines. The decision to hedge Delta's oil exposure proved brilliant as prices rose steadily over the next five years from less than $20.00 per barrel in 1999 to more than $60.00 in 2005. The hedges saved the company $684 million in 2000, $299 million in 2001, and $136 million in 2002. As oil prices climbed, Delta gained a significant advantage over its unhedged competitors.

However, this benefit became a liability when Delta executives failed to appreciate what generated its profits and how sustainable they were. In 2000, the hedge gains represented almost half of Delta's net income. The next year, senior managers signed an expensive new contract with the pilots, using the profits from their financial decisions to fund ongoing operational expenses. Effectively, they bet that the gains from their hedging activities would be replicable throughout the five years of the pilots' contract, even though the hedges covered only three years. Had they fully appreciated what produced their profits, Delta executives would have realized they could ill afford pay increases when industry oversupply was pressuring every airline's operating profits. In the previous five years, U.S. airlines had grown their plane fleets at record levels. By early 2001, it was apparent that excess capacity was going to send the industry into a downturn. It was not a time to be increasing costs. Had Delta's executives considered how much profit came from financial devices and how unsustainable those profits were,

Delta might have avoided bankruptcy. Certainly the 2001 pilot contract would not have been as costly to the airline (and ultimately detrimental to the pilots of the bankrupt carrier).

Inside Information

- Remain vigilant. Even when your numbers are good, periodically dig into the reality underlying the numbers.

- Apply the "smell" test to assess what's happening to produce the numbers. Sniff around and ask yourself if they really make sense.

- Separate the factors that drive your number: isolate financial from operating factors, cyclical upswings from long-term growth, and so on. View the numbers from these distinct perspectives to predict how sustainable your results will be.

FOLLOW THE MONEY

As an equity analyst, I have to ascertain the reality underlying a company's financial reports, whether a company's reported numbers fairly represent its sustainable earnings, understate them, or are misleading due to limited-time benefits, as in the case of Delta. When digging into the numbers, I always adhere to one essential rule: Follow the money. When interpreting information, I remain cognizant of each source's economic incentives—for instance, rivals rarely say good things about their competitors, so when they do it's especially meaningful. Similarly, sell-side analysts' opinions are suspect when their firms are doing investment banking for the companies they are recommending.

I also pay more attention to what people do with their money than to what they say. When a top executive is cashing in his options, that information is far more valuable than the executive's arguments about why his company's stock is undervalued. As a business leader, you should leaven what your people, customers, and partners tell you with their behaviors. An employee may tell you he can't meet objectives without adding staff, but if he never asks anyone to work weekends or after five, that's a disconnect you should heed.

Stay aware of the economic realities underlying the information you receive. When direct reports tell you things are going well in their areas, it behooves you to dig further. Your employees have powerful economic incentives to present a rosier picture than exists. When a customer says it is postponing an order, investigate whether the delay is a prelude to a cancellation while maintaining whatever pricing concessions it has. In general, when assessing the underlying reality, always:

Watch what people do with their money, not what they say.

By building its decision-making systems on the economic bedrock of customer transactions, Lowe's used this rule to outperform its fiercest competitor. For years, The Home Depot ruled home improvement retailing, having pioneered the big-box concept in this category. Lowe's was historically the wannabe, the second player in the industry. In 2004, that started to change when Lowe's installed its Rapid Response Replenishment (R3) system. The R3 system advanced inventory planning and management by basing replenishment shipments on the prior day's sales, rather than the forecasts that most retailers use. Only educated guesses, forecasts require planners to incorporate history, seasonality, and gut feelings to decide what should be shipped to stores. They are often wrong, since they are removed from what customers are doing with their money today. With its new system Lowe's turned inventory ordering over to its customers, freeing up forecasting resources and at the same time getting more accurate information, since customers have no problem letting store managers know that their pet product is not selling.

R3 eliminated forecast errors, improved in-stock positions, and reduced overstocks. More inventory now traveled through Lowe's distribution centers, offering flexibility (e.g., to try unconventional products), more cost-efficient shipping, and lower investment in safety stocks. In 2005, the first full year after the R3 implementation, Lowe's improved its gross margins by 0.6 percentage points, to 34.2 percent. Inventory, 27 percent of total assets, grew by only 13.5 percent despite a sales increase of 18.6 percent. Better inventory turns led to better returns on investment. Lowe's shareholders noticed; in 2005, Lowe's stock price outperformed The Home Depot's by 22 percent.

Lowe's experience shows that the actions of external customers are the most reliable sources for short-term information. When people put their own money to work, they act on reality (or their view of it), not on a desire to please the boss or to avoid bearing bad news. People's actions—particularly parting with money—are generally far more telling than their words. Finding ways to drive daily decisions based on outsiders' actions, rather than your own beliefs about customers' behavior, produces better results and will enable you to join the ranks of the moneymakers.

While Lowe's used sophisticated information system technology to follow customers' money, Commercial Metals Company (CMC) tracks customer actions with a more basic approach. An $8.3-billion-revenue, vertically integrated steel company, Commercial Metals has achieved profitability in each of the last thirty years despite operating in a low-return, boom-and-bust industry. It offers recycling (scrap metal procurement), milling, fabrication (bending rebar, the product of the milling step), and marketing/distribution. Each of its four divisions not only supplies other CMC operations but also sells externally. In the recycling division, the company buys scrap for its own needs and for others as a scrap dealer serving other steel mills. Following the money from these external sales gives Commercial Metals reliable insights into the current state of the steel market. By knowing where the market is in its boom-and-bust cycle, CMC managers can adjust their business appropriately. In 2003, markets for finished products were weak; Commercial Metals shifted its resources to the earlier stages in the steelmaking process, and its recycling division had a banner year. In the strong economy of 2005, the company reallocated toward later-stage processes generating record profits in fabrication. In 2007, marketing and distribution led the way, and in 2008, high prices returned leadership back to the recycling segment. Access to external customer transactions gives Commercial Metals the information edge that enables it to outperform in good markets and bad.

Inside Information

- Evaluate the potential bias behind every source of information. Customer transactions provide the most reliable sources of short-term information.

- Build feedback loops around actual customer transactions to access this information as close to the transaction time as possible.

- Sell externally throughout your product creation process. The value of the information will justify the effort.

Skin in the Game: Rely on Partners with Their Own Money at Risk

Customers provide valuable, unbiased information through their purchasing decisions. This data, however, can lead to mistakes if projected too far into the future. Customer transactions are best used to guide short-term decisions, as Lowe's did in developing its inventory plans. But for longer-term decisions, customer purchasing data can be misleading. Just because demand is high today doesn't mean it will sustain that level a year from now. Therefore, it's wise to integrate other "follow the money" sources into the mix, and some of the best are those who put up their own money for a shared venture.

Independent partners who invest their own capital provide tremendous value. They are more likely to offer brutally honest and reliable feedback because their own fortunes rise or fall with the success of the shared enterprise. With their own "skin in the game," they have a powerful incentive to make you aware of problems and opportunities. Dealer, bottler, and franchisee relationships are the most common form of investment partnerships, but there are many ways to structure them. Corning has repeatedly and successfully formed joint ventures, including Dow Corning and Owens Corning, to bring in investment partners. The advertising and marketing services company Omnicom Group, which regularly acquires smaller marketing agencies, usually encourages the entrepreneurs whose businesses it buys to retain a minority equity stake so that they have a significant economic interest in the success of their agency even after it's been sold. Though the form of investment partnership varies from industry to industry and business to business, attracting investment partners can allow you to benefit from the information advantages they offer.

McDonald's has become the world's largest and most global restaurateur largely due to the partnership it has formed with its franchisees. Independents own and manage about 80 percent of McDonald's restaurants. They provide regular and compelling feedback to McDonald's managers, ensuring that information gets through to decision makers. Though it can take some time before the information penetrates, the importance of franchisees to McDonald's operations means that leaders have to listen.

In early 2003, this feedback mechanism did its job and saved the company a billion dollars. McDonald's was struggling operationally, and the stock had fallen from a high near $50.00 a few years earlier to around $12.00. Though the overall stock market had fallen too, McDonald's stock drop was mostly self-induced. The company took more than $1.6 billion in reorganization and asset impairment charges between 2001 and 2003; earnings per share dropped from a 2000 high of $1.46 to $1.25, even excluding these charges. Management had lowered its earnings expectations repeatedly, and new operational challenges continued to surface. In the face of these grim results, McDonald's executives continued to add locations, sticking with the strategy that had propelled growth through the 1990s. Only the approach wasn't working anymore.

Even worse, pursuing location growth had McDonald's managers taking their eyes off executing operationally. Customer dissatisfaction scores rose to uncomfortable levels. In response, CEO Jack Greenberg and his team devised a big solution. They developed a new front counter team service system that reengineered the ordering function. Historically, McDonald's cashiers have performed all the customer-facing tasks. The new system had one person take customers' orders and another fill them. The handoff required McDonald's to develop expensive new software and franchisees to spend heavily to buy new hardware (monitors, printers, etc.).

But this new approach failed to solve the customer satisfaction problem. Fortunately, the franchisees, who had their own investment dollars on the line, provided feedback. They complained that the system was expensive and did not produce meaningful gains in service efficiency. Their actions supported their words; franchisees were slow to implement the new system in their locations.

Still believing in their grand solution, Greenberg's team started offering U.S. franchisees $2,000 per restaurant to mitigate the equipment costs. Still franchisees resisted. Finally, franchisees' actions and frank feedback enabled the executives to see the cockroaches. McDonald's pulled the plug on the new system in early 2003. Management took a $170 million write-down on the software development expense, in addition to the $22 million already spent to help franchisees. While this roughly $200 million loss hurt, it was far less than the $1 billion needed for a complete rollout of the ineffective system. The checks and balances of the parent-franchisee relationship enabled McDonald's to avoid a significant capital investment with dubious operational benefits and subpar returns.

Following this experience, the new CEO, Jim Cantalupo, led a team that turned around McDonald's performance by refocusing on managerial basics. Rather than develop one grand, expensive solution, they implemented numerous small improvements. They slowed location growth but reinvigorated the company's "mystery shopper" program to enforce cleanliness and other standards. They lowered prices on the least differentiated menu items and introduced new higher-profit products. Customer satisfaction scores started to improve, and in short order revenues, profits, and the stock price followed.

Investment partners who are smaller and/or privately owned are particularly valuable because they are more attuned to the cost of capital. For the most part, the money required for investments comes out of their personal bank accounts. They also tend to be closer to day-to-day operations than larger organizations are and can more readily identify when additional focus on operational details is needed or when there is a market opportunity that you are not capitalizing on. Of course, if you expect your investment partners to keep you informed about problems and opportunities, you need to treat them fairly and ensure that they earn an adequate return on their capital.

Caterpillar, the machinery and engine manufacturer known for its bright yellow construction machines, has discovered new market opportunities through its symbiosis with its independent partners. Cat sells its products through strong independent dealers who make their own decisions to buy its equipment; they then resell and service the machines for the end customers. Caterpillar devotes significant time and resources to managing its 181 dealers. Unlike many companies that hobble their partners (e.g., the movie studios with the movie theaters), Caterpillar prices its products so that its partners earn solid profits. As a result, its dealers are economically sound and well capitalized.

Leveraging its dealers' financial strength enabled Caterpillar to build an equipment rental business quickly and successfully. It learned about the untapped rental opportunity from a few dealers who were dabbling in rentals. Seeing the dealers' success with a basic offering, Caterpillar developed the Cat Rental Store concept in 1996. It required dealers to establish separate locations, but it allowed them to stock other manufacturers' products in lines where Cat did not have products, and it encouraged shorter rental periods than what dealers were initially offering. In 1998, Cat further supported the rollout by making financing available for dealers to purchase equipment for rental and by launching a new line of compact equipment more suited to renters' needs. Because the concept provided a good return for the independent dealer-owners, it took off quickly. By the end of 2000, a quarter of Cat's dealer body ran rental stores. Expansion of the concept did not stop there; by 2005, more than 40 percent of dealers operated rental outlets.

Inside Information

- Seek partnerships with independent entities that bring both capital and information to the table; their capital commitment makes their information much more valuable.

- Take full advantage of the insights partners offer, rather than bemoaning how difficult they make it for you to maneuver. Speed is an advantage only if you're pursuing a sensible course. Consider investment partners' protests against new initiatives seriously and determine if the protests are valid (or, conversely, if the investment partners are missing their own information roach motels).

COMPARE, COMPARE, COMPARE

Companies constantly try to "sell their stories" of why their stocks are undervalued to me as an investor. I find it pays to be a skeptic, to remain mindful of the biases and incentives of the speakers, and to seek additional sources when evaluating information. I reach conclusions about companies only after comparing the information I've received from companies, their suppliers, and their customers over a period of time. Most professional investors have learned the hard way not to trust a single "insider," no matter how much information this person possesses. Similarly, you can be the most brilliant executive in the world and have terrific insight into your company and industry, but if you rely only on what you know, you're going to lose out to a competitor who may not be as brilliant but has the benefit of comparative information.

Comparing different sources allows you to maintain a healthy skepticism about any single-source information you receive. Employees' feedback can be compromised by their desire to agree with the boss; they may also be too close to the issues. Customers' feedback has limits because they see only part of your operation and can also be myopic. The best managers recognize that any single source of information is inherently flawed, and they build multifaceted, independent feedback systems. These systems provide a diversity of ideas and information, and, more important, they allow for comparison.

Gannett, the United States' largest newspaper publisher, has created such a feedback mechanism through "management by template." Each month, all of its 100-plus divisions (corresponding roughly to each of its daily newspaper operations) prepare a summary of their previous month's results according to a predefined template. The template requires key operational metrics, a profit-and-loss statement, and a brief discussion of market conditions. While each publisher has incentives to present his or her performance in the best possible light, the standardized format and focus on numbers leave little room to distort the reality. Though numbers can lie, it is hard to do so with predetermined metrics.

Gannett's senior managers then compare the results across various regions and markets. The uniformity of data makes it easy to see trends across geographic areas or different types of markets. It also allows managers to quickly identify where results are particularly poor or good. They can then focus their attention and probe deeper to identify the root causes of these outliers. Once the source of the exceptional performance is known, senior managers and local leaders work together to solve problems or spread successful practices throughout the organization.

For instance, a local-market publisher might attribute soft help-wanted revenues to a weak job market. Armed with everyone's reports, senior managers can quickly ascertain if other markets are experiencing the same softness. If not, they will investigate to find the real cause of the weakness since the comparative information disproves the suspected cause. After further questioning and comparing, they might discover that the job market is indeed weak but a few publishers are performing well because they have new products or sales tactics. These best practices can then be spread to other markets.

From 2002 to 2005, Gannett rolled out new products—nondaily shoppers, job sheets, and other free niche publications—across the company's far-flung operations profitably and quickly. Gannett discovered the power of these line extensions after it acquired Newsquest Media Group, a regional newspaper publisher in the United Kingdom. Through the monthly reports, Gannett CEO Doug McCorkindale and his team saw the power of Newsquest's nondaily offerings. Company leaders then became evangelists to persuade U.S. publishers to launch similar products. Select publishers volunteered to lead the experiments. Among the first nondailies were two youth-oriented publications, *Thr!ve* in Boise, Idaho, and *Noise* in Lansing, Michigan; both launched in October 2002. The new products took off. Through the monthly updates, other publishers tracked the progress of the experiments and could determine which nondailies were best suited to their markets. Through this comparative information sharing, Gannett built nondailies to 13 percent of newspaper advertising revenues by 2005. This growth helped newspaper profitability immensely as the newspaper division's operating profits grew by 12 percent from 2002 to 2005. Over the same period, Gannett's two biggest counterparts, Tribune and Knight Ridder, saw their newspaper profits decline by 11 to 13 percent.

Management by template works so well because:

- Its comparisons allow managers to ferret out the underlying reality.
- Managers can quickly identify which results are most unusual and know how to prioritize their efforts.
- Creating a friendly rivalry between divisions can spur greater effort and achievement.
- The numbers, based on what clients actually spent, make it easy to follow the money.

Benchmarking is another, better known way to access the benefits of comparison, though I urge you to exercise caution with it. Some managers will use it when the components of their businesses are too integrated or too different to set up effective internal comparisons. They hire consultants to compare their performance to that of their competitors. While benchmarking has many well-documented success stories, I'm far more cautious about its usefulness since it relies on second-hand, mediated data. Often the consultants who collect and interpret the data have limited access to competitors' numbers and have strong incentives to tell managers what they want to hear.

In 2000, Holly Becker, a veteran sell-side analyst at Lehman Brothers, began researching a new sector, the Internet. To get up to speed, she commissioned a consulting firm to study the future of Internet advertising. Swept up in the "new economy" vogue of the time, the consultants' initial results suggested unending growth for Internet advertising. However, Becker was skeptical. For years she had followed the consumer packaged goods companies and knew that they were not pouring money into Internet advertising. She expressed her skepticism to the consultants and pushed them to dig deeper. After reexamining, they came to the opposite conclusion: that Internet advertising was driven by unprofitable start-ups that were spending their venture-capital funding recklessly to "get big fast." Since these companies were mostly unprofitable, the supply of ad dollars was not sustainable. Becker launched her coverage of the Internet companies with a negative stance and was quickly proved right when Internet advertising crashed.

The telecom industry during WorldCom's ascendancy also suffered from benchmarking mistakes. From 1999 to 2002, many telecom CEOs browbeat their employees to match the low costs of WorldCom. Companies reengineered, restructured, and laid off thousands of employees but still couldn't achieve the mark set by WorldCom. Only when it came out that WorldCom's numbers were fraudulent was it apparent why. The WorldCom experience illustrates the dangers of relying on just one source, particularly a secondhand source, of information. Both managers and investors should evaluate results through comparisons with multiple sources of information, both internal and external, and must apply common sense when drawing conclusions.

Inside Information

- Build feedback systems that supply comparative information from multiple, independent sources.

- Accord more weight to firsthand data sources. Use secondhand data with caution, and routinely consider the incentives and biases of your information sources.

(continued)

- Read what your competitors are saying in their earnings releases and analyst conference calls; plenty of comparison information can be gathered from competitors without expensive third-party studies.

- Apply common sense when drawing conclusions from comparisons.

FOLLOW THE VALUES

Creating robust information flow is not just about following the numbers and the money. Though the right metrics bring fresh and useful information throughout an organization, they can't prevent other types of roach motels from forming. Comparisons have limited use if, when you investigate what's going on, your people are reluctant to raise problems with you. Advocating and rewarding a collective purpose, beyond merely making money, encourages employees to share bad news that might otherwise remain unarticulated. A shared goal provides cover for employees to raise problems or disagree with superiors. Organizations that balance values and returns generally deliver superior long-term results. When employees share nonmonetary ideals, they create greater value for shareholders and themselves, in large part because information can flow more freely.

At Pixar, the animation studio behind *Toy Story, Finding Nemo,* and *Cars,* employees valued creating the highest-quality films above all else. Driven by this shared goal, the company created a truth-telling, self-critical culture that produced the best hit ratio in the film industry's history.

Making movies is difficult, involving the efforts of hundreds of specialists who often are personally vested in what they are producing. Films can easily devolve into crass, money-losing propositions when contributors worry about the repercussions of being honest about what's working and what isn't. Too often, compromise and expediency lead studios to settle for low-quality solutions. As a result, only 40 percent of films ever recoup the money put into them. Many studios talk about improving financial returns by making only good movies, but none has been able to do it.

Until Pixar. As an independent company from 1984 to 2006, the studio had a 100 percent hit rate with the six feature films it produced. Pixar achieved this enviable record because everyone in the company, from top animators to finance department secretaries, was charged with protecting the quality of the product. Anyone could attend in-process screenings and make comments. Decisions were ultimately made by the "Brain Trust," Pixar's eight film directors, but input from all was actively solicited and incorporated.

By holding film quality, rather than collegiality or hierarchy, as its highest ideal, Pixar kept producers from getting too close to the product and losing their judgment. The broad-based and honest feedback engendered by the employees' shared goal kept this all-too-common problem from surfacing.

To keep the culture of honesty from devolving into lip service, Pixar extended it to all aspects of the business. Management held quarterly meetings for the entire staff. Employees were encouraged to ask pointed questions and rewarded for doing so, even when leaders might be embarrassed in front of a large group. Senior leaders had to develop thick skins, but they expected questioners to have them as well. CEO Steve Jobs pushed people to argue their positions with him. The emphasis on quality also enabled strong-minded experts to work together by setting an ideal above their individual careers or those of senior managers.

Pixar's quality focus produced outstanding financial results. In 2005, its last full year as a stand-alone entity, Pixar had a net profit margin of 53 percent and a return on tangible assets (total assets less cash and financial investments) of 43 percent. The results were so good that in 2006 the Walt Disney Company acquired Pixar for $6.3 billion, or forty-one times the prior year's earnings.

Employees at Goldman Sachs, a premier institutional financial services firm, share the goal of being the best. Though many firms say they strive for excellence, Goldman makes it happen through a rigorous 360-degree annual review process. This process ensures that Goldman has the best and most collaborative people, which is the key to success in its people-based business. It certainly produces financial results. When Goldman went public in 1999, the average partner received a paycheck of $160 million, and in the following five years the stock price almost doubled.

I should emphasize that it's more difficult to make values-based feedback processes work than number-based ones. As many as 60 percent of Fortune 500 companies do 360-degree reviews, yet few of them achieve the success of Goldman Sachs. Goldman makes the process work because:

- Employees spend more than thirty hours annually filling out evaluations of their subordinates, colleagues, and superiors. The company devotes considerable resources—in this case time rather than money—to show how serious the firm is about the feedback.
- Management actively encourages truly candid feedback, taking issue with evaluations that lack any negative or uncomfortable information.
- Leadership uses the evaluations to run the firm, particularly to determine employees' opportunities for advancement.

In contrast, executives I know at another financial services firm had their secretaries write up the annual peer reviews so they could fulfill their requirement without expending any effort. As one would expect, the results were far less useful for steering the firm, which was eventually swallowed in a merger.

Inside Information

- Foster shared cultural values to create an atmosphere in which employees feel safe sharing criticisms that will improve your performance.

- Create and reinforce feedback systems that support the shared values.

- Make sure you apply the values to every part of your organization. If not, the shared values will quickly devolve into meaningless slogans.

- Look at how much negative or uncomfortable information comes out of your values feedback system. If not much is forthcoming, the process isn't working. You'll need to investigate where the roadblocks are and communicate both publicly and individually that identifying problems is the first step in fixing them. Show that it's safe to be honest by inviting and accepting criticism—lead the way in the behavior you want your people to adopt.

RECRUIT AND REWARD TRUTH TELLERS

Ever mindful of people's tendency to paint a pretty picture, I am always surprised and delighted when I come across a business leader who is resolutely honest. And I'm not the only one. Invariably, leaders who "tell it like it is" draw the largest crowds at investor conferences. Their willingness to highlight the mistakes they've made, the risks they've taken, and the weaknesses in their business models earns them great esteem among investors and great results in their businesses. Of course, they also point out the things they're doing right, but it's the combination of their successes and their honesty about what went wrong that elevates them as leaders and moneymakers.

Many executives view truth tellers as cranks and complainers; they see them as creating more work for them and impeding their pet projects. This response is unfortunate, because what's bad for the individual is great for the organization. When supported, truth tellers foster an environment where honest information flows and problems can be identified and addressed.

Emerson's Charlie Peters is a rarity in a world where truth tellers rarely advance. As senior executive vice president, Peters is one of the top four executives at this $22-billion-revenue industrial conglomerate. While the other three top leaders have typical titles (CEO, COO, and CFO), Peters has responsibility "for helping Emerson businesses and divisions develop innovative global business models and strategies that build the company's capabilities to support and create value through its customer relationships." What does this mean? Peters effectively functions as Emerson's chief truth teller. He is charged with seeking out problems and opportunities facing Emerson. To do so, he seeks fresh perspectives constantly, devoting considerable time to listening to customers, lower-level employees, and investors. When he finds an opportunity, he raises awareness about it throughout the organization. Because of the honest, self-critical eye that Peters helps Emerson apply to its business, the firm has effectively seized opportunities as market conditions have changed. Peters's truth telling is Emerson's secret weapon to stay ahead of the curve.

Peters is also a doer. He identifies challenges and then spearheads efforts to turn them into opportunities. In 2001, Peters drove an initiative to consolidate purchasing. Like many large organizations, Emerson had let its business units develop their own supplier relationships. Unit heads wanted control over their supply chains, and liked the freedom to purchase from suppliers who tailored products to their preferences. They were extremely wary of headquarters meddling in what was working. But as Peters discovered from his many discussions, the system wasn't really working. Emerson was paying far too much, because it wasn't accessing volume discounts by consolidating its purchasing. Though he might have kept quiet to avoid rocking the boat with division heads, Peters knew the opportunity was too big to pass up. He began talking frequently about the size of the potential savings and ferreting out which of the units' concerns affected the business and which were merely people being territorial. With this information and a passion to improve Emerson's overall results, Peters worked with programmers and others to implement new information systems and standardized reporting. The team injected transparency into the now-centralized purchasing systems, so everyone could see the savings. Through this work, Emerson became a pioneer in strategic sourcing.

Then, in November 2003, Peters turned to pricing. Even

contemplating raising prices was a major cultural shift for Emerson. For years the company had been a price taker (i.e., it let the market dictate the prices it could sell its products for). Managers concentrated on what they could control—cutting costs and improving productivity—to generate acceptable profits at prevailing prices. In late 2003, Peters set about trying to change what many thought was set in stone. With the support of CEO Dave Farr and his compatriots in the office of the chief executive, Peters first led Emerson to purchase, install, and customize software that allowed salespeople and sales managers to manage pricing. Using the new tool, the sales department began experimenting with pricing, tailoring prices to each customer's situation, and being more aggressive where it could. To support the more dynamic pricing, departments from customer relations to financial forecasting had to make changes. The work paid off. By 2005, Emerson had realized 1 percent price increases companywide, the first gain in years. Due in part to the pricing strength, the company had record earnings in 2005, finally surpassing a high-water mark set five years earlier. The stock also surpassed the peak set in 2000.

Inside Information

- Recruit new truth tellers and cultivate the ones you have.

- Fight your natural instinct to marginalize them as complainers.

- Put them in charge of fixing whatever problems they identify.

• • •

Prevent Cockroaches from Multiplying

Because no one likes to be the bearer of bad news or particularly wants to hear it, information roach motels are easily built and almost impossible to recognize until the cockroaches are too numerous to hide.

But there is another option, one that I've seen moneymakers use to solve problems before they multiply. These exceptional managers know that comfortable is the enemy of successful. They actively seek challenges and challengers because problems are much easier to overcome when identified early. To make sure you have the information you need to run your business, answer the following questions:

- When was the last time someone told you something surprising, particularly something negative?

- Do your employees regularly tell you about problems they're having or roadblocks on a big project?

- When employees say something negative, is it really just a mild criticism to create the illusion of candor?

- When was the last time you asked your employees where the problems are? Did you create an environment to allow them to answer without fear?

- Do you ever feign ignorance so that employees, customers, suppliers, and outsiders feel free to share information, or do you project such mastery of your business that they are too intimidated to share information?

- Are you able to hear bad news without killing the messenger or blowing up in some other way? When was the last time you rewarded a bearer of bad news?

- Do you consider the personal motivation of the person sharing information with you when evaluating that information?

- What are the primary metrics by which you judge your business, and how did you settle on them? Do they incorporate the trade-offs inherent in your business decisions?

- Do your numbers make sense? What value edge drives the numbers? Are your costs appropriately aligned?

- When was the last time you looked at customer transactions? If it was more than a week ago, you need to improve your reporting. How do you incorporate customer data into your decision making?

- Do you seek out investment partners? Do you integrate their information into your business perspective?

- Do you ever make a list of the sources from which you get your information and evaluate how independent they are or whether they are all recycling the same information to you?

- Do you make a consistent effort to communicate the importance of your company's values? Does this effort motivate people to share ideas and information in line with these values, even if it's not in their best interest or has negative connotations?

- Do you recruit and reward people who are relentlessly honest, who call things as they see them, even if they make you uncomfortable?

CHAPTER 3

AVOID THE TRAP OF PROFITLESS GROWTH

N OT ALL GROWTH IS GOOD. REVENUE AND INCOME growth that use more resources than they generate do not advance economic profit and do not create value. This profitless growth is a constant source of misunderstanding between executives who have worked hard to produce the growth and investors who only see value destroyed. A few years ago at an investor meeting, the CFO of a major oil company was arguing that his company should be valued as much as the leader in the field. Armed with a list of twelve metrics, he showed his firm outperforming the competitor on ten of the twelve, including revenue growth, reserve replacement, and income growth; the only two where his firm lagged were return on investment and growth in ROI. Investors were astounded that the executive didn't know that without better ROI, the other metrics didn't matter.

You can avoid the trap of profitless growth by remaining focused on ROI, and by not taking a top-down approach to improving it. Most executives devote too much effort to increasing their profits, the numerator of the equation. However, in my observing dozens of companies striving to improve their value, I've learned a secret shared by moneymakers:

When managing ROI, focus on the I.

Because so few focus on the denominator, minimizing the capital and assets that go into your business is the surer way to improve your returns. Moneymakers make every investment dollar produce the maximum return. Let's look at some of the strategies they use to boost their ROI.

MINIMIZE THE MONEY THAT GOES IN

Southwest Airlines, in its first three decades, was possibly the best-managed company of all time. It invented a better mousetrap in a cutthroat, mature, capital-intensive industry. Though many factors contributed to the company's success—its warm culture and famed employee relations, low prices, and frequent flights—the company's greatest value edge lies in making its investment dollars work harder than its competitors'. On any given day Southwest's planes spend 50 percent more time flying passengers than do those of Delta, United, and other full-service competitors. Consequently, Southwest effectively has 1.5 planes for the same cost as its competitors' one.

The people at Southwest make their assets work harder than competitors' by substantially reducing the time its planes sit unproductively on the ground. While most competitors' planes spend an hour (or more) between flights parked at airport gates, Southwest turns its planes around in twenty-five minutes. To achieve this feat, *everything* at the airline supports the overarching goal of reducing ground time. Southwest serves only peanuts and sodas because that simplifies the unloading and loading of food service containers, a time-consuming ground activity. No seats are assigned, so passengers arrive early at gates to be in the best possible boarding group. Passengers board and seat themselves more quickly because they have to snag seats before someone else does. The airline flies primarily from secondary airports, because they are less crowded and have shorter takeoff lines.

Though Southwest's secret is simple to describe—improve airplane productivity by reducing ground time—implementation requires enormous discipline and focus. Every operational detail is judged based on how it impacts turnaround times. Whenever one of the full-service airlines starts a low-fare competitor to Southwest, it always does it with a twist: "We'll be low fare, but we'll offer assigned seating" or "We'll sell meals for purchase on the plane." However, these twists generally doom the upstarts. They require additional ground time and reduce asset productivity. For instance, in 2003, shortly after Delta launched its low-fare subsidiary Song, I was traveling through an airport and observed a couple Song planes at their gates. Looking at the posted information, I saw the planes were at the gates more than an hour before departure. I knew then that Song would have no meaningful competitive impact on Southwest.

Most people attribute Walmart's success to its low prices, but the company's breakthrough was devising a logistics system that reduced its investment in inventory. CEO Sam Walton then passed some of those savings on to customers, spurring the growth that built the world's largest retailer. Cross-docking—whereby employees at distribution centers break down suppliers' single-product truckload shipments and reassemble them into multiple-product truckloads that head to the stores daily—reduced Walmart's inventory investment and expense by counterintuitively *adding* an additional layer of handling and labor. Since replenishments arrived frequently, local stores could shrink their safety stocks (extra inventory kept as a cushion in case of unexpected demand). Suppliers could also ship more often to larger, consolidated distribution centers. So powerful was this innovation that Walmart eclipsed Sears and Kmart as America's largest retailer in the 1990s. The incumbents' superior retail locations, name recognition, and other advantages were not sharp enough to offset the power of Walmart's low-investment value edge.

Over the years, successful retailers have generated exceptional value by turning stocks faster, thus reducing the investment and obsolescence risk inherent in inventory. As I mentioned in the last chapter, Lowe's overtook its rival The Home Depot with a more efficient inventory system. The clothing retailers Gap, Benetton, and Zara achieved their initial successes through shortening product cycles to minimize inventory investment.

Then there is Toyota. By working closely with suppliers and redesigning its processes, Toyota reduced the stocks of components that its factories held from several days' supply to several hours'. This "just in time" manufacturing process is the company's biggest value edge and another demonstration of how minimizing investment can propel a company's success.

As commonsensical as all this is, you probably don't do it. If you're like most managers, you focus on creating breakthrough products or services or otherwise increasing sales. Or you look for product line extensions or acquisitions. Or you plan and execute innovative growth strategies. There's nothing wrong with any of these activities—and there's a lot right about them if done effectively—but as satisfying as they may be for you as a leader, they can lead you, particularly if you're not careful with investments, into the trap of profitless growth. If your strategies are growing the top line but are not improving or even diminishing ROI, it's wasted effort. Instead, consider concentrating on reducing investment as an alternative or adjunct to your growth strategy. As an added bonus, powerful business innovations often flow from these reductions.

Inside Information

- Judge operations not only on profitability but also on the investments required to produce those profits.

- Be disciplined about reducing investment levels in your business; evaluate all changes based not only on the additional profits they produce but also on the resources they require. Consider when *not* making an improvement will benefit ROI more than making it will.

- Think creatively about ways to tamp down capital. Ruthlessly reduce time and expenses that customers don't see.

STANDARDIZE, STANDARDIZE, STANDARDIZE

Conventional airlines tend to follow conventional thinking: they maintain fleets of different aircraft types so they can deploy the best airplane for each flight's "mission." They use smaller planes for short-haul flights and 747s on longer or more popular routes. When analyzed flight by flight, this approach appears to maximize efficiency. However, the efficiency gains achieved by tailoring each flight are more than offset by the additional operational complexity and investment required companywide. Tailoring equipment and processes to specific situations costs more in the long run; greater effort is often required to devise the just-right solution than to work with a standardized one. A custom-tailored suit fits better, but it costs more (in time and money) than one you pick off the rack. The same principle holds true in business. As useful as it might be to individualize your equipment and processes to each situation, it's a luxury you cannot afford.

Rigorous standardization is another technique that Southwest has used to reduce the "I" in its ROI equation. The airline flies only one type of equipment, Boeing 737s, whereas competitors fly many different models. Using 737s for both its busiest and least popular routes, for its transcontinental flights and its short hops, Southwest does not operate each flight at maximum efficiency. The 737s on less popular routes fly relatively empty. In fact, Southwest's load factor (the percentage of seats occupied per flight) is a full 10 percentage points below that of American Airlines, which operates twelve different airplane types.

Airline executives, like most businesspeople, have an efficiency mind-set. They don't want to transport empty seats. They believe that eliminating waste in each part of their business will maximize the efficiency of the whole. But this is often not true. Suboptimal solutions in individual segments can frequently deliver a simpler and more efficient whole.

At Southwest, spare parts inventories can be kept low because all the planes use the same parts. Pilot training is simplified and costs less. The airline also benefits from greater flexibility when problems occur, as anyone who has suffered through being rebooked onto a new plane with fewer seats will appreciate. Furthermore, standardizing equipment facilitates faster turnaround times when planes are at the gate. So although the plane for an individual trip may be suboptimal, the networkwide savings far outweigh this inefficiency. Despite flying with 10 percent more empty seats, Southwest's operating margin was 8 percent in 2007, double American's 4 percent margin.

Achieving the benefits of standardization requires discipline and the fortitude to work with individually suboptimal solutions. At the energy and petrochemical giant Exxon Mobil, discipline is a hallmark of the company. One cannot read its financial reports or attend its analyst meetings without hearing the word repeatedly. Its prodigious discipline enables Exxon to standardize effectively, reduce investments and expenses, and achieve some of the best long-term returns in its business. In capital spending, the company's mantra is "Design once, build multiple." This credo extends from drilling platforms to processing plants. For its Kizomba project off the coast of West Africa, Exxon has built three drilling platforms from the same design, and in Qatar, it is constructing its third liquefied natural gas (LNG) plant from the same plans. Not only does reusing plans save on design time, but construction is more efficient because builders don't need to reinvent the wheel each time.

Exxon extends the standardization discipline to its operations and processes as well. Its "retail-site operating initiative" starts by measuring productivity at its gas stations. It then standardizes systemwide on the most cost-effective practices. As a result, Exxon no longer develops individualized designs for each retail site. Instead it has created and implements a handful of off-the-shelf designs (allowing a constrained set of options for different situations). The retail initiative also standardizes how the stations are run, an effort that Exxon started in 2003 and that has saved the company more than $100 million a year. Moreover, this effort hasn't restricted innovation but has actually accelerated the deployment of improvements. For instance, the initiative has led Exxon to become a leader in self-service locations.

Understanding the larger benefits of standardization across its company has been a boon for Exxon Mobil. In 2005–06, when a boom in oil exploration was driving costs up by 50 to 60 percent for most oil companies, Exxon experienced an increase of only 10 percent due to the discipline and cost advantages that standardization provided.

Inside Information

- Be disciplined to improve the productivity of your capital investments and your operations. Don't reinvent the wheel every time a variation crops up.

- Accept that the cost of standardized solutions is often suboptimization in individual situations. Learn to work with standardization, because it is almost always the right decision for the business.

- Standardize whenever possible, and even sometimes when it doesn't seem possible, to reduce investment and, as an added benefit, improve flexibility.

OTHER PEOPLE'S MONEY

Entrepreneurs are regularly counseled to use someone else's money when starting their businesses. This is good advice for even the largest corporations. Tapping other people's money allows you to spread your capital across more opportunities. It brings in partners whose success is aligned with yours and who will therefore provide information and perspective to run your operation better. Despite the benefits, executives often shy away from tapping into others' capital to maximize their own returns.

They worry about the loss of control, but, as illustrated in chapter 2, having independent, financially involved partners can spur better performance in addition to increasing your returns through lower investment levels.

Franchisee relationships are a classic example of how you can tap into other people's money to grow your business and enhance your returns. Typically, franchisees are small-business owners who have more limited opportunities, fewer funds available, and different capital return requirements than larger public organizations do. As a result the partnerships are a "win-win," with both sides improving on the returns available to them otherwise.

Franchisee relationships aren't appropriate for all businesses, but other options exist for capitalizing on other people's money. Genentech has become a leading biotechnology firm in large part by being a paragon of partnering; it accesses others' capital, resources, and even ideas. Its founders, Bob Swanson and Herb Boyer, started a collaborative approach early on because Genentech's resources were very limited. On the advice of their venture capital backer, Tom Perkins of Kleiner Perkins, they subcontracted out their initial research. They recognized that the trade-off—sharing trade secrets with "outsiders" versus having to invest significant amounts of time and money by keeping research in-house—was worth it. The partnering worked; Genentech became one of the first profitable biotechs and the first to go public. Swanson and Boyer continued to follow Kleiner's advice, even when capital became readily available. Partnering is a core tenet of Genentech's corporate culture. It collaborates with other biotech companies, pharmaceutical firms, the National Institutes of Health (NIH) and other government institutions, hospitals, nonprofits, and even individual researchers through postdoctorate fellowship and reagent supply programs. These collaborations have contributed immeasurably to Genentech's success. Moreover, the benefits are not a one-way street. Genentech's partners have also gained enormously.

Genentech's work with the Cystic Fibrosis Foundation illustrates how it has creatively tapped other people's cash and resources to generate better returns for itself and benefits for its partners. The partnership came at a particularly crucial time for Genentech; in 1987, it suffered a crisis when an expected FDA approval did not come through. Shortly thereafter, the company began work with the Cystic Fibrosis Foundation on a drug to alleviate the symptoms of cystic fibrosis (CF), a rare genetic disorder in which mucus builds up in the lungs of sufferers. An enzyme from cows, DNase, had been shown many years earlier to thin the mucus that plagues CF sufferers, but the bovine enzyme caused an immune response in people. Genentech scientists envisioned artificially producing a modified enzyme that did not trigger the adverse side effect.

Yet the company could not justify developing artificial DNase by itself because the market opportunity was too small. CF affects only 80,000 people worldwide; developing a drug and bringing it to market typically costs half a billion dollars. However, partnering with the CF Foundation made the economics work; the foundation provided financial support and assistance in setting up trials. Providing capital to Genentech enabled the foundation to achieve its goal of alleviating the suffering of those afflicted with CF by capitalizing on the biotech firm's resources and expertise.

The partnership was a great success. Genentech developed a product, Pulmozyme, and received FDA approval for it in less than half the usual time required for drug development. Because the partners shared the expense, they could afford to fund the development and approval process aggressively even when obstacles were encountered. In the midst of the human trials, the FDA requested a meaningful increase in the number of patients participating in the trial. With its partner, Genentech was able to easily locate additional trial participants and bear the increased expense, so it readily agreed to the FDA's request. In December 1993, the FDA approved the drug. In its first year of sales, Pulmozyme represented 15 percent of Genentech's product sales and 11 percent of its overall revenues. Genentech's ROI also certainly benefited from the shared cost of development and the shorter time to market. Overall, in 1994, Genentech's net income more than doubled on a modest (20 percent) increase in net assets.

ProLogis, a real estate investment trust (REIT) specializing in warehouses, has found its own way to access other people's money. As with Genentech, business challenges compelled the company to think creatively about finding capital. REITs, in exchange for highly favorable tax treatment, pay out 90 percent of their net income to shareholders every year. They can retain almost no operating profits to purchase or build new properties. Consequently, for REITs to grow, they need to raise fresh capital; typically they do this by issuing additional common equity or preferred stock. Yet in 1999, REIT stocks experienced a market swoon; at the bottom, REITs were trading as low as 80 percent of the value of their net assets, making raising additional equity a nonstarter.

Yet ProLogis, eyeing market opportunities, did not want to just wait out the downturn. So CEO Dane Brooksher, Chief Investment Officer Irving Lyons, and their team found an alternative method to access the capital they needed: they turned to pension funds, insurance companies, and other institutions that have money to invest. ProLogis's first fund was a fifty-fifty joint venture with the New York State Common Retirement Fund, which manages about $130 billion to fund pensions for state and local government employees in New York. ProLogis transferred

eighty buildings and some land into the fund. NYSCRF contributed cash. About a month later, the REIT launched a second
fund, the ProLogis European Properties Fund, which partnered
with other pension funds and insurance companies on twelve
properties in Europe.

These ventures were a success for all the partners. The fun-
ders got steady, predictable cash flows from the ProLogis properties to fund the pension checks and insurance claims they
had to pay out, as well as the diversification the real estate assets added to their portfolios. For its part, ProLogis became
largely self-funding, no longer needing to tap the equity markets in order to grow. Maintaining a management contract for
the facilities, the REIT continued to earn revenues from them.
More to the point, ProLogis managers could concentrate their
own capital on the riskiest but highest-return portions of the
business: designing, constructing, and leasing up new warehouse facilities. The partnerships have been so successful that,
eight years after launching the first fund, ProLogis manages seventeen funds with $22 billion in assets.

GIVEN THE ATTRACTIVENESS of using other people's money to
improve returns, why don't more businesses do it? Consider
why you may have not done it—or done enough—by reviewing
the following list of reasons typically offered for not using other
people's money:

- It has to be too good to be true.
- I don't want to lose control.
- Partnerships never work.
- My operations will be too complicated with partners
  poking their noses into what I'm doing.

- Why should I share my good returns?
- Partners will steal my trade secrets.

There are all sorts of excuses for why it's impossible to bring in outside funding. Generally they boil down to worries about the additional operational risks and complexity. I understand why managers worry about these risks and the additional work, but in reality, the rewards in most cases far outweigh whatever chances you think you're taking.

Force yourself to think creatively and broadly about financial partnering. For both Genentech and ProLogis, their partnerships worked because their partners had different goals and return requirements. Synergies result when you open your mind to partnership possibilities. And they can occur at all sizes and levels of businesses. For instance, in 2001, Sean McManus, Tony Petitti, and others running CBS Sports asked corporate for extrabudgetary funding to lease new equipment to produce the Saturday football games in high definition (HD). CEO Sumner Redstone, COO Mel Karmazin, and CBS president Leslie Moonves agreed that an HD telecast was a good idea but weren't willing to fund the extra expense. They told the division managers they would have to find someone else to foot the bill. This response didn't stop CBS Sports. Instead, McManus and his team went to work and convinced Thomson Consumer Electronics to pay for the additional HD broadcast costs in exchange for on-air promotion as the HD sponsor. Both sides benefited handsomely, and over the years CBS Sports has successfully secured numerous partners to fund its expansion into HD.

Many times, you don't tap into other people's money because you don't consider all the options. To that end, here are eight possibilities that might work for your business:

1. **Small businesses.** Many individuals want to run their own businesses, but with help from a larger organization. Franchisees, bottlers, and dealers are prime examples. Individuals' return requirements are generally lower. This source also offers the added benefit of sweat equity and local expertise. Can you carve out smaller, localized portions of your business?

2. **Governments.** With goals to benefit the commonweal, government entities do not assess the deployment of capital by the same return metrics as most companies do. Thus, there are win-win opportunities. The best examples are research funding—Genentech and other biotech firms have collaborated with the NIH and accessed government funds. How does your business create value? Do any of your activities align with voters' priorities or governmental goals?

3. **Nonprofits.** Again, their priorities are not cash returns. Like the Cystic Fibrosis Foundation, many of these organizations have cash to spend to achieve their mission, and nonprofits pursue a wide variety of missions. If your business creates societal good in some way, what not-for-profit would make a natural partner?

4. **Pension funds, endowments, and other institutional fund investors.** The recent trend among these large asset managers has been to diversify from traditional asset classes like stocks and bonds. ProLogis tapped into this. Do you have distinct assets or operations that others can own with you? Do these assets produce reliable cash flow, or are they ventures that are extremely risky but offer an enormous payout in success? Asset managers interested in both types of businesses exist. Recent examples of assets funded by institu-

tional investors have included timberlands, oil fields, shipping containers, and film libraries.

5. **Wealthy individuals.** Individuals' personal interests often guide where they invest their dollars. Filmmakers have successfully solicited sizable investments from affluent people who were attracted to the glamour of the entertainment business and access to stars. A medical device firm raised start-up money from individuals whose lives had been impacted by the illness the start-up was targeting.

6. **Sidelines.** Other organizations may pay you for work that is adjacent to your main endeavor. Pixar worked on commercials to pay the bills while it was developing its first full-length feature. Genentech's cystic fibrosis drug was never going to be a blockbuster, but it enabled the company to get its momentum back. (But use your judgment when pursuing sidelines to make sure you aren't spread too thin.)

7. **Other businesses.** Do you have assets that cost you relatively little that you can trade for cash or for something you need? CBS exchanged promotional support for funding of its HD initiative. You don't have to be a media company to offer promotional support. Starbucks has promoted movies in its stores, which has cost the coffeehouse chain little but allowed it to negotiate a participation in the films' profits.

8. **Customers and suppliers.** The timing of when customers pay you and when you pay them can result in substantial contributions to the capital available to fund your business. Can you encourage customers to pay, at least partially, up front? Can you delay payments to your vendors without having an undue impact on the relationships?

When using other people's money, do not abuse the privilege. The partnerships that provide access to this money must be approached responsibly, and opportunities for one side to "pick the other's pocket" must be resisted. Certainly ProLogis might have been tempted to put all its underperforming warehouses into its partnerships, and hold back the best assets to own exclusively. But over time potential partners would figure this out and withdraw their capital. Even in the best of circumstances, partners sometimes disagree on the split of profits. Don't let this risk dissuade you, but do take pains to treat your partners fairly.

Inside Information

- Think creatively about where your business can tap into outside pools of capital. What organizations adjacent to your business may share your goals and be willing to partner with you?

- Understand your partners' needs (which may differ from your own) and find ways to meet them. Seek nonmonetary opportunities to help your partners.

- Resist the temptation to "pick your partners' pockets." If you are larger than your partners, eschew using your size to force them to accept unfair deals. Sharing the upside with your partners (in line with their own needs) will improve your returns over the long haul by providing continuing access to other people's capital.

High Margin Is Not High Return

Which has better returns on investment:

- Clear Channel Communications, which owns TV, radio, and outdoor assets and has an operating margin of 24 percent, or Omnicom Group, an advertising agencies holding company, with a 13 percent operating margin?
- Union Pacific, the nation's largest railroad operator, which has a 21 percent operating margin, or C.H. Robinson Worldwide, a freight broker that places cargo on trucks and railroads and generates a 7 percent operating margin?

Perhaps surprisingly, the lower-margin companies have the superior returns. Omnicom's return on invested capital is 21 percent, compared to Clear Channel's 6 percent. Likewise, Union Pacific earns an 8 percent return on its invested capital, whereas C.H. Robinson generates 33 percent. Confusing high margin with high return has caused more than one otherwise savvy leader to fall into the trap of profitless growth. Though margin is easier to impact in the near term, in the long run, return on investment is what counts.

Distinguishing between high margins and high returns helped turn around IBM in the early 1990s. When Lou Gerstner joined as CEO in 1993, Big Blue was struggling. Revenues had declined two years in a row and were poised to fall again in 1993. Sales of high-profit mainframes were dropping as personal computers became popular. Earnings fell in 1992 and 1993 as the company restructured and laid off thousands of workers to recalibrate its cost base to the new reality. Some pundits even questioned whether IBM would survive.

The computing giant not only lived but thrived by embracing the services business. Previously services had been largely an afterthought, viewed as necessary extras to support the more lucrative mainframe business. Services' margins paled next to the 38 percent gross margins of the hardware division. Nonetheless, Gerstner and his team vastly expanded IBM's consulting, integration, and outsourcing work. During Gerstner's tenure from 1993 to 2001, services accounted for 80 percent of the company's revenue growth.

Expanding services came with a cost; over the first five years of Gerstner's tenure, IBM's margins stagnated. Though services provided the company with plenty of revenue growth, they dragged down its overall operating margin. Shareholders generally devalue stocks of companies that experience negative shifts in the mix of divisional profits like this, and IBM in its annual reports and communications with shareholders was almost apologetic about its struggling operating margins.

Nonetheless, IBM's stock soared during this era. An increasing proportion of services negatively impacted gross margins, but it also reduced the investment necessary to generate those margins. Largely people- and information-based activities, services required far fewer assets than did IBM's traditional manufacturing businesses. As a result, returns on investment increased, and the improvements in this measure swamped the negative impact of lower operating margins. IBM's stock price more than tripled while the broader market only doubled. Understanding the importance of returns and capital requirements, rather than focusing solely on margins and profits, enabled IBM to grow both its returns and its stock price.

Inside Information

- Concentrate on high returns, no matter how tempting high operating margins might be.

- Accept that high-return businesses can generate low margins. Because many other companies are fooled into avoiding such businesses, high-return businesses often have less competition.

THE HIGHEST-RETURN ASSET: KNOWLEDGE

Low-margin, high-return businesses almost always capitalize on knowledge. IBM's service business is a consulting/integration business in which Big Blue's employees leverage their knowledge of technology and products. Omnicom's ad agencies sell their people's creativity and knowledge of how to promote products. C.H. Robinson's truck brokerage thrives on its employees' knowledge of shippers who need to move their products and truckers who need to fill their trucks, especially for backhaul (i.e., if a truck is at point A and its next load is at point B, the truck has to drive from A to B anyway, so the driver will take a load for minimal payment). Finding opportunities to exploit your people's knowledge is often the easiest route to improving returns.

Knowledge management has become a buzzword at many companies, but its ability to improve ROI is still often underestimated. I've repeatedly seen businesses achieve better returns through activities that increase their knowledge base. Contrary to what you might think, my investor colleagues and I don't view knowledge management as a "soft" tool. We have seen how effective programs produce better returns; we know that in this information age, knowledge is more than power—it's money. At IBM the services business gave the company a direct view into all their clients' needs. To shift services from an activity that supported other IBM businesses to a business in its own right, Gerstner and his team decided to support competitors' products when they were the best solution. IBM's consultants helped their clients solve all sorts of problems, often problems that no one had seen before. They developed a comprehensive view of the information technology market and how it was evolving; IBM's leaders then used that knowledge to steer the firm. As a result, IBM became an early proponent of network computing (putting most of the intelligence on servers on the network as opposed to locally on desktop computers) and made a successful move into middleware, software that facilitated the move to network computing.

Google, the well-known search engine company, is another organization that capitalizes on its knowledge to advance its business. The company has one of the world's best business models, earning high margins and high returns from selling ads alongside its search engine results. Though the ad business is lucrative, Google's greatest asset is its free search engine. It provides a front-row seat on Internet users' online activities. Leveraging this knowledge has allowed the company to make some terrific acquisitions and avoid "not invented here" problems.

Like many others, Google recognized that video would be the next frontier of Internet content; in 2005, it started up a subsite, video.google.com, to allow users to upload video online. Earlier that year, two entrepreneurs, Chad Hurley and Steve Chen, recognized the same trend and launched their own video-sharing site, YouTube. YouTube took off while Google Video didn't. Looking at their user logs, Google observed how many more people were going to YouTube's site than to its own. Armed with this knowledge, Google didn't react defensively and pour money into its uncompetitive site. Instead the company swallowed its pride and acquired YouTube. In terms of traffic, the acquisition has been highly successful, with YouTube continuing to increase the number of users and the time they spend on the site. (Whether the YouTube acquisition will ultimately earn an adequate return on investment for Google is still undetermined, but certainly YouTube has met Google's first goal, delivering a huge audience.)

Inside Information

- Recognize how valuable your intellectual property is and how it can produce outstanding ROI due to its limited capital requirements.

- Leverage your employees' specialized knowledge to offer differentiated products for your customers and to guide how you run your business.

- Consider the value of knowledge gained when deciding which activities to pursue. Factoring in the value of market insights or other knowledge gained can make seemingly low-profit activities more attractive.

If You Don't Need It, Give It Back

As an investor, I love when companies buy back their own shares using cash on their balance sheets or adding debt when their debt levels are too low. The press and popular opinion often excoriate companies that undertake such share buybacks. Managers are accused of trying to prop up their share prices or manufacture earnings. Even august publications such as *The Wall Street Journal* report negatively on companies that have increased their debt loads to fund major share repurchases.

My professional investing colleagues and I applaud share repurchases not because they prop up share prices (short-term pops often fade) but because they reduce the investment in a company, thereby raising returns. We also appreciate that returning cash to shareholders means that it won't "burn a hole in executives' pockets." Buying back shares uses companies' financial capacity, thus limiting executives' ability to make acquisitions. Since many acquisitions—particularly big ones—fail to achieve their promised returns on investment, corporate managers who remain focused on their core business generally produce better results for shareholders. Moreover, when repurchasing their own shares, leaders are effectively buying their own business, which they understand better than any acquisition.

Henry Singleton of Teledyne pioneered corporate share repurchases in the 1970s. Not coincidentally, he is regarded as one of the best company leaders ever by many investment luminaries, including Warren Buffett of Berkshire Hathaway and Leon Cooperman of Omega Advisors, one of the longest-running hedge fund managers and previously the head of Goldman Sachs Asset Management for twenty-five years. Singleton started Teledyne in 1960 and successfully steered it for more than thirty years. While Singleton had numerous accomplishments and offered the rare combination of a leader with exemplary skills in both operational and financial management, one of his most crowning achievements was his use of share repurchases to raise returns for shareholders. From 1972 to 1984, while a bear market was depressing the company's stock price, Singleton bought Teledyne stock from shareholders through eight formal offerings. Altogether these tenders reduced Teledyne's shares outstanding by 90 percent.

With less investment in Teledyne and its profits split among fewer shares, Teledyne's stock rose from $6.00 a share when Singleton did his first buyback in 1972 to more than $400.00 (adjusted for splits and distributions) fifteen years later.

More recently, the truck manufacturer Paccar has generated strong returns by reducing the investment in its business through share repurchases, regular dividends, and special dividends. Best known for its Peterbilt and Kenworth brands, Paccar is a century-old company that builds medium- and heavy-duty trucks. In 2004, sales rose by 40 percent as a strong economy and upcoming stricter EPA emissions regulations encouraged truckers to increase their equipment purchases. With strong sales generating strong cash flow, CEO Mark Pigott and his team initiated a share repurchase program, in addition to their regular and special dividends. Repurchases accelerated in 2005 and 2006. In 2007, with revenue growth slowing, the Paccar team reduced the share repurchase program but continued to return cash to shareholders by increasing the special dividend.

Paccar not only repurchased shares but it also retired those shares, rather than create a bank of shares available for reissue. Paccar returned $2.1 billion to shareholders from the beginning of 2004 through the end of 2006, a period when the company made $3.5 billion in net income. Discipline and judicious use of the capital that it did deploy helped Paccar produce returns on equity of 36 percent, and its stock price rose by 71 percent over the three years.

Returning unneeded capital is always a positive, but what really distinguishes Henry Singleton and Mark Pigott is how savvy they were in deploying their capital. In the 1960s, when his stock was flying, Henry Singleton did not buy back Teledyne shares. Instead, he used his high-priced currency (i.e., stock) to purchase companies. He bought more than a hundred during that period. Only when the bear market took the company's stock price to levels well below its intrinsic value did he aggressively repurchase shares. In 2004, with Paccar's stock price around $15.00 and a big jump in business on the horizon, Mark Pigott accelerated share repurchases. In 2007, with the business entering a slowdown and its stock in the mid-$50s, the company shifted from share repurchases to special dividends.

It seems as obvious as ABC (or ROI), yet many executives keep too much capital in their enterprises. Since it's impossible to know exactly how much investment your business will require, it's tempting to maintain a generous cash cushion. Though this cushion may comfort you, it will also impede your business from achieving its full potential, and not just in financial terms. If you've ever been through a leveraged buyout (LBO), you have experienced this principle firsthand. When you squeeze every extra penny to make interest payments, you quickly learn which expenditures really matter to your business and which do not. My investing colleagues and I see repeatedly that:

Running tight on capital forces astute decision making.

Limited capital requires you to approach your business more creatively and to devise capital-light solutions. ProLogis developed its high-return funds strategy in response to the capital constraints of the 1999 REIT bear market. Southwest Airlines perfected the twenty-five-minute plane turnaround, and Toyota Motor Corporation developed just-in-time inventory because they couldn't afford anything else in their early years. Though you may worry that good ideas will languish because you can't find the dollars they need, I've seen the opposite: good ideas can attract funding from all sorts of unconventional sources. Even though the CFO might say, "There's no budget for that," superlative concepts generate sufficient enthusiasm that organizations find ways to fund them. Thus, there's no need to maintain a "safety stock" of capital. Just as businesses have benefited from moving to just-in-time inventories, you can achieve superior returns by using just-in-time capital. The capital constraints of the post-2008 environment will undoubtedly bear this out as businesses become more innovative in devising capital-light solutions and moneymakers find ways to distinguish themselves.

Inside Information

- Give back excess capital to supercharge your ROI.

- Recognize that you can probably run the business with less capital cushion than you think. It just requires some creative thinking.

CHARGE IT

Many executives have a tendency to hoard capital because it seems costless. Moreover, adding assets is often the easiest way to hit revenue and earnings growth targets. If you have two machines turning out widgets rather than one, it's likely that you'll have more revenue and income. But if the annual cost of the second machine is equal to the additional income it generates, all you've achieved is profitless growth.

Consider your own attitude toward growth. Perhaps you have introduced new products, orchestrated a headline-making acquisition, or opened a series of new plants—whatever strategies you have executed, your efforts resulted in increased profits.

Naturally, you expect your accomplishments to be acknowledged by your shareowners.

However, as I noted earlier, these efforts don't create value if there isn't an equally impressive return on your investments. It's easy to lose sight of this fact if you don't interact regularly with shareholders or measure the cost of the capital you use. To avoid falling into the trap of profitless growth, follow these recommendations:

- Measure the net investment in your business. How much equipment, working capital, and other assets does it use?
- Calculate the cost of capital in your business. Take an average of your cost of debt and your cost of equity weighted for the amount of each that funds your business. If you don't know your cost of equity, use 15 percent. If you don't have access to your borrowing costs or percentage of debt to equity, use 10 percent as your cost of capital.
- Charge yourself and your people for the assets you use when calculating your business's profits. If the people to whom you report don't calculate a capital charge, suggest that they credit 10 percent of any investment dollars saved to your P&L.*
- Include this capital charge in bonus payment calculations whenever possible.

---

* If your operation typically requires $1,000.00 in capital equipment to operate, a typical capital charge included in your P&L would be $100.00, or 10 percent. If you can double your profit with only $400.00 in additional equipment, then you deserve only a $140.00 charge to your P&L if the capital is explicitly expensed. If it isn't, you deserve a $60.00 credit to your P&L for using assets more efficiently. Likewise, if you maintain your profit but use only $500.00 worth of equipment (perhaps by stretching the useful life), you deserve a $50.00 credit if capital is not explicitly charged.

This quick process will help you institute a charge that makes you and your people aware of the assets you use, which is more important than being precise about how much to charge.

By including a charge for assets used when determining its bonuses, the office furniture manufacturer Herman Miller has focused the attention of everyone from senior managers to factory workers. With its people acutely aware of the cost of its assets, the manufacturer has achieved substantial improvements in asset utilization and waste reduction. Shareholders noticed its profitable growth, and the stock price doubled over five years from the end of 2002 to the end of 2007.

Dayton Hudson, the predecessor of Target Corporation, devised its own asset-usage measure called Return Against the Curve in the early 1980s. It assessed a capital charge (the curve) for each of its stores. The leadership team charged different rates for each of its retail concepts (the bookseller B. Dalton, the traditional Dayton Hudson department stores, and Target) to reflect the life-cycle characteristics of each (B. Dalton stores achieved maximum profitability quickly, whereas Target stores started more slowly but then had longer periods of growth). Instituting these metrics helped the company to focus on where it generated returns, with low-return spending cut quickly. It also led ultimately to the company's disposing of the challenged B. Dalton and department store businesses. Focusing on its highest-return concept enabled Target to outpace its rival Walmart from 2003 to 2007.

Inside Information

- Explicitly account for capital used in your business; this is a crucial management task.

(continued)

- Devise a charge for capital appropriate to the characteristics of your business, but don't overthink it. The charge is more important than the exact amount.

- Consider other scarce resources your company possesses and whether you should charge for their usage.

•   •   •

THE PATH TO PROFITABLE GROWTH

Return on investment is what drives value creation (and stock appreciation) over the long run. Unfortunately, accounting standards and conventional practices induce many managers (and sometimes investors) to focus on earnings per share, revenue growth, and other components of ROI without focusing on the whole. In particular, the amount of investment required to generate returns is often underappreciated. Thus, lowering investment is a much easier way to improve ROI and avoid value-destroying traps.

To achieve profitable growth, consider the following questions:

- Do you pay attention to the capital deployed in your business? Do you measure and charge people for the capital they use?

- Have you thought creatively about how you can reduce the investment in your business while maintaining or even improving your operations?

- Whom can you partner with to reduce your capital needs? Have you adequately considered their needs to ensure that it will be a good, long-term relationship?

- Where can you standardize to improve capital efficiency? Have you fought the urge to tailor solutions for every situation when a good-enough solution that works for all situations will provide overall higher returns?

- Have you confused high margins with high returns? Are there opportunities in your business to reduce margins but increase returns?

- What specialized knowledge can you deploy to earn additional returns? Are you shying away from knowledge-based businesses due to the difficulty of managing people even though these often have the highest returns?

- What assets or capital in your business are not necessary? Why not give them back? Can you find a way to get credit for the capital you haven't used?

CHAPTER 4

DON'T BE A CUSTOMER FANATIC

L ISTENING TO YOUR CUSTOMERS IS OVERRATED. Do your customers know more about your operation than you do? Are they better able to predict future trends than your experts are? Do they ever say they want one thing but their buying behavior demonstrates that they want something else? And what customer doesn't want your offerings at lower prices?

Many organizations confuse listening to their customers with paying attention to their behavior; the latter tells you much more than the former. Though you certainly need to understand what your customer is saying, my experience with moneymakers shows that asking customers about your business, particularly new-product innovations, often leads to mistakes. Many of the most successful companies rely on their own insights and instincts much more than customer feedback, which can be short-sighted and tradition-bound. These high-return operations don't ignore customers, but they aren't slaves to the feedback they receive. Ironically, moneymakers serve customers better by not listening to what they ask for. Let's look at some of these

successful "nonlisteners" and the alternatives they've implemented to serve customers better.

YOUR CUSTOMER KNOWS NOTHING (ABOUT YOUR SYSTEMS, PROCESSES, AND CULTURE)

Illinois Central (IC), a freight railroad running from Chicago to
the Gulf of Mexico, radically improved the economics of its
business *and* the service it offered clients by ignoring what its
clients were asking for. In the usual relationship between railroads and their clients—generally factories, mines, and other
producers of bulk products that need to be moved long
distances—clients call the railroad to pick up loaded cars as soon
as they are ready. The railroad, being responsive to its clients,
picks up the cars as quickly as possible.

Let's say the cars are going from a chemical plant on the Gulf
Coast to a factory near Springfield, Illinois. The plant finishes
loading the chemicals into tank cars on Monday and calls the
railroad for pickup. The railroad sends a locomotive to collect
the cars, taking them to the nearest rail yard for holding until it
has enough cars going north to justify running a train. While
the cars are in the yard, they are usually shuffled around a few
times as crews pull other cars off the same holding tracks for
trains headed elsewhere. Finally, on Wednesday, the railroad
has enough Illinois-bound cars and the yard crew assembles the
long-haul train. If all goes well, the crew finds the cars picked
up on Monday and doesn't have to move too many other cars to
get at them. Running the railroad in this manner is highly responsive to clients but requires great investment in manpower
and track capacity.

In 1989, after it was taken private by the buyout firm the
Prospect Group, Illinois Central couldn't afford the investment

in tracks or people that this standard operating procedure required. To service its enormous debt load, CEO Ed Moyers had most of IC's double track and excess yard capacity ripped up. This move reduced long-term maintenance costs and provided salable assets to raise cash, but it also decreased the railroad's flexibility and capacity.

IC had no choice but to take the risky path of being unresponsive to its customers. Now when a client called on Monday to say cars were ready, IC replied that it would send a locomotive on Wednesday to pick them up, no doubt angering clients who felt the railroad wasn't listening to them. On Wednesday the railroad picked up the cars, took them to the yard, connected them to the train going to Illinois, and away they went. The cars arrived at their destination earlier than they would have using the more "customer-responsive" approach because the yard didn't have to move them as often. Moreover, IC reduced the odds of misplacing or forgetting cars, thus providing customers with better service.

Illinois Central endured some customer criticism in the short run to achieve better client service in the long run. Understanding its own operation (the cost and potential for error inherent in additional yard time) enabled the railroad to create improved service. It could also be argued that IC understood its clients' needs better than the clients themselves. Though clients may have yelled at IC about not taking their cars away when asked, IC recognized that the clients' main goal was getting their cars to their destinations when promised and removing cars from their premises quickly was less important. By ignoring clients' requests to pick up their cars immediately, IC was able to offer a service that met their real priorities. In the process, it also attained the lowest operating ratio (i.e., the best margins) in the business and the best return on capital, because it engaged in less unproductive work and maintained less surplus track. After

becoming a publicly traded company again in 1990, IC was acquired by the Canadian National Railway Company in 1998.
The IC operating system was implemented across the larger
railroad and produced another substantial reduction in operating costs and improvement in service for clients.

In the late 1990s, well after IC's approach had produced remarkable and well-known gains, I found myself in the offices of
a different railroad company. The company was just recovering
from gridlocking its entire network, which had caused substantial outcry from clients and politicians. To improve its operations, the chief operating officer explained, the company had
entered into an agreement with selected clients in the Houston
Gulf Coast region to pick up cars from their chemical plants
only when it could build a train's worth and send them directly
to the Northeast. Though the railroad's executives expected
pushback from clients, they were pleasantly surprised by how
quickly clients (most likely, they were also clients of Illinois
Central) grasped the new operating plan's value. The COO was
thrilled at how well the new approach was working.

"Hallelujah," I thought to myself, "they've finally figured it
out." Excited by the potential for improved service and profits if
the company reduced its unproductive effort of storing and
shuffling cars, I asked how he was going to implement these
new practices across the entire railroad. After some hemming
and hawing, he explained that the chemical coast was an iso-
lated opportunity and the entire railroad's operations were far
too complex to roll out this plan. Shortly after that meeting, I
sold the company's stock, disappointed that the company wasn't
going to act on this huge opportunity. Perhaps its executives
feared that other clients would object to the seeming unrespon-
siveness of the new approach. Perhaps they didn't trust the evidence in front of their eyes—they refused to believe that the
new plan, which had been implemented so successfully on the

chemical coast, could be implemented in other areas. As well as they knew their business, they were afraid to abandon traditional operating practices and potentially upset customers.

The art of not listening to customers effectively requires that you:

Understand what your customers need rather than what they're asking for.

Illinois Central knew its customers wanted on-time, fast delivery, not just quick pickups. The customers asked for quick pickups because they assumed that the sooner their freight was taken away, the sooner it would arrive. Most customers, lacking knowledge of (and frankly interest in) their suppliers' operations, focus on the obvious "solution" rather than the right solution. The most effective "nonlisteners" meld a sophisticated understanding of their customers' true requirements with a thorough knowledge of their own operations.

Boeing has been highly responsive to its commercial airliner customers and suffered the consequences. It offers customers a wide variety of options when purchasing airplanes, everything from class configuration and paint colors to where lavatories and galleys are located. Customers take full advantage of what Boeing offers and customize their plane layouts to their own preferences. However, this customization introduces enormous complexity into the production process. Though changing where the lavatories are located on a $50 million plane may seem like a minor alteration, the lack of standardization significantly reduces Boeing's manufacturing efficiency. Customers, not knowing the intricacies of plane production, probably don't realize the operational cost of these adjustments. Boeing's customer responsiveness encourages customers to continue to ask for customized designs. Boeing is responsive and in the process subverts customers' real need: to make planes as inexpensively as possible.

Certainly, some variations are necessary: Cathay Pacific doesn't want its planes painted the same color as United's. But do passengers choose an airline based on where the galleys are? By limiting its customers' choice in nondifferentiating items, Boeing could greatly improve the efficiency of its airplane assembly and share some of the benefit with its customers in the form of lower prices. Moneymakers know that they have to sometimes say no to customers and make astute trade-offs when the cost to their system outweighs the benefits to the client (lavatory placement) and when it doesn't (plane colors).

Before I tell you a related story about Cisco Systems, let's pause for a moment and test the premise that customers don't know much about your business. Look over the following list, and place a check next to each statement that you feel applies to customers and your business. Our customers:

- Don't understand the costs and additional work required to make changes/improvements in a product.
- Prefer the traditional way of doing things.
- Are unaware of marketplace trends that impact the types of products and services we offer.
- Don't know much about our larger organizational aspects—our culture, our processes, etc.—that affect our ability to provide customer service.
- Do not have access to the economic and market data that helps us anticipate emerging trends.
- Assume that we are making a larger profit than we are because they don't appreciate all the costs that go into the research, manufacture, and marketing of products.

I bet that you placed check marks next to at least half the statements. Doing so isn't customer bashing but recognizing that there are times when you—rather than your customer—know best.

The networking equipment provider Cisco Systems provides another example of why relying on your own judgment and not blindly listening to clients is a smart move. Cisco rolled out a program called The Network Is the Platform in 2006. The program, which had been in the planning and testing stages for years, offered products that facilitated computing over networks rather than on the desktops of individual users.

In 2002, Cisco CEO John Chambers started floating the concept of network computing when he met with clients. They generally rejected the idea. Following the dot-com bust, most of Cisco's clients were choking on excess capacity (Cisco itself took a $2.25 billion charge for excess inventory in 2001), and many were just trying to survive. They were skeptical of new innovations after so many broken promises from "new economy" companies such as Cisco. Despite customers' negativity, Chambers directed his R&D organization to develop the middleware and other products necessary to fulfill his vision of "the network is the platform." The following year he broached the concept again. Again customers rejected it, but he kept research resources focused on it. In 2006, customers were able to look forward, and Chambers finally received a positive response. Cisco quickly moved the products out of R&D. When it launched the product suite, customers were ready to buy.

I should add that Chambers told this story at an investor conference to illustrate how well Cisco listens to its customers. Positioning his remarks like this was probably Chambers's natural reflex in our customer-centric world. It illustrates that even when we don't listen to customers, we like to say we do. To his credit, Chambers listened selectively. In directing Cisco's research efforts, he understood that he had as much or more insight into the evolution of networking as his clients, who were suffering from an overinvestment hangover that colored their views of what they needed. Chambers identified the megatrend that customers missed and incrementally put resources toward it (more on that in chapter 9) so that Cisco would be prepared when the market was ready. Where Chambers did listen closely to clients was in the implementation. Cisco did not roll out products until the market was ready for them. In effect, Chambers listened, but he filtered what he heard with his own knowledge. When customers' voices and his knowledge jibed, Cisco acted swiftly.

Inside Information

- Refuse to accept the conventional wisdom that customers are always right; you know more about your business than they do.

- Make an effort to discover what your customers' customers want; when you grasp the demands your customers face, you can understand the why behind their requests and address their real requirements. Weigh the cost for you to fulfill customers' requests against the benefit they and their customers receive.

- Devise solutions for customers that address their ultimate need rather than their immediate one, even if your solutions seem to contradict customers' feedback; devise these solutions based on your superior knowledge of your business.

- Be willing to cause customers short-term pain if they gain in the long run; conduct small tests and build your way into the new operations or products incrementally.

- Listen perceptively and selectively to customers; take their objections seriously, and communicate to them why you're taking a given action; learn as much as you can from them and then consider whether you should make changes.

THE VALUE OF VALUE: RESPONDING TO CUSTOMER PRICE DEMANDS

Ask customers in any industry what they want, and most will ask for lower prices. Nothing illustrates more starkly the danger of listening too closely to your customers. Giving in on price demands often satisfies customers in the short term but risks your business in the long term. While certain situations may require you to lower prices, don't let this decision be driven by customers. My experience, as well as the experiences of other professional investors, reveals that the best metric to guide pricing decisions is internal return on investment, not the customer-centric metrics that most pundits promulgate.

Sometimes risking alienating customers with higher prices is the right strategy for both your business and your customers. I know that remaining tough on prices is difficult. It often feels as if you'll lose your customers if you don't give in to their price demands. In reality, there's a reason customers are buying your products: they often lack acceptable alternatives. You have a value edge. A competitor's price may not be significantly lower than yours. Your superior quality or differentiated offering may keep them buying even if they don't like your prices. The key is not to panic when customers start to complain that your prices are out of line, and to consider whether you are charging enough for your effort and capital and whether it's feasible that anyone else could be doing it for less.

The experience of Cypress Semiconductor Corporation shows how beneficial taking a tough line on pricing can be for you and your customers. Led by its outspoken founder CEO T. J. Rodgers, the company has thrived by innovating and finding fresh niches within the semiconductor industry. To execute this strategy, Cypress has had many "science experiments" going at any one time—small products that often weren't profitable. In summer 2005, Brad Buss joined the company as CFO and set about evaluating Cypress's product lineup. At the same time, profits were down from the previous year as less profitable products had become a larger portion of sales. Rodgers, Buss, and other senior leaders decided to raise prices on the unprofitable products, intending to drive away customers and get out of the negative-return niches. A funny thing happened, though. Many customers chose to pay the higher prices. They had no other viable alternative sources for the chips, so they bit the bullet and paid up. Cypress's revenues and profits—with some help from strong markets for its top products—improved dramatically the following year.

Cypress Semi underestimated the value it was offering to its customers. At the same time, customers didn't let on about how good a deal they were getting. In fact, if Cypress had conducted a survey of its customers, I bet a majority would have complained that prices were too high. Only through a strategy designed to kill off unprofitable products did Cypress management discover its pricing power. Heeding its customers' actions, rather than their words, led Cypress to better decisions and better profits for its employees and shareholders.

Of course, not all companies are in Cypress's situation; many operate in broader markets where customers have more choices. How do the best companies prosper in the face of their customers' requests for lower prices?

First, they remember that customers buy value, not price. Focusing on price may be an easier strategy to execute, but it usually is far less profitable. Moneymakers find all sorts of ways to focus their clients on value. The most basic is to offer additional goods that equalize the value of the competing offerings. One of the classic examples of equalizing value occurred during the early days of Southwest Airlines.

An interloper in the then-clubby airline business, Southwest began flying in 1971 with a no-frills service between three cities in Texas. The company saw itself as competing with car travel rather than with other airlines. However, it wasn't long—two years, to be exact—before the incumbent airlines, notably Braniff, responded aggressively to Southwest's low price of $26.00 per ticket. Hoping to drive the upstart out of business, Braniff dropped its fares to $13.00 on routes where the two competed. Southwest could have responded by lowering its own fares, but without other routes to subsidize the fare war, it would soon have been bankrupt. Instead it responded by offering its customers a choice: they could fly for $13.00 or they could pay the full $26.00 fare and receive a gift, generally a bottle of liquor (it was the 1970s). Chairman of the board Herb Kelleher and his team backed the offer with a major advertising campaign that painted the fare war as a battle between David and Goliath. Not only did Southwest not lose business, its traffic surged because it offered more value to its customers than Braniff did. Since many fliers were traveling on business, the cost of the airfare did not come out of their pocket, whereas the gift was something they could use personally. Moreover, by buying liquor in bulk, Southwest could get lower prices than its passengers could, so the value of the gift to customers was greater than the cost to Southwest to provide it. The promotion was a huge success, and Southwest has since become one of the United States' largest airlines. Braniff, as you probably know, has ceased to exist.

Gifts can be a surprisingly effective alternative to capitulating to customers' price demands. Estée Lauder sells cosmetics in department stores and its own free-standing shops for far more than similar products sold by Maybelline and Revlon in drugstores. Most purchases come with a "gift" that increases the value to the customer and enables Estée to maintain higher prices than its competitors'. In addition, this gifting tactic serves as an effective sampling program. If customers really like the gifted product, they may purchase it in the future.

Bloomberg L.P. is another company that sidesteps price criticism through a value-added approach. Though it's not a company studied by public-market investors, since it is privately held, it is a well-known provider of financial data and news services used on trading floors and in investors' offices. The Bloomberg service is eye-poppingly expensive, yet financial companies pay up because it includes a full package of data services and analytics, as well as high-touch customer service, for one set price. Its competitors—financial data providers such as Thomson Reuters and McGraw-Hill—offer their products in a piecemeal fashion; each separate data set has a separate cost. Bloomberg, on the other hand, charges one price whether you use one of its data streams or all of them. For a customer who uses more than two or three streams, the offering quickly becomes price-competitive.

Moreover the pricing matches the economics of the Bloomberg organization. Developing each data set requires a fixed up-front investment regardless of whether one customer or a million customers buy it. By requiring customers to buy a full suite of offerings, Bloomberg earns good margins on all the data sets it develops. Though customers are aware that Bloomberg is expensive and at times protest the cost, they also appreciate the value delivered by the all-service package—when they suddenly need a yield-curve history or some other data that they would not have purchased (because it would be used so infrequently), they are able to access it because of Bloomberg's approach. Suddenly the price does not seem so high relative to the value provided.

Inside Information

- Respond to customers' complaints about price selectively. Test the market, particularly if your profits do not cover your cost of capital, to see if you can charge more. If you can't, exit the business.

- Focus on the value you offer rather than the price you charge. Be creative about what "extras" you might provide customers to bring the value proposition into line.

- Consider your cost structure in determining additional offerings. Find products where your incremental expense is less than the value accorded to them by your customer.

MAKING THE LONG-TERM COMMITMENT

Maintaining price discipline is difficult, particularly in the short term. The pain of lost orders and share losses happens early on, while the gain of higher returns and a smaller but more profitable business usually takes time to become apparent. Yet the payoff of price fortitude is enormous, not only for you but also for your customers. When your pricing actions let your customers,

employees, and investors know that you won't chase unprofitable business, you benefit in unexpected ways.

Paccar, the $16 billion truck manufacturer I mentioned in chap-
ter 3, demonstrated the value of price discipline for customers as
well as itself when it refused to engage in a price war initiated
by its primary competitor. In 2000, as the economy softened,
Freightliner, a division of Daimler, lowered prices to stimulate demand for its trucks. Rather than match its competitor and ensure
that its profitability would fall, Paccar held its pricing and allowed
its market share in the United States and Canada to drop from
21.4 percent in 2000 to 19.6 percent in 2001. Given the weak
economy, the share loss was particularly painful; Paccar's sales in
the North American heavy-duty truck market fell by 40 percent.

Yet Paccar understood a secret that moneymakers grasp but
many others miss:

Your pricing actions tell your customers what your product is worth.

When Freightliner dropped the prices of its new trucks, the
residual values of all trucks bearing its nameplate dropped in
tandem. These secondary declines hit Freightliner customers
hard as the net worth of many owner-operators, dealers, and
fleet operators fell with the residual values. For many individual
and corporate owners, their trucks represent the bulk of their
assets. The residual value of Paccar trucks was far less affected,
since Paccar hadn't dropped the prices of its new trucks. By
holding the line on prices and ceding market share, Paccar
helped its customers in the long run, something they remem-
bered when the slowdown ended.

Paccar's pain was relatively short-lived. By mid-2001, Freightliner raised its prices, and in 2002 Paccar's market share in the

American and Canadian heavy-duty truck market rebounded to 23.6 percent. With the increased market share, Paccar's profits returned that year to the third highest level in the company's history.

Inside Information

- Recognize that though customers ask for short-term price decreases, what is more important is creating long-term value for you and them.

- Price your products and services based on how you want customers to value them; if their prices are too low, it will lower their perceived value.

- Keep the lifetime value of your product in mind when deciding whether to endure short-term pain for long-term gain.

INTANGIBLES MAKE CUSTOMER DISSATISFACTION DISAPPEAR

If customers always ask for lower prices, they almost never request intangibles. You can conduct focus groups from now until doomsday, and you're unlikely to hear someone demand better design or stronger branding. When questioned about design, most customers will refer to features of competitors' products. They don't have the time or inclination to think about unusual innovations for your product. As for branding, consumers have been saying since the 1960s, the supposed Golden Age of Television, that commercials didn't affect them. They disavow the power of marketing and branding even though plenty of evidence suggests that these efforts have an impact. If you listen to your customers regarding intangibles, you are likely to ignore them or assign them too low a priority.

Even if your customers do voice opinions on your intangibles, you can be led astray, as customers tend to gravitate to the comfortable and familiar. Yet here is another area where money-makers have discovered a valuable paradox:

> *Many of the most successful products are driven by strong marketing or design perspectives that alienate customers, at least initially.*

Apple's iPod is probably the best recent example of this phenomenon. On the most basic level, the iPod is just an MP3 player, indeed a late-entering, more expensive, and less fully featured version. Imagine how a more customer-responsive organization might have objected to bringing out the iPod. No doubt someone would have noted that customers cannot load other MP3s onto their iPods; only songs downloaded from iTunes, the music-purchasing service that Apple provides, or songs ripped from their own CDs work on the device. Salespeople would have been aghast at the pricing. "Who will buy a product with such limited use and at such a high price point?" might have been a question that prevented the iPod from seeing the light of day and becoming the best-selling digital audio player in history, with more than 100 million units sold.

Steve Jobs and his team at Apple recognized how intangibles could create value that swamped other aspects of the product that were less consumer-friendly. They knew people would pay for a product that was aesthetically pleasing, sported a price that said it was worth it, and was supported with a strong marketing campaign. They saw that the value offered by the simplicity of a closed software-hardware environment was more important to customers than their desire to download MP3s purchased elsewhere. An additional benefit to Apple of the closed system was that it diminished competition and led to profitability better than almost any product in the consumer electronics business.

It is easy to underestimate the impact of intangibles, especially in relation to price. At most corporate headquarters, the assumption is that intangibles can only do so much and that customers will rebel if prices are raised too high. This certainly can be true in specific circumstances, but my investing colleagues and I frequently find companies that undervalue and underprice their offerings. These firms so fear a customer price rebellion that they don't ask for what their products or services are worth.

Though Tiffany and Co. has had some well-publicized management problems in recent years, the retailer has been extraordinarily successful at using branding and a reputation for high prices to generate sales. Many Tiffany purchases are intended as gifts, and the giver wants to communicate to the recipient that he or she spent a lot of money. Tiffany helps customers with this underlying need by charging high prices and wrapping the gifts in distinctive packaging. Buyers often shop at Tiffany merely to obtain the robin's-egg blue box that announces how highly the gift giver prizes the recipient. By focusing on intangibles, Tiffany achieves operating margins in excess of 23 percent in its core operations.

At this point, you may be thinking that intangibles thwart customer price objections only if you have superpremium products such as those offered by Tiffany or a once-in-a-lifetime phenomenon such as the iPod but won't do much good for more mundane products and services. Staples would prove you wrong. The big-box retailer uses branding to create value for its customers and itself even though it is selling generic products such as pens, paper, and other basic office supplies.

Started in 1986 by Thomas Sternberg, who was inspired by his inability to buy supplies for his printer one Fourth of July holiday, Staples has transformed the retailing of office products by focusing on branding. Operating in a business where conventional wisdom said the only thing its hard-nosed small-business customers cared about was price, Staples took the opposite tack. The company hired marketers from consumer products companies who brought a deep understanding of branding. The Staples marketing team developed the "Yeah, we have that" and the "That was easy" tag-lines and spent heavily on television commercials and other advertising. Staples even sponsored a sports arena in downtown Los Angeles. It worked fabulously. Customers appreciated Staples' branding so much that the company has even been able to sell the "easy button" from its television commercials, a red piece of plastic that says, "That was easy," when pushed (profits from the sale of these buttons go to the Boys and Girls Clubs of America).

More important for the bottom line, Staples uses its powerful brand to generate strong sales of its private-label products. While most retailers offer private-label products only at starting price points, Staples succesfully offers good, better, and best products in its own name because the branding enables customers to trust its quality. Private-label offerings made up 22 percent of the company's sales in fiscal 2007, and operating margins in its U.S. operations were a healthy 10 percent, in the top tier among large retailers.

Inside Information

- Have faith that customers value intangibles, no matter what they might say to the contrary.

- Allow returns to drive what product features you offer and what markets you pursue (or cede).

- Capitalize on your intangibles; use them to sell products and services at higher prices than your competitors do.

Price Decisions: When to Raise and When to Lower

Not every organization can or should immediately raise prices to raise value. Though the strategy is too seldom considered, it is not always appropriate. If the value edge of your product or service is relatively limited and you raise your prices, you will precipitate a disaster. In some situations you need another "trick" to stimulate sales and profits: lower prices so they are better aligned with the value you are offering. This doesn't mean blindly following customers' requests for lower prices. You need to know your product's value to your customers—admittedly, not an easy thing to discern. It also requires being disciplined about the value you earn for your business. Lower prices for lower value generating good returns on investment is a wise move; lower prices that generate subpar ROI mean you should get out of the business.

Sometimes organizations overestimate the value they offer. It's especially true with companies that have been market leaders but failed to maintain their edge. When Anne Mulcahy took over at Xerox, she directed the company to take a fresh look at the pricing and value that it was offering its customers. The company's copiers came with all the bells and whistles; customers, however, didn't need them. They were only too happy to purchase cheaper, less robust machines from Xerox's competitors. While Xerox was maintaining its price discipline, it wasn't offering sufficient value. Customers may have said they wanted certain features, but their actions showed that they didn't value them enough to actually pay for them. In response, Xerox brought out slimmed-down versions of its copiers that were far more price-competitive. It also restructured its manufacturing operations so that it could still earn decent returns with the new lower-value offerings. With products that reflected what customers would actually pay for, as opposed to what they said they wanted, Xerox was able to reverse years of market share losses and avert bankruptcy.

Microsoft uses a lower-price, lower-value strategy when entering new markets. To compete with Sun Microsystems in servers and Oracle in databases, Microsoft developed cheaper solutions with less functionality than the incumbents' but that are good enough for a large number of customers. As in the price-leading strategies that I talked about earlier, this strategy requires knowing your customers' needs intimately. Microsoft had to determine which functionality was absolutely necessary and which was dispensable. By developing slimmed-down products for these new markets, it has garnered a 30 percent share in the Web server market, while Sun's shrank to 2 percent in 2007. In databases, Microsoft has grown faster than competitors since 2000.

Inside Information

- When considering lowering prices, first determine if you can earn returns greater than your cost of capital at the lower prices. If not, you have to either raise prices or get out of the business.

- Be very cautious if you decide to lower prices. Make sure you offer less value for the lower price. Never lower prices as a short-term tactic; customers will get anchored on the lower prices, which makes it nearly impossible to raise them again.

● ● ●

KNOWING HOW TO LISTEN

Knowing how to be responsive to customers without being fanatical is as tricky as knowing when to raise and when to lower prices. To develop the confidence to accommodate what your customers are asking for, while looking out for their best interest and your bottom line, answer the following questions:

- What are my customers doing (as opposed to what they're saying)? While customers' feedback can be misleading, their actions are usually a good guide. If your product has a long life cycle, like Paccar's trucks, you need a longer period to assess customers' actions. Tracking their spending habits on your offerings versus those of your competitors over time is the best approach.

- What is your position in the industry? If you are a challenger or your product does not have a significant edge, you generally are better off going with a lower-value, lower-priced product.

- Are you earning your cost of capital? If not, you need to make a radical change. Raise the price of your product. If customers won't pay for it, you should exit the business.

- Have you tried experimenting with pricing? While rolling out higher prices, develop a lower-priced but less featured offering. If raising prices doesn't work, roll out the cheaper product. If raising prices does work, consider rolling out the lower-value product under different branding.

- What are your costs to develop products? If their features are relatively fixed (i.e., the cost is the same whether you sell one or a million), you should favor a higher priced, full-featured offering. If costs are more variable, you can consider lower-value offerings.

- Will short-term pain for your customer offer long-term benefits? Use your knowledge of their business to prioritize their needs and the demands on them. Use this ranking as a guide to determine how to best serve them.

- What are you not? What part of the market will you not go after? Trying to be all things to all prospective customers is the road to disaster.

- Have you thought about your customers' customers, either internal or external? If you can please your customers' customers, you will generally succeed.

CHAPTER 5

GET MORE REWARD FOR
THE RISK YOU TAKE

SEMGROUP WAS AN OIL STORAGE AND DISTRIBUTION company that went bust in 2008 because CEO Thomas Kivisto thought he'd found a riskless way to increase profits: arbitraging the price of oil (selling oil where it commanded a higher price than it did in Cushing, Oklahoma, where the firm stored its oil). SemGroup was insulated from oil prices in its main business and Kivisto underestimated the risk in his location-arbitrage strategy. In the first half of 2008 when oil prices spiked, SemGroup's trading partners required considerably more collateral, cash that it didn't have. Kivisto attempted to make up the shortfall by placing ever larger, more speculative bets on oil prices, and got in over his head. SemGroup filed for bankruptcy in July 2008. While most companies' results are usually not so dire, many business executives underestimate the risks they take that produce the rewards they enjoy.

Professional investors have extensive experience with this risk-reward balance. Every day, I make decisions based on the amount of risk an investment entails versus the amount of reward it might yield. I'm far from perfect—I've taken bad risks and missed out on big rewards, like everyone else—but I try to learn from my mistakes. I've found that the best investors develop a sixth sense that tells them if the risk-reward equation justifies an investment—or if it doesn't.

As a business leader, you too deal with risk and reward, but in a different way. For one thing, you do it far less frequently than those of us in the investing community. You don't make dozens of separate decisions daily where you're taking significant risks for significant rewards. In addition, your risks and rewards aren't often quantifiable. You may decide to pursue risky strategy A and it yields a profitable result, but it's difficult to know how much the strategy was responsible for that result or the economy or a hundred other factors. It's also nearly impossible to know what would have happened if you had pursued strategy B instead.

The lack of frequency and measurability makes it difficult to learn from your risk-reward experiences. Professional investors, on the other hand, can easily measure their results. As an investor, I know every minute the market is open if I made the right decision when I bought stock A instead of stock B. I can easily calculate how much more (or less) money I would have made with different choices. I also see the value of my decisions fluctuate constantly. Because risk is so measurable in the investing world, we spend a lot of time thinking about the risk-reward equation and how to earn a little more return than the risk we are taking would warrant.

If you can understand the risk-reward equation as investors do, you can avoid a lot of costly business mistakes. You can stop yourself from taking huge risks in pursuit of rewards that aren't as significant as they may first appear. And you can learn that avoiding risk too much means you will never enjoy adequate rewards. Better yet, you can learn the secrets investors and moneymakers use to get more reward for the risks we take. Finding ways to minimize risk without eliminating reward leads to great returns; let's look at some of the ways you can do so.

FLEXIBILITY AND FEEDBACK

One of the first lessons I learned as a green equity analyst was the benefit of reducing risk, even if it required spending a little extra and suboptimizing your operations. On one of my first on-site company trips, I went with a senior portfolio manager to the High Point, North Carolina, area to meet with some furniture manufacturers. First we toured the factories of Ladd Furniture, which manufactured midpriced furniture. Then, over dinner, the company's CEO and CFO explained how they ran their business. Each year they began their annual planning process by gathering economic forecasts from the major brokerage houses. They averaged these numbers to arrive at a consensus view on what the economy would do in the upcoming year. Next, they determined how much they expected their business to grow based on the historic relationship between the broad economy's growth and demand in the furniture business. With their forecast for the next year's growth in hand, they planned the next year's production, ordering raw materials and scheduling work shifts accordingly. It was all very logical and well thought out.

The next day we visited with Albert Prillaman and Doug Payne, CEO and CFO respectively, of Stanley Furniture, a company that produced wood furniture in the middle-to-upper-middle price range. When my colleague and I asked how they planned their business, it sounded as though they did it by the seat of their pants. They waited until orders came in and then purchased raw materials and scheduled work crews as needed. They even put on extra shifts and paid overtime as necessary to keep up with the order flow when business was strong. Prilla-man explained that their approach had been born of necessity after a near-disastrous LBO in 1989. The company had taken on extensive debt to go private near the top of the economic cycle. The debt, already heavy, became crushing when the economy went into a recession and orders and profits dropped. The company could no longer afford to tie up cash in inventory, so Prillaman and his team redesigned the business. They streamlined their assembly processes so they could ship orders as quickly as competitors did even without stocking inventory. They maintained this strategy even after they had repaid their debt and gone public again.

As a young analyst, I was more impressed with Ladd Furniture's highly systematic approach to planning its business, but my more senior colleague explained why Stanley's approach was superior. Stanley had done a far better job of eliminating economic risk from its business (at least as much as possible, given how economically sensitive demand for furniture is). Though Ladd's approach would produce better profitability if the economic forecast that underpinned the production plans was correct, what were the odds that the forecast would be correct? As anyone who has even a couple years of experience listening to Wall Street economists knows, their forecasts are less reliable than the weatherman's. Stanley's approach would be more expensive on paper—with its reliance on overtime to handle business surges—but in practice would be far more economically sensible. The company would never be caught with excess inventory that could be sold only at a deep discount. Because raw materials were not stockpiled (with some exceptions), Stanley's investment in inventory was far less for the same amount of sales than Ladd required. The results proved my portfolio manager right. A few years later Ladd disappeared when it was acquired by La-Z-Boy after a period of subpar performance. Meanwhile, Stanley continues to be one of the best-managed independent furniture companies around.

It's a mistake to rely too heavily on your ability to anticipate the economy and other future developments. The experience of moneymakers, on the other hand, mandates the following principle:

Don't go meet the future; let it come to you.

This is more than just semantics. Of course, you must be aware of and prepare for trends and events that will impact your business (more on that in chapter 9). What you don't want to do is assume too much precision in your forecasts. When you bank on your predictions, you raise the risk in your business while reducing the odds of reward. On the other hand, when you keep your options open so you can respond to whatever scenario the future throws at you, you tip the risk-reward equation in your favor. Moneymakers achieve the latter goal not only when setting production levels, as Stanley does, but also in another risk-fraught activity: developing new products.

Google, the search engine company and perhaps the youngest organization ever to crack the top fifteen highest-market-capitalization companies, has been particularly adept at letting the future come to it in product development. It leaves the generation of new-product ideas to its employees in a bottom-up process and the evaluation of those concepts to its audience. For the former, Google gives all employees "20 percent time"—a fifth of their time is to be spent working on their own innovations. These ideas can be completely unrelated to the work they do the remaining 80 percent of their time, but Google expects its employees to create these ideas within a process. The employees report on what they are working on during their 20 percent time and receive guidance on how to flesh out their ideas. Once sufficiently developed, ideas obtain an "official" status and are integrated into an employee's (and often a team's) regular work schedule. Many of the new ideas address problems that employees face in their daily lives. Thus they tend to be more cutting-edge and forward-looking than what generally comes out of a more traditional product development process.

Google further improves the risk-reward balance by soliciting user feedback when the product is new—real user feedback, not the artificial focus-group findings that so often lead companies astray. Engineers develop a workable version of a new offering and then post it on a section of Google's Web site called Google Labs, where customers can start to use it. Observing actual usage, the team can reliably identify which new features are winners and warrant full-blown development, which should be killed, and which are inconclusive and should receive some inexpensive tweaks and more time. One product that the company killed was Google Answers, which allowed people to post questions for other Google users to answer. The company created the offering in 2002. It never got significant traction, and it stopped accepting new questions in 2006. Though the theory—users who went to Google to find information would sometimes like to have another person, hopefully an expert, answer their question—made sense, users didn't see the need. Because Google did not expend a lot of resources making a big, risky bet on the new product, it could easily kill the product; there was not a lot of lost investment to justify when it didn't work.

Orkut, Google's social networking offering, has seen middling success. Created by an engineer whose first name is Orkut during his 20 percent time, the service was launched in 2004. While its rivals MySpace and Facebook have surpassed Orkut in the United States, it is the top social networking site in Brazil. The company has kept a "beta" tag on the site to indicate that the product is not as refined as other Google offerings. Google

Maps, on the other hand, has been an unquestionable success. Launched in 2005, maps.google.com was initially offered for only two browsers (Internet Explorer and Firefox), but as usage grew, the company added additional functionality. As I write this, a link to the maps site is featured on the sparse Google home page, and the offering is no longer tagged "beta." Indeed, Google Labs now features Ride Finder and Mars, new offerings that advance upon the now-core Google Maps product.

Certainly Google has an advantage in developing products rapidly—it doesn't have to tool up factories to develop working prototypes—and it has more than 100 million users in the United States alone. Nonetheless, companies and managers across a broad spectrum of industries can find ways to reduce risk and obtain market feedback on products more quickly. To make sure you're exploring all your options in this regard, ask yourself the following questions.

- Do you provide time and encouragement for employees to develop their own new product or service ideas? In the manufacturing realm, 3M has long promoted skunkworks projects among its employees, and a surprising number of its most successful products (most famously the Post-it note) have come from these efforts.

- Are you spending money to reduce risk? Smaller product lots and faster development generally cost more per unit to produce, but the ability to get market feedback and reduce the risk of new-product development will more than compensate.

- Have you moved a promising but imperfect product to market fast? Use the Google strategy of labeling the imperfect product a "beta" or "prototype." This strategy is preferable to expending lots of time and money perfecting something that the market ultimately rejects. Customers understand that you are not always perfect and will appreciate the innovation, especially if they fall in love with one of your new products.

- Do you refuse to allow "it can't be done" thinking to stand in the way of getting new products out? Despite protests that it couldn't be done, U.S. car manufacturers have cut in half the development time for new models. Contract manufacturers can help develop prototypes and do production; they cost more than doing it in-house, but getting customer feedback as soon as possible is worth it.

- Are you using the Internet to gather customers' responses to new products? You may not have Google's traffic, but you most likely have enough to obtain meaningful feedback. Create your own version of Google Labs to talk about new products under development. Offer the product, if feasible, or describe it as concretely as possible. Solicit customer feedback; you'll be surprised how involved customers will get and how much they will want to help you succeed.

- Are you willing to offer products for sale before they are ready? Naturally, you want to be up front about the lead times on delivery, and this will work only for relatively shorter-lead-time products. Magazine publishers, for instance, often offer special holiday books to subscribers that they create only if there is sufficient demand.

- Do you test and learn regularly? For variations on offerings, segment your population by geography or another variable and make the new offering (say, a different price point) available to that portion of the population. Compare the results with those of a control group.

For companies such as Cisco, new-product development requires more research and development and longer lead times. So its challenges with getting prototypes to the customer quickly are greater than Google's. But regardless of your industry, you can find ways to have the future come to you. You might have to spend more money, but the risk reduction more than offsets the spending and usually produces higher returns. Cisco is the paragon of one such method: R&D through M&A (research and development through mergers and acquisitions).

Cisco, the leading networking equipment company, operates in an industry of constant change. Catching market transitions in technology is the key to remaining successful, or even relevant, in the networking business. Most companies in the industry are like prototype rocket ships—innovative vehicles that zoom into the stratosphere and then flame out when they fail to catch the next product cycle. Cisco, on the other hand, has remained the industry leader for a remarkably long time. Its secret to staying ahead is that it mitigates the risk associated with catching new-product cycles by supplementing its own R&D, which runs between 13 percent and 15 percent of sales, with acquisitions. CEO John Chambers has laid out a very clear methodology on innovation and acquisitions: if Cisco is not one of the first five entrants into a new market that it needs to be in, it will buy one of the companies that is. If the companies are too big, Cisco will find a way to partner with one of them. With a 70 percent success rate on acquisitions Cisco achieves better success than on its own R&D.

The difference in the probability of success—i.e., the risk— justifies Cisco's "R&D through M&A" strategy. Conventional wisdom argues that companies generally destroy value through acquisitions, and for years Cisco was criticized for its aggressive buying sprees. Acquisitions always cost more than developing something in-house because a premium must be paid to the owners to sell out. However, since Cisco buys a company or a technology only after it has achieved some success, Chambers and his team can see how a market will develop before they commit investment dollars. They keep their options open far longer than with in-house R&D, where lead times are lengthier. Though Cisco is spending more, it has reduced its risk considerably. This strategy has enabled it to remain current as new technologies evolve and to create one of the most valuable companies around, with a return on invested capital in excess of 21 percent.

Inside Information

- Manage the risks inherent in your commitments, be they production schedules or new-product development. Don't be so optimistic about your endeavors that you fail to consider the possibility of setbacks.

- Build as much flexibility into your system as possible. Pay extra for that flexibility if it adequately reduces your risk.

- Focus your efforts on designing systems that can respond rapidly to change. By reducing risk through flexibility, you can generally produce better returns than by focusing single-mindedly on maximizing efficiency (which generally leads to fixed systems that cannot respond to change).

- Solicit customer feedback—actions, not opinions—as early in the process as practicable. Then look again to find a way to make it even earlier.

Payback Should Be Fast and Sweet

When making investment decisions, many business executives—and the investment bankers, consultants, and academics who advise them—rely on projections of the cash flow that a new product or piece of equipment will generate throughout its useful life. Derived from the discounted cash flow (DCF) analysis that every business student learns, these forecasts are generally dominated by the cash flows that an investment generates in later years, when it has achieved a mature state. As a newly minted MBA steeped in this conventional thinking, I was surprised that the more senior professional investors I worked with were skeptical of this approach. But, as I began to study companies as an investor, I realized they knew something the business schools overlooked:

> *The more time between investment and payback, the greater the risk.*

Using an analysis that relies on estimates of earnings more than three years out is inherently risky. Things change, and the more time between the start of a project and when it produces revenue, the more likely change will occur. The assumptions that fueled the original investment may no longer be valid when conditions change. Because of this risk element, I have found that the best companies concentrate on projects with quick paybacks.

The faster a new piece of equipment or new product recoups its initial outlay, the lower the risk. While I can hear my old professors and more than a few CEOs I've met argue against emphasizing the near-term impact of spending to the detriment of long-term cash flows, I've witnessed repeatedly how the best-laid plans can go awry. Betting on far-off cash flows invites steep odds. Even if a short-payback project is less attractive based on long-term cash flow projections, it is often the better option from a risk-reward perspective.

Apache Corporation is among the largest independent energy companies. Unlike the better-known Exxon Mobil, Royal Dutch Shell, and other "majors" that do everything energy-related from drilling to refining to running corner gas stations, Apache specializes in exploration and production (E&P), finding and drilling for oil and natural gas. Frequently started by wildcatters trying their luck drilling holes in remote parts of Texas and Oklahoma, E&P companies occupy the riskiest part of the energy industry; either they earn phenomenal returns by striking "black gold" or, more typically, they go broke. Investing in wildcatters has a risk-return profile not much better than buying a lottery ticket. Yet by understanding the trade-off between risk and reward, Apache's team built a durable company with $10 billion in revenues.

In 1954, Raymond Plank, an accountant, along with Truman Anderson and Charles Arnao, started Apache not to fulfill their love of exploration and the wildcatter spirit but to exploit oil-drilling tax shelters. In the early years, the company used other people's money, a moneymaker technique I discussed in chapter 3, to tip the risk-reward balance in their favor. Plank and his partners created oil-drilling partnerships that allowed investors, mostly individuals, to realize tax benefits. In 1981, Apache created the first master limited partnership (MLP), which allowed it to consolidate its limited partnerships while retaining favorable tax treatment.

The Tax Reform Act of 1985 took away many of the tax benefits of these partnerships, so Plank and his team had to find a new strategy. Other oil companies, both majors and E&Ps, searched for the "big" find, drilling where they were likely to tap huge reserves with years of production potential. Their investment models, with projections of decades of cash flows, easily justified large up-front expenditures to find those big strikes. Apache took another route, focusing instead on drilling opportunities with quick paybacks but steep decline rates and short lives (of course, everyone would like to find opportunities with quick paybacks and long lives, but such opportunities rarely exist and are snapped up as quickly as a hundred-dollar bill lying on the sidewalk). Apache sought projects requiring six to twelve months of investment, a two- to three-year payback, and an additional three years or so of high-profit production before running dry. Throughout the 1990s and early 2000s, it acquired cheaply a number of assets, primarily in the Gulf of Mexico, that Amoco, Shell, and BP deemed too short-lived to bother with.

Apache's strategy required more work than the "megastrike" approach. With wells that depleted quickly, Apache had to acquire new assets constantly just to maintain its reserve levels. Employees understood the need to produce returns quickly, and the company's culture stressed "a sense of urgency," which reinforced the strategy. Apache sacrificed long-lived revenues for high returns, and the strategy worked beautifully. From 1985 to 2005, its stock averaged a 14 percent compounded annual increase, besting both the Standard & Poor's 500's 9 percent and what other oil companies achieved. Even the constant need to replace reserves proved manageable; revenues grew thirtyfold from 1990 to 2006. And best of all, from my investor viewpoint,

Apache did it while achieving a high 17 percent return on capital in 2006. (While the high oil prices from 2003 to 2006 certainly helped, Apache's outperformance relative to its energy company peers validates the success of its strategy.)

SUCCESS THROUGH QUICK payback works for all sorts of investments, not just big oil field projects. The newspaper publisher Gannett moves its older printing machines from high-volume to lower-volume locations. Though the used equipment has a limited remaining life, the cost to move it is so much less than to buy new equipment that this tactic produces far greater returns. Gannett also retains greater flexibility than it would with a thirty-year investment in new presses, which is particularly valuable at a time when newspaper circulations are falling. A number of food purveyors capitalize on the quick-payback concept in their new-product development by creating limited-edition varieties. Heinz with its green ketchup, McDonald's with its limited-edition sandwiches, and Starbucks with its holiday coffee drinks have all earned high returns through quick-hit new products. Just as Apache knows it has to replace reserves constantly, these companies grasp that quick-payback projects require continuous reinvention for continuing success. With the returns so high, the effort is well worth it.

Inside Information

- Prioritize projects with quick paybacks.

- Don't be seduced by huge payoffs looming far on the horizon. Be especially skeptical of any project that requires a huge up-front investment with attractive returns coming in years five and beyond. You have no idea what alternatives will be available to your customers then.

- Keep time frames in perspective: quick paybacks depend on the life cycle of your industry. They will be far longer in oil exploration, for instance, than in quick-serve dining. Moreover, I certainly do *not* want to encourage quick fixes (such as cutting spending) to make a quarter.

Speed Kills, Especially Reckless Speed

Some companies confuse short paybacks with speedy action. It may seem like a paradox, but you can seize quick-return opportunities without rushing into them. There's a difference between opportunities that offer inherently quick gains and forcing speed in a misguided effort to manufacture quick gains. Moneymakers combine quick-payback projects (that often draw on years of experience in the business) with pacing appropriate to each project and its participants.

In our current environment, though, executives sometimes rush projects in an attempt to accelerate their returns. Conventional wisdom prizes the "first-mover advantage" and endorses speed, but I have seen too many wrecks from executives pushing through changes, particularly strategic changes, too quickly. Though pursuing projects with fast paybacks tilts the risk-reward balance in your favor, steamrolling through strategy changes, particularly ones that impact customers, often results in risk with no reward.

In December 2004, the nation's largest radio station owner, Clear Channel Communications, introduced a new strategy called Less Is More that reduced the commercial time on its stations.

Responding to listeners' and advertisers' disillusionment with the average eighteen minutes per hour devoted to commercials, Clear Channel's management team sought to move advertisers to thirty-second ads from the industry standard of sixty seconds. CEO Mark Mays, CFO Randall Mays (both scions of the founding family), and radio division head John Hogan promoted Less Is More as a win-win-win: for listeners, advertisers, and shareholders.

Clearly they needed to do something, as commercial time had been creeping up while time spent listening to radio had been eroding for years. The bursting of the dot-com bubble, with the evaporation of so many companies and their ad budgets, had hit radio ad sales particularly hard. To maintain revenues, station managers had added more spots in ever-longer commercial breaks, which gradually drove listeners away. Advertisers also complained about clutter: the abundance of ads was keeping their particular ad from being heard. Being the seventh ad in a ten-ad pod (set of ads) almost guaranteed it would go unheard as listeners learned to turn the dial as soon as ads started. Shareholders were unhappy because radio revenues and profits had been stagnant since 2000.

Clear Channel's top executives promised that its ad-time reductions would help everyone. Listeners would receive more entertainment with fewer ads. Advertisers were more likely to have their ads heard, as shorter commercial breaks meant that listeners were less inclined to switch stations when ads started. Even shareholders would benefit, as management expected to generate similar revenues despite the reduction in ad time. The shift from sixty-second to thirty-second ads would enable them to sell as many ad units as before, and a better listening environment would improve ratings, which would allow them to charge more per unit of ad time.

Less Is More should have been a resounding success, but it flopped because Clear Channel pushed the changes through too fast, alienating advertisers and shareholders and making a sensible strategy unpopular and risky. Having announced the new program in fall 2004, it switched (or "cut over" in industry parlance) all its radio stations to the new "clocks" (ad/programming schedules) a couple months later, on December 15, 2004. Advertisers were unprepared and furious. Many had sixty-second ads already produced. Some couldn't fit their message and legally required disclaimers into thirty seconds. Yet Clear Channel's salespeople had a mandate to move quickly and pushed advertisers to provide them with thirty-second spots. The results were ugly; Clear Channel's radio revenues dropped by 6 percent in 2005, when the overall industry was flat. Most radio operators reported revenue growth as advertisers shifted their budgets away from Clear Channel stations. Over the course of the first year, the company had to backtrack, allowing more sixty-second commercials on its air. In time, Less Is More will prove to have been the right strategic move—revenues recovered in 2006, when the company had 5.6 percent growth in radio revenues compared to an industry increase of 1 percent—but had it phased in the implementation, Clear Channel would have seen less disruption in its revenues and might have even taken share from competitors with heavier commercial loads.

GANNETT, THE LARGE newspaper company, understood the risks of moving too fast when it addressed the dot-com challenge in the late 1990s. During this period all companies were being exhorted to "obsolete" their business models, seize the "first mover advantage," and embrace the new economy yesterday. The impact was keenly felt in the media industry, where Yahoo!, Excite, AOL, and others seemed to rise out of nowhere to become major players and amass market capitalizations that surpassed those of stalwarts like Disney. Numerous media companies panicked, with

Disney and GE's NBC paying tens of millions of dollars to buy the Internet companies Infoseek and Xoom.com respectively (to say nothing of the well-known debacle, Time Warner's sale of itself to AOL for stock whose value soon cratered).

Gannett, however, approached the challenges of the Internet in a more measured fashion. Senior managers, led by CEO John Curley and President Doug McCorkindale, directed the company's newspapers to create Web sites incrementally and on the cheap. With centralized servers and technologies, the company produced effective Web sites without making a big-splash acquisition. Even more important, at a time when everyone else was more worried about getting big than making money, Gannett's Web sites were actually profitable in 1999. When the dotcom crash came, Disney, GE, and Time Warner had to write down their Internet investments, while Gannett was able to continue to make strides in its Internet portfolio, acquiring substantial stakes in the online sites CareerBuilder.com and ShopLocal.com after the hype had died down.

Inside Information

- Don't move too quickly, particularly when outside participation (e.g., of customers or partners) is required. Excessive speed can waylay even the best strategy.

- Look for ways to respond to trends with smaller, cheaper (quicker-payback) steps to shift the risk-reward balance in your favor.

- Wait watchfully in high-risk situations; prepare to move on targets, but allow others to make first-entry mistakes and learn from what they've done wrong.

Share the Upside

The next piece of moneymaker advice comes not from a spirit of magnanimity but rather from a desire to improve the risk-reward trade-off.

Greed is risky. Share the upside.

Sharing some of your upside with strategic partners can give greater certainty to future cash flows and returns, thus reducing risk.

Exxon Mobil, the oil major, has a well-deserved reputation as a hard-nosed, no-nonsense, return-focused company; socially conscious critics have demonized it as rapacious. In reality, though, Exxon has succeeded in large part because it understands how to share the upside. Not only does the rigorous standardization I discussed in chapter 3 contribute to its superior returns but Exxon also generates strong returns by operating in locations where others cannot or dare not. Many of the world's oil reserves lie under countries lacking traditions of capitalism, property rights, and consistent rule of law, so managing political risk is crucial for a multinational oil company. Exxon has excelled at managing this risk because it shares profits and understands well that 40 percent of something is worth far more than 100 percent of nothing.

Though many multinational oil companies recognize that sharing revenues is required to drill in many countries, Exxon Mobil takes this sharing principle further. In 2007, it signed a joint venture with Sinopec and Saudi Aramco to invest $5 billion to build the first fully integrated refining, petrochemicals, and fuels marketing project with foreign participation in China. A division of Sinopec owns 50 percent, Saudi Aramco 25 percent, and Exxon Mobil 25 percent. By sharing the profits with both the consuming and the producing countries' national oil companies, Exxon has secured a stable interest in a deal with the world's largest oil exporter and second-largest importer.

An added benefit to sharing the upside is that Exxon also lays off some of the downside, tilting the risk-return balance in its favor in two ways. First, because partners contribute access, assets, and capital, Exxon can pursue more projects than if it had to pay for all the access and assets itself, thus reducing risk through diversification across multiple projects. Second, it can often negotiate downside protection in exchange for sharing the upside. For instance, its deal with the Indonesian oil company Pertamina to develop the Cepu oil field in eastern Java gives Pertamina 55 percent of the profits unless the price of oil falls below $45.00 a barrel, in which case Exxon's share will increase. For Exxon, gaining steadier cash flows warrants giving up some of the upside.

CONVERSELY, BANKRUPTCY GROUNDED Delta Air Lines because it didn't share its upside. As with Exxon's success, Delta's bankruptcy had multiple causes. I referred in chapter 2 to how hedging masked the company's true unprofitability, but management's shortsighted greed also contributed. In 1996, following years of losses, Delta's management gained wage concessions from its pilots, the company's only unionized workforce. The pilots agreed to a 2 percent reduction in their pay from 1996 through 1999 in exchange for a share of profits if the company's pretax profit margin went over 2 percent, capped at 10 percent. When the airline's revenues improved, as they inevitably do in this highly cyclical industry, Delta's profits increased dramatically. It went from losses in the early 1990s to earning almost $7.00 a share in calendar years 1998 and 1999. Soon the company bumped up against the cap on the pilots' profit sharing, and management decided to enforce the limit, thus improving its reported profitability even more. The only problem was that enforcing the cap infuriated the pilots, who felt they had fully shared the pain but had not participated fully in the gain. Union-management relations soured dramatically. The pilots dug in their heels and by 1999 had negotiated an interim contract to convert their profit sharing to a 6 percent across-the-board pay increase starting January 1, 2000. Then, in 2001, the pilots secured further pay increases at a time when operating profitability was declining precipitously (despite the illusion of profitability due to the company's successful fuel hedges).

I'm not suggesting that Delta pay its pilots extra out of the goodness of its heart. But triggering the cap was an excellent opportunity for Delta management to improve the risk profile of the company. The airline industry is notoriously cyclical, with large profits in good times and large losses the rest of the time. The industry's biggest expense is labor, with the pilots earning the most among the frontline employees. Delta could have dramatically improved its risk profile by making some of its labor expense variable. Why not negotiate a deal to make the profit sharing permanent (i.e., no snapback in wages) in exchange for eliminating the cap on the upside? When the company was making healthy profits, shareholders wouldn't have minded giving up some gains to improve the ability to stay solvent in the bad times. Instead management opted for the riskier strategy of fixed pay, augmenting profitability when the industry was flush but ultimately leading Delta to bankruptcy court in 2005.

Too many organizations are like Delta, believing they need to squeeze every penny out in order to please investors. In reality, they are penny-wise and pound-foolish. Companies must think about sharing the upside as a fiscally prudent business decision rather than as a concession to placate their employees and other partners. Costco, the warehouse club operator and one of the world's largest retailers, perpetuates its success by sharing its upside. Costco pays 40 percent more to its store staff than does its primary competitor, Walmart-owned Sam's Club. It also subsidizes health care premiums more than its rival does. Yet Costco's stock trades at a significantly higher price/earnings (p/e) multiple than Walmart's does; at the end of 2007, shareholders paid twenty-eight times earnings to buy a share of Costco's stock compared to sixteen times for Walmart's. A large part of this discrepancy is due to the companies' differing risk profiles. By sharing more of its profits with its employees, Costco has a cushion to absorb surprises. Indeed, as health care costs have ballooned, it has been able to increase the share its employees pay from 4 percent to 8 percent. Moves like this have helped Costco keep its sales, general, and administrative (SG&A) costs flat as a percentage of revenues. At the same time, Walmart has come under fire for its employee health care policies, result-ing in a political backlash against it that most likely hurt sales. Walmart's SG&A costs as a percentage of sales have also been rising. Clearly, adopting a "squeeze every penny" approach to profits has negative repercussions in more ways than one.

Inside Information

- Share the upside in good times to minimize the down-side in bad times.

- Don't look to maximize every dollar of profit; instead, use some of your profitability to reduce long-term earnings variability or create a cushion to mitigate cost shocks.

- Never become complacent and assume that bad times won't recur. Implementing risk mitigation strategies is far easier and more effective when profits are flush.

- Align your key partners' interests with yours by sharing your upside and paying fairly; it's an excellent way to mitigate risk.

•   •   •

Maximize Your Reward

To tilt the risk-reward balance in their favor, moneymakers understand where their risks lie and willingly pay to minimize those risks. If you identify and address risks such as time, speed, and greed, you can generate more return for the risk you do take. To adjust the scales to your advantage, consider the following questions:

- How much of your business plan relies on forecasts? Because forecasts are ultimately just guesses, they are inherently risky. Can you find ways to replace those forecasts with actual market data based on real customer actions? Can you make decisions after receiving the hard data rather than anticipating outcomes?

- Are you relegating quick-payback projects to the back burner because they don't have the large forecasted returns of longer-term projects? Have you considered the projects' returns on a risk-adjusted basis? Remember, the further out you go, the riskier the projection. If you are using discounted cash flow analyses, are you reflecting the risk in the out years? Have you considered that an alternative product could emerge that would make your out-year profits zero?

- Are you willing to spend to reduce risk, or do you seek to maximize your efficiency? Over the long term, spending to reduce risk generally produces better results than striving for maximum efficiency, which requires everything (and every partner) to act according to plan.

- Do you consider profit sharing with strategic partners, including employees? Are you willing to give up some of your upside in order to minimize your downside, or are you so convinced of success that you fail to prepare for a rainy day? Reducing volatility in profits is an important component of risk reduction.

- How quickly can you implement new projects and strategic changes? Can you break large projects and major strategy changes into smaller pieces that offer quicker returns or that enable you to sell the change to some of your partners? Do you seek ways to establish proof of success with new efforts in order to build a case to take your efforts further?

- Do you consider how much buy-in you will need from partners to get a project going? Determine pacing by the demands of the project, not your demands for quick results. Have you considered ways to pare down or phase in a new effort to increase speed without rushing and introducing unnecessary risk?

- Are you willing to take chances? Do you allocate some of your budget and time to pursuing new initiatives? Without risk there is no reward.

CHAPTER 6

ECONOMICS TRUMPS

MANAGEMENT

E CONOMICS 101 OFTEN TAKES A BACKSEAT TO MANAGE-
ment 101, since your days are filled with the details and
demands of running a business. Unfortunately, if ignored,
broad economic factors can have a dramatic impact on your
results.

Professional investors like myself are often surprised by business managers' lack of attention to economic factors, since we
focus almost entirely on them. When I decide which stocks to
buy, I examine the structure of an industry, the competitive dynamics, the macroeconomic trends that drive sales, and other
factors beyond the control of corporate executives. The quality
of management is generally a secondary or tertiary considera-
tion, because even the most brilliant CEO can do little in the
face of powerful competitive forces and current trends. As Warren Buffett has said, when a good manager joins a bad business,
the latter usually retains its reputation.

Though we investors sometimes underestimate the power of
good managers (poorly managed companies frequently trade at
higher earnings multiples because investors expect they will
catch up to others in their industry), many executives forget

inviolate economic laws when executing strategy and tactics. Too often, managers rely on growth plans or pursue strategies that work in the short term but are ultimately torpedoed by the laws of supply and demand or the inevitability of competition. Remaining in sync with Economics 101 enables moneymakers to keep their businesses thriving over the long run. Let's look at the economic principles that can help you prevent managerial pitfalls and capitalize on opportunities that less economically savvy executives may miss.

SUPPLY AND DEMAND

The most fundamental principle in economics, akin to the law of gravity in physics, is the law of supply and demand. If supply exceeds demand, prices and profits will drop, maybe not immediately but inexorably. Despite this fundamental law, organizations regularly overproduce even though it will hurt prices and profitability. In the heat of the moment—as customers call for more— it's easy to forget basic economics and increase production.

The dot-com boom was a classic example in which managers— and many investors—got caught up in the euphoria of the boom and ignored supply and demand. Many convinced themselves that the dot-com revolution overthrew traditional economic rules. They expected that Internet-based start-ups could add capacity to industries without feeling any price- or profit-lowering impacts; only hidebound traditional companies were supposed to be hurt. It worked for a few years, while venture capitalists were pouring money into start-ups. Eventually, though, the rules of economics reasserted themselves and dot-coms everywhere began failing.

A more quotidian example of the damage caused when companies ignore supply and demand principles also occurred in the late 1990s, when the U.S. airline industry was riding high. Continental Airlines was particularly confident; it had gone "from worst to first," as a book about the company was titled. Having narrowly averted a bankruptcy filing earlier in the decade, it had become one of the most profitable airlines in the industry. The management team, led by CEO Gordon Bethune, deserved a lot of credit for the transformation. To capitalize on its success and to expand its operations, management began buying more planes and offering more flights. When questioned about the impact this increased capacity might have on the notoriously cyclical airline industry, Bethune argued that Continental and other airlines had transcended these cycles. He suggested that because airlines had organized themselves around hubs, they were not truly competing with one another and therefore could add capacity with impunity.

For a while this theory seemed to work, but eventually supply overwhelmed demand. For a New Yorker, a direct flight from Continental's Newark hub (just outside New York City) to San Francisco was no more compelling than a direct flight from a New York airport to United's San Francisco hub. At the same time, with its own empty plane seats to fill, American made flights from New York to San Francisco through its hub in Chicago compelling by lowering prices to compensate for the hassle of changing planes. Even more competitive was the choice for those flying from Bozeman, Montana, to Boston, Massachusetts. They could choose between connecting through Delta's Salt Lake City hub, Northwest's Minneapolis hub, or United's Denver. By mid-2001, the impact of the additional planes all the airlines had been adding was apparent. The industry headed into one of its periodic swoons, with American, Delta, Northwest, and United all losing money in the first half of 2001. The downturn was exacerbated by the national fear of flying that ensued after the September 11, 2001, terrorist attacks, but the oversupply of flights had already set the airlines on a loss-making path.

The response of Ford Motor Company and the other U.S. auto producers to the economic slowdown after September 11 reveals another way organizations disregard the laws of supply and demand. In October 2001, the U.S. auto companies, concerned about a potential slowdown and with union contracts that made it nearly impossible to reduce workers' hours during a period of slack demand, decided to stimulate car buying with aggressive price cuts. General Motors started the effort with its Get America Rolling campaign, which offered no-interest loans on purchases. Ford and Chrysler followed quickly with their own no-interest campaigns, effectively cutting several hundred dollars (and most of the profit) from the price of a new car. As predicted by economics, the price cuts stimulated demand and cars flew off the lots. Unlike in the early 1990s recession, when U.S. auto sales had fallen by 37 percent, auto sales dipped only 12 percent from 1999 to 2000 and by 2001 were back to peak levels.

Though initially all seemed good, management at the Big Three U.S. auto companies only postponed and exacerbated the day of reckoning. They made the mistake of trumping economic principles with economic optimism. In 2002, I attended a meeting with Ford's leadership where this optimism was in full display. Ford's senior management was in New York, meeting with investors to update them on the company's plans and strategy, with an eye to keeping their current investors and encouraging some new buyers. At the meeting, senior managers expressed their conviction that once the recession was over, they would be able to raise prices and sell the same number of cars at a profit (with the current low prices, they were not making money on the cars they sold). Even though U.S. consumers bought almost 18 million cars in 2002, as many as Ford had ever sold in one year and a third higher than in recessionary 1992, Ford's management expressed no concern about their price cuts pulling demand forward and reducing future sales. Instead, they expected that when the broader economy strengthened, it would bail them out of their losses. Executives at GM and Chrysler must have been thinking similarly, because their actions (price cuts, no production cuts) were the same. Toyota took a different route; the fourth-largest seller of vehicles in the United States (at the time) did not offer zero-interest deals and discounted less. Its market share dropped more than a point.

In the end the law of supply and demand won out. After a few years of stimulating the market with low prices, Ford was on the verge of bankruptcy. It then realized it couldn't rely on an economic boom to rescue it. There was only so much demand at profitable prices, and Ford needed to cut production to match that demand. After years of overproduction and with the pressure of a potential bankruptcy, the cuts were particularly painful. In 2006, Ford lost $12.6 billion and announced plans to eliminate a third of its workforce. The following years were no better, with a loss of $2.7 billion in 2007 and more than $10 billion in 2008.

The industry would have been much better off today if the Big Three had recognized the law of supply and demand, and addressed the oversupply issue in 2001. Their price cuts would not have undermined the resale value of their used cars, which further devalued their new cars. The cuts in 2001 would have been painful, but not as painful as what the company had to go through after 2006, when it could no longer ignore the law of supply and demand.

Cisco Systems' response to the 2001 economic downturn demonstrates how a business can benefit by respecting the principles of supply and demand. No industry was more impacted by the dot-com implosion than telecommunications. During the late 1990s, lots of impressive—and often erroneous—statistics suggested that demand for telecom and Internet equipment would grow exponentially to handle the expected dramatic growth in Internet usage. Everyone in the industry repeated the well-known axiom that Internet traffic was doubling every hundred days. The telecom industry, both incumbents and start-ups, rose to the challenge of this growth, laying fiber-optic cable across the country and the oceans to handle the coming tsunami of Internet traffic. Cisco provided WorldCom, Global Crossing, and others with the routers, switches, and other equipment necessary to build out these networks. Then the telecom bubble burst along with the dot-com bubble, and it turned out that Internet traffic wasn't growing as fast as the oft-repeated adage suggested (it was doubling about once every year). After attempts to disguise how weak their financials were, Global Crossing and WorldCom filed for bankruptcy in 2002. Every telecom company drastically cut back on its capital spending, which meant far fewer orders for Cisco.

Rather than try to stimulate the market as the domestic automakers had, Cisco bit the bullet. The company laid off more than 10 percent of its workforce and took a $2.25 billion charge to write off excess inventory. The write-off was not just an accounting adjustment; the company actually scrapped more than half its inventory. In this way Cisco reset its operations to the now-prevailing level of demand. Though the charges and layoffs hurt, they set the company up for a better future. In 2006, when Ford was just coming to terms with its oversupply, Cisco earned $5.6 billion in profit. Its quick but painful actions to align its supply with the new reality of demand allowed it to return to health quickly.

Inside Information

- Never doubt the law of supply and demand. Recognize how rare it is for supply to be added without a downward impact on pricing or sales volume.

- Accept that the underlying demand for your class of products is largely out of your control (certainly you can take share with better products or lower prices) and tends to grow at a relatively steady rate.

- Determine the underlying level of demand growth by considering what drives demand: population growth and greater penetration within the population. If you are growing at above-trend (above-average) levels, continue to pursue that growth but also make contingency plans for when growth might slow (e.g., it's probably not the best time to increase production by building an expensive new plant).

- Respond to the demand that exists. Even if you expect demand to return, you should adjust production downward in the short term.

- Never lower prices to stimulate demand unless you can structurally lower your costs. It may appear to work in the short term, but it will fail in the long term.

Pigs Get Slaughtered

Corporate executives often complain about Wall Street's insatiable demand for ever-greater returns. I understand why executives complain, and I'm sure some professional investors are relentless in this regard. Most of us, though, don't believe that continually raising prices and increasing returns is the best way to build long-term value. I always remain mindful of this bedrock rule of capitalism:

Excess profits attract competition.

Or, in the more graphic way to put it: "Pigs get slaughtered." If you consistently drive product profits ever higher, you violate this rule and you effectively send an invitation to your competition to enter your market. Entrepreneurs, expanding companies, and other new entrants tend to follow Willie Sutton's rule and go where the money is. They enter businesses where profits are high, usually with a pitch that says "If we only get half the profitability, we'll still make outstanding returns." Don't encourage them to focus on your business.

For many business leaders, taking a step back from increased profitability is counterintuitive. Most executives have convinced themselves that they must always strive for a more attractive profit picture, failing to realize that at some point they're placing a target on their backs. A much more economically sound policy is to shoot for the sweet spot between strong returns and excessive, competition-inviting ones.* This can be done by lowering

---

* Strong returns are those that are one percentage point or more than your cost of capital (see pages 98–100 for a discussion on how to calculate cost of capital). If your business is not able to earn at least this level, it's not worth it: increase prices and see what happens, restructure the business to make it profitable, or exit the business. Excessive profits are those that invite competition, for which unfortunately there is no standard answer. You'll need to consider the cost for competitors to enter your business (e.g., new oil refineries are almost impossible to build, while new Internet sites can be put up overnight). However, if you are earning five percentage points or more over your cost of capital, you should consider very seriously the potential for new competitors.

prices or increasing investment; your new financial results will fend off most potential competitors.

The tobacco company Philip Morris, now known as Altria Group, was one of the most profitable companies on the planet until 1993. Even though consumers were smoking less and its taxes had increased, Philip Morris had preserved its superb profitability by regularly raising prices. The business seemed immune to the law of supply and demand as customers paid the higher prices. When your consumers are addicted to your product, little price sensitivity exists. However, Philip Morris hadn't considered that its continued high profits would attract competition. In the early 1990s discounters came aggressively into the market and, with packs priced as much as 60 percent less than Philip Morris's flagship Marlboro brand, began taking a meaningful share. Their share gains accelerated when a tough economy made customers more price-sensitive despite their addiction. Marlboro's market share fell from a high of 30 percent down to 22 percent.

Philip Morris's management realized that the price umbrella it had created had become too tempting to competitors. On April 2, 1993, known as Marlboro Friday, the company cut its prices dramatically, lowering the cost of a pack of Marlboros by 20 percent. Managers in another industry might have opted for raising the cost of doing business—increasing the advertising budget, for instance—but this avenue wasn't open to Philip Morris because of restrictions on cigarette advertising. So it dropped prices dramatically.

The tactic worked. Some discount players, such as American Tobacco, exited the market, and by 1995 Marlboro had regained its market share. Though operating margins never returned to the 43 percent the company achieved in its domestic tobacco operation in 1992, Philip Morris maximized its long-term cash flows by lowering profits to a level (33 percent in 1995) that provided solid returns for shareholders without attracting excessive competition. More to the point, it avoided the continuing market share losses that a high-price strategy would have guaranteed.

NEWS CORPORATION HAD a similar experience with News America, its free-standing insert (FSI) division. This less-known division of Rupert Murdoch's media conglomerate publishes *SmartSource,* booklets of advertisements—mostly coupons—that it distributes through newspapers. Though not glamorous, FSIs are a solid, cash-cow business. With only two meaningful players in the industry, News America and Valassis, the industry's stable structure allowed for good profitability—good, that is, until Valassis suffered a case of economics amnesia.

The problem began in 1992, when Valassis's operating margin jumped from 18.5 percent to 23 percent, as price increases allowed it to increase returns markedly. Sullivan Graphics, a contract printing company with a large business in printing inserts for single advertisers, noticed the attractive profits and decided to enter the multi-advertiser FSI business. As Sullivan sought to establish a foothold in the market, a brutal price war ensued, with all the players dropping prices to secure contracts with advertisers. Valassis's operating margins fell to 5 percent in fiscal 1994 (based on contracts written in 1993). With the lower prices, industry profitability eventually became insufficient to support a new entrant, and Sullivan exited the business in February 1994. It took four years before the incumbents' profitability returned to levels similar to those before the price war.

Despite this experience, Valassis did not learn the perils of overly high profitability. In 2001, it sought to raise prices again despite FSI margins of 28 percent, above the levels that had attracted competition in 1992. Moreover, paper prices—which represent about a third of costs—declined that year. News America, mindful of attracting new competitors with excessive profits, did not follow Valassis's price lead. As a result, it gained share. A period of price and share instability followed as Valassis tried to encourage News America to raise prices and News America refused. Through 2005, News Corporation's magazines and inserts division, which is dominated by FSIs but does include other businesses, maintained operating margins in excess of 20 percent and close to 28 percent during much of this period. Even Valassis's FSI segment had margins between 19 percent and 34 percent from 2001 to 2005. In a business with relatively modest capital needs, these margins produced strong returns. News America was right not to follow Valassis's price increases, because doing so would only have invited competition and reduced cash flows over the long term. With News Corp maintaining the sweet spot of good but not competition-attracting returns, the health of the industry was preserved.

As I MENTIONED earlier, you have other options besides lowering prices to discourage new entrants. Increasing investment in your business lowers returns and expands the moat that protects you from competition. In 2000, when Yahoo! posted a terrific 27 percent operating margin (excluding the cost of stock options), equity analysts exhorted the company to invest more in the business, particularly marketing, to cement the portal's lead versus other Internet sites in a business with relatively few barriers to entry. The company didn't heed this advice and soon faced significant competition from Google and MySpace.

Google, on the other hand, has lowered its returns through aggressive capital investments, making it more difficult for competitors to succeed. Google's core business, paid search, is one of the best businesses of all time—it's large, has extraordinary returns, and requires modest capital investment. In 2004, its first year as a public company, Google had revenues of $3.2 billion, generated operating margins of 26 percent, and began the year with less than $1 billion in total assets. A business with returns that good cannot help but attract competition. Google didn't have the option of lowering prices, since an auction determines the price its clients pay. So it opted to invest heavily in its business. Beyond the basic, ongoing work of continually refining its search algorithms and ad presentation, Google invested in making its search box ubiquitous, cutting advantageous deals with its Internet site partners (such as AOL) and others (such as Dell) that share revenues in exchange for encouraging use of Google search. Even more important, it spent heavily on servers and other equipment to ensure that it offers the fastest and most comprehensive search. In 2006, the company devoted $1.9 billion to capital expenditures. To put this into perspective, Yahoo!, which was somewhat larger in terms of page views and time spent by users on its sites, invested less than $700 million in new property and equipment in the same year. The investment worked; through 2008, Google continued to gain share in the search market despite numerous competitors targeting the business.

Inside Information

- Do not issue an invitation to competitors by squeezing the most out of your margins.

- Consider not only your current competitors but also potential new entrants as you evaluate how much to invest in your business.

- Reinvest in your business rather than lower prices, if it can be done effectively, i.e., the investment involves something that customers appreciate rather than spending just to spend.

• Find a balance between investment and pricing, and periodically calibrate this balance based on the changing dynamics of your environment and the levers available to you.

A Time to Be Born, a Time to Die

Just as business profits will be competed away if returns are too attractive, so too—and even more assuredly—will the profitability of individual products. Every successful product follows a life cycle, and eventually becomes commoditized. The speed of that process varies enormously based on the dynamics of the industry and how easy it is for competitors to offer rival products (especially when there are low barriers to entry). Despite all that has been written on this phenomenon, I can almost guarantee that every year numerous companies will be unprepared when their core products no longer earn superior returns. It's human to be lulled into thinking that a stalwart product will always provide excellent returns. Nonetheless, recognizing the inevitability of commoditization represents the type of economic realism that causes moneymakers to thrive.

Over its long history E. I. du Pont de Nemours and Company has created innovative products that earned exemplary returns precisely because they weren't commodities. DuPont has insulated its products from the erosive power of competition through patent protection and branding. Product names such as Lycra, Stainmaster, and Corian are well known because the company has marketed them to consumers despite operating in businesses where they do not sell directly to consumers. However, even with its branding efforts, DuPont's products eventually lost their competitive edge to knockoffs.

Take the example of Lycra. Invented by a DuPont scientist in 1959, Lycra (DuPont's brand name for spandex or elastane) was a marvel, both for its elasticity and for the 30 percent return on equity the business earned. By the late 1990s, though, the thirty-five-year-old product had become commoditized and numerous competitors were offering comparable products.

Yet DuPont did not manage Lycra as the undifferentiated product it had become; the company continued to invest behind it, rather than shift gears into a strategy more appropriate for a commodity business. Though the word "commodity" has a pejorative sound, such businesses can be highly successful *if they're run as the commodities they are rather than the innovations they were.* This means having the lowest costs to earn profits at the price the market sets. Continuing to invest in anything other than cost reduction projects at this point in a product's life cycle is money poorly spent. Some companies, however, eschew the cost-obsessed strategy necessary to manage a commodity business successfully. In this instance, leaders should sell off these businesses. Eventually, DuPont managers came to this conclusion, and they divested Lycra and their other textile businesses in 2004.

Unfortunately, it looks as though they are making a similar mistake with another iconic but long-in-the-tooth product, the countertop material Corian, for which the company is keeping prices high, attracting numerous competitors to the category. As a result of decisions like these and the poor results they have produced, DuPont stock struggled throughout the 2000s.

AMYLIN, A TOP biotech firm specializing in diabetes and other metabolic disorders, has achieved continuing success because it remains attuned to product life cycles and knows how early it needs to start working on rejuvenating products to keep competitors from catching up. In October 1996, Amylin acquired the rights for exenatide, a compound first derived from the venom of Gila monsters, that showed promise for glucose control, a major concern for people with diabetes. With the long development process for new drugs, it took until June 2005 before Amylin introduced the drug, now called Byetta, to the market for patients to use in twice-daily injections. Even as the company was conducting clinical trials and filing with the Food and Drug Administration (FDA), CEOs Joseph Cook and Ginger Graham and their team recognized the need to start preparing for the next wave of products. So, in May 2000, with the original drug in Phase 2 (of 3) trials, management signed an agreement with another firm, Alkermes, to develop a long-acting-release (LAR) formulation, which would require only once-weekly, rather than twice-daily, injections. Due to the company's early planning for product cycles, the more convenient LAR version will be ready—barring any unexpected problems in research—within four years of the original version, fast by the standards of the pharmaceutical industry. Due to Amylin management's farsightedness, the stock price continued to rise by more than 50 percent two years after the announcement that Byetta had been approved by the FDA. Investors appreciated the company's foresight in planning for its product's full life cycle.

No doubt, as you consider product cycles and investing money in unproven products, you weigh the risks of making such an investment. There is risk. But here's a truth I see every day when studying companies:

> *Two types of risk exist—the risk of going out on a limb and the risk of holing up in a safe place—and success comes from balancing between the two.*

If you try to squeeze every drop of profit out of a product, you are taking a big gamble that there will always be profit to squeeze. At the other end of the spectrum, if you invest in the development of a follow-on product even as you're rolling out a relatively new product, you double your risk if the new product doesn't work. Finding a balance between these two extremes can be tricky, but moneymakers are brilliant at mastering the challenge.

Generally, mastery involves astute assessment and planning about how to develop follow-on products and manage risk. The following tips will help:

- Force yourself to quantify the probability of success for your initial product. That number will not be absolutely correct, but it will foster discussion as you outline how you came up with the number. Then assess the probability with your team very honestly; don't let your enthusiasm for the new product overwhelm your judgment.

- Determine the cost savings of concurrent development of follow-on products. The more savings there are, the lower the risk. Amylin was able to leverage some of the research and other resources for the original version of Byetta to reduce the cost of developing the LAR version.

- Remain mindful of the length of product development cycles in your business, and plan accordingly. Though this may seem obvious, I have seen some leaders become so enthusiastic about follow-on products that they fail to plan for the costs that development will require or, conversely, so confident about how long an initial product's advantage will last that they don't allow enough time to develop new versions.

- Explore the feasibility of sharing the product risk with a
  partner to spread your risk and give yourself the ability to
  invest in more products. In the case of Byetta, Amylin
  brought in Eli Lilly as a partner on developing exenatide.
  By sharing the cost and the risk with Lilly, Amylin was
  able to continue to invest in the LAR version of
  exenatide and thus prepare for the long term.

Of course, not all businesses have the decade-long product
development cycles or massive up-front costs of the pharmaceutical industry. And most industries lack the pharmaceutical
industry's patent protection and long periods in which products enjoy profits above the cost of capital. In the financial
services market, Goldman Sachs knows that its product innovations will enjoy superior profits for no more than four years before becoming commoditized. This awareness drives it to
continue to innovate so it can replace the profits from maturing
products with new innovations. Monsanto, a leading agricultural-
biotech firm, has also managed its innovation pipeline well by
mapping out each of its key areas (cotton, corn/maize, soybeans,
etc.), and the cascade of new products that it will develop and
roll out.

Inside Information

- Prepare for the inevitable loss of profitability to competition. Product cycles are moving faster than ever before, and patents and copyrights are no longer an
  ironclad guarantee of continued profitability.

(continued)

- Adapt to aging products. If a product has become a commodity, treat it as such and focus exclusively on cost efficiencies. If your culture cannot adapt, sell the product and reinvest in new-product development.

- Create a map/timeline of your new product development and period of competitive advantage. Be rigorous about how long a product will remain profitable (undoubtedly a shorter period than it used to be). Use the map to identify gaps and potential opportunities. Redraw the map periodically to update for changing conditions.

• • •

LIVING IN THE (ECONOMICALLY) REAL WORLD

An airplane's ability to fly doesn't disprove the laws of gravity, though a naive observer might think so. Similarly, just because your product has no competition doesn't mean that it never will, or because additional supply hasn't impacted prices yet doesn't mean it won't. The laws of economics may be superseded temporarily, but they always reassert themselves. Therefore, moneymakers ensure that their strategies are consistent with economic realities.

Admittedly, this wisdom can be difficult to adhere to in the heat of business battles, when appearance often belies reality. Further complicating matters, following a given economic principle can mean doing one thing in situation A and the opposite in situation B—i.e., sometimes lowering prices (e.g., Altria) and other times holding the line on prices (e.g., Ford).

To make sure your business isn't tripped up by the laws of economics, consider the following questions:

- What are your overall returns on invested capital? Are they higher than your cost of capital? Meaningfully so? If returns are below or close to your cost of capital, do not lower prices. You need to shrink your business to a profitable core. If returns are meaningfully above your cost of capital, act now to lower prices or invest in the business; otherwise you might as well issue an embossed invitation to potential competitors.

- Where are you in your industry's cycle as well as that of the broader economy? Lowering prices to maintain demand during slower economic times or to maintain unusually high levels of sales only postpones and exacerbates the pain. Don't try to fight against the natural level of demand in your industry (one exception is if you have a product that still generates acceptable returns at lower prices; then you may be able to generate a new level of demand in your industry).

- How much supply are your competitors, direct and indirect, adding to the market? If a lot, start investing today to differentiate your business from theirs or shift into a new business where you can leverage your expertise. Hoping a transgressor will cut back or leave the business because it's "your rightful share" or certain customers are "yours" results in heartache.

- How easy is it for new competitors to get into your business? How much capital is required for competitors to enter? Will they require employees with specialized skills or knowledge? How hard are those employees to find? Do you have big customers or big suppliers that have an incentive to help competitors start in your business? How rational are potential competitors? What are their motives? Do you have different return requirements than you do? Do they have other imperatives to get into your business (e.g., their core business is dying)? Are regulatory approvals or licensing required that can slow competitors' entry? Are there economies of scale in your business? As you ask yourself these questions, be sure not to overestimate how protected your business is. If the returns are good enough, competitors will find a way in.

- Have you excluded sunk costs in your analysis? Don't! Over the long run, all costs are variable. Do not let attractive incremental returns justify price cuts. If your overall returns are subpar, shrink the business through pricing up or paring back.

- How can you expand the competitive moat around your business if you are earning attractive returns? Will additional marketing, maybe even to the ultimate consumer and not your direct buyer, cement your position? Can you strengthen your brand (a strong brand is an often underestimated competitive edge)? Are there additional property, plant, or equipment purchases that can lengthen your lead over competitors? Are there up-and-coming companies that you should acquire?

- Have you prepared for the inevitable erosive impact of competition on your products' returns? Have you drawn a map/timeline of your product pipeline?

- Are you prepared to reorient how you manage business lines as they become commoditized? Once a product has become commoditized, it is very rare that the situation can be reversed; in this circumstance, shift gears in how you manage the business. What are your current trends indicating? Even if a product is still earning good returns but they are eroding, you need to prepare now.

- Do you take time at least once a month to consider the impact of economics on your business?

CHAPTER 7

THE BEST COMPANIES TO INVEST
IN ARE THE WORST TO WORK FOR

T HE MANAGEMENT THEORY TRUISM THAT HAPPY EM-
ployees make for effective workplaces has it backward.
The truth is:

High-performing workplaces make for happy employees.

Please don't misunderstand me. I'm not suggesting that we should become a nation of sweatshops. Nor do I believe that the more miserable you can make your employees, the happier your shareholders will be. But what I have seen repeatedly is that companies must create an environment where productivity and performance come first. Not everyone will prosper in or enjoy such an environment, and those who don't generally avoid such companies or quickly leave when they realize they're in the wrong place. On the other hand, those who enjoy steep learning curves, taking risks, and working hard self-select for such companies.

Much has been written about the war for talent and how some companies are adept at attracting a cadre of top-level leaders, but the real trick is attracting and keeping a wide range of employees who prize performance. If you fill your business with employees at all levels who are eager and excited to compete, you're likely to produce far better results than an organization run by a few superstars. Here are some of the best practices moneymakers use to recruit, retain, and motivate high-performance employees.

WHEN INTERESTS ARE MISALIGNED

Conventional management theory teaches that for organizations to be effective, employees need to cooperate; it further postulates that to foster cooperation, you should reward everyone based on the same metric to align interests. Following this logic, many large corporations set bonuses based on the profitability of the entire company. They believe that, when bonuses are aligned, all employees will work together to advance the cause of the broader organization. It sounds great, but unfortunately it doesn't work.

Rewarding a large group on a shared metric may align interests, but it has a more pernicious impact: it decouples pay from performance. In large organizations, most workers outside top management have no ability to impact the overall profitability of their corporation. They can put in extra hours and produce stellar results, but if elsewhere in the organization results are poor, they'll see no additional reward for their better results in a shared-bonus environment. It works the other way too: poor performers are sheltered from their ineffectiveness, receiving rewards based on their team's (or larger group's) performance. In such a setting, employees quickly learn not to exert themselves.

The following are five faulty assumptions that encourage businesses to reward everyone equally; see which ones your organization subscribes to.

- By rewarding group rather than individual performance, we will motivate strong teamwork (and we're a team-based organization).
- Individual rewards work against the decision-making consensus that we're trying to achieve.
- If we reward only the best performers, we encourage our people to hoard, rather than share, knowledge.
- We are trying to depoliticize our culture, and individual rewards cause people to jockey for position and curry favor to achieve these rewards.
- Individual performance yields only short-term gains.

The best companies recognize that the pluses of individualized rewards—based on clear and quantifiable metrics—far outweigh the minuses. Even if customized bonuses cause one person to hoard knowledge in the mistaken belief that this is how to become a star, it will cause five others to exchange knowledge to improve their individual performance. These latter five people recognize that they need to give up some information in order to receive crucial new data and ideas.

The savviest organizations tailor the metrics on which bonuses are paid to quantifiable actions that are meaningful for their profitability; they make these metrics simple to understand; and, most important, they focus the metrics on something that the individual employee (or sometimes a small group) can control.

Lincoln Electric manufactures arc welding equipment and materials, as well as other industrial products. At a time when other companies in similar rust-belt industries are struggling and even declaring bankruptcy, Lincoln has thrived. Much of its success comes from its incentive compensation system, which rewards shop floor employees based on their individual output; it's essentially a piecework system. Factory workers receive credit for attendance and for all their output that passes quality checks. If a customer rejects a product, pay is deducted from all the individuals who worked on it, tapping into workers' self-interest narrowly enough to ensure that good work is done throughout the factory.

The system has worked well for workers and shareholders alike. Lincoln Electric's factory workers are well paid, with the top performers able to earn well above $100,000 in a good year. However, that pay is variable; around half comes from individual output and half from annual bonuses that are allocated based on individual performance. When sales are tough and less product is needed, employees make less product and are paid less, though anyone with more than three years of tenure is guaranteed at least 75 percent of his or her base pay. The system allows workers to share with shareholders both the risks and the rewards of the enterprise.

It also leverages workers' self-interest to overcome their reluctance to raise problems with managers; as discussed earlier (in chapter 2), having systems to encourage people to "speak truth to power" is crucial to managing any business well. With their pay determined by their output, Lincoln's workers have a powerful incentive to push managers to fix any problems that limit their ability to produce. An advisory board of elected worker representatives that meets with management twice a month, as well as management's open-door policy, provides the avenues for workers to speak up about problems. Overall, this system aligns interests between workers and shareholders more effectively than systems that mandate top-down cooperation through shared rewards; it has produced stellar results for both Lincoln's employees and its owners.

Inside Information

- Tie pay to individual or small-group performance to create the maximum benefit for your whole organization; this is Adam Smith's "invisible hand" of individual self-interest producing collective good for businesses as well as economies.

- Share business rewards fairly, and employees will be willing to share the risks, including downtime or reduced pay as necessary.

- Use high pay for high performance to attract employees who embrace the initiative and hard work required to succeed in a performance-oriented environment.

- Avoid incentives based on the performance of your entire organization except for those at the top who can truly affect the entire organization.

BUILD SHAREHOLDERS' GOALS INTO REWARD SYSTEMS

Not only should compensation metrics measure what employees can personally impact, they also need to reflect the goals of owners, a.k.a. shareholders. Employees who generate strong sales but overuse resources fail to create value. Metrics have to be designed very carefully so they incorporate what's good for shareholders *and* attainable for employees. For instance, salespeople should be paid commissions for profitable revenue, not simply dollars generated. Rewards also need to be targeted so they focus employee efforts. Just as metrics based on the performance of too broad a group disenfranchise individual effort, too many opportunities to receive rewards encourages employees to hit the easy targets and ignore the rest.

When Clear Channel Communications, the radio operator, instituted its Less Is More initiative (see page 139), the company greatly improved its sales commission structure to achieve the best results for the company overall. If only the implementation of the change had been more measured, the results would have been extremely effective.

Less Is More was Clear Channel's attempt to improve the radio experience for its listeners by reducing the amount of commercial time. As part of this initiative, the company changed the commission structure from one that rewarded employees based on sales dollars to one that rewarded them based on revenue adjusted for the airtime required to generate that revenue. In other words, thirty-second spots earned higher commission rates than sixty-second spots, because they detracted less from the listener's experience. Over the long run, less commercial time produces higher ratings and allows Clear Channel to charge more per spot and generate more revenue. Clear Channel did not move to reward its salespeople based on ratings, because they had only minimal control over ratings, which are the bailiwick of program directors and on-air talent. Salespeople, though, did have direct contact with advertisers and could convince them to switch from sixty-second to thirty-second ads. By structuring its compensation system to reflect not only revenue generated but also the use of its most precious resource (listeners' attention), Clear Channel fostered the return goals of shareholders.

MOST COMPENSATION SYSTEMS don't motivate employees to stretch for "extra credit" profitability—for example, revenue generated after a salesperson hits a bonus-linked revenue target. Yet time and again, I have seen how this revenue is critical to a business's success; it provides the push that lifts an organization above the competition. General Electric has been broadly praised for the success of its "stretch targets." On a more operational level, Viacom's MTV Networks has designed a compensation system that encourages salespeople to reach for every last dollar of revenue. To receive their bonuses, salespeople must meet a revenue target, but unlike in most reward systems, Viacom pays its salespeople larger commission rates on any revenue brought in that exceeds their annual target. Viacom grasped that running down sales leads and generating an extra sale becomes progressively more difficult after hitting the first target. Yet many compensation systems offer equal or smaller rewards for any results beyond budgeted targets. MTV counteracted this mismatch between work and reward by making each additional sale personally more valuable to salespeople than the previous one. Motivating salespeople to stretch for every dollar of revenue contributed greatly to MTV Networks' success; from 1997 through 2004, the division grew its revenues by 140 percent, or more than 13 percent each year.

THE ENERGY EXPLORATION and production company Apache has adapted the principle of ever-greater rewards for ever-greater accomplishment to the dynamics of its company and industry. With a strong entrepreneurial culture, Apache awards bonuses for its managers based on the ROI that they generate in the oil fields they operate. Since the industry is highly capital-intensive and Apache's managers determine how much capital is allocated to their individual fields—each manager can have as much as he wants—Apache bases managers' rewards on the returns produced on that capital. Bonuses are calculated on a sliding scale; managers earn only token bonuses for a 12-percent return, but the rewards accelerate as returns increase.

To ensure that managers are paid for what they control,

Apache calculates project returns using the long-term prices of oil and natural gas. Managers neither benefit from nor are penalized by oil prices—a factor beyond their control. Moreover, this approach counteracts the natural, and unfortunate, tendency to follow the crowd and overinvest when prices are high and underinvest when prices are low. Since there is a long lead time on investment decisions, prices will certainly change between when an investment is approved and oil is available for sale. Because commodity prices tend to revert to a mean (i.e., return to an average price over time rather than rise or fall consistently), the contrarian approach that Apache's system encourages produces superior returns over the long run. Moreover, Apache's managers are incentivized to maximize the oil their wells produce, rather than gamble on commodity prices.

Inside Information

- Build incentives that not only reward people for their production but also incorporate factors that support your business's long-term profitability. When in doubt, err on the side of making incentives narrower and more within employees' control.

- Structure rewards for each level of your organization; managers who control capital spending should have return on capital as a primary metric in their evaluations, while workers who cannot impact capital should not.

- Structure rewards on a sliding scale, so employees are motivated to strive for more than an initial bonus; make it even more desirable to achieve increasingly ambitious targets.

Show Me the Money

Paying as many employees as possible in stock is an article of faith to both corporate leaders and people in the investing community. I risk being branded as a heretic, therefore, when I say:

> ### *Don't pay employees in stock except those at the highest levels.*

Investors advocate paying in stock, because we want employees to share our pain when their stocks are not doing well. A shareholder revolt ousted CEO Bob Nardelli from The Home Depot in 2007 due to his indifference to the stock price, which had been stagnant for years. Those at the most senior levels of an organization, the top five to ten folks, certainly need to be responsive to shareholders, and receiving a large piece of their compensation in stock or options ensures that they will pay attention when the stock isn't doing well.

However, to pay anyone else in the organization in stock or options separates pay from performance. Over the long term, stock prices are determined by the earnings and returns that employees generate, but in the short and intermediate terms stocks can move for reasons entirely unrelated to a company's performance. Nothing makes investors cringe more than when a CEO or CFO predicts how high a company's stock price is going. As people paid to forecast where stocks are going to go, we know how inherently unpredictable the stock price for any one company is; too many exogenous factors influence prices.

These influences disconnect pay from performance. Throughout the 1990s, many CEOs and other option holders enjoyed huge increases in their compensation despite mediocre or poor performance. They benefited as the stock market rose more than fourfold over the course of the decade. As interest rates fell and risk tolerance rose, investors paid higher price/earnings multiples for stocks. This rising tide lifted all stock prices, even those of poor performers. In 2007–08 executives have seen the reverse impact as the global credit crisis has taken down all stock prices, even for those companies with no exposure to the subprime mortgage market meltdown that precipitated the crisis.

Changes in market conditions decouple the performance of stocks from underlying companies' earnings and return results. For employees below the upper echelon, the disconnection between stock price and individual performance is even larger. These folks not only don't impact the multiple of earnings that their stock trades at, they don't impact the overall earnings. Just as rewarding employees on companywide metrics doesn't work because most employees can't impact the whole, so too rewarding employees with stock is ineffective.

The United Airlines debacle with its employee stock ownership plan should serve as a warning to any corporate executive who thinks freely awarded options or ownership will align the interests of his or her employees. In 1994, UAL Corporation, the parent of United Airlines, signed a historic deal with its pilots' and mechanics' unions, giving them majority ownership in the company in exchange for wage and work-rule concessions. United represented the perfect test case of aligning employees' and shareholders' interests through stock ownership.

Instead, they proved to be woefully misaligned. The original deal had the pilots, mechanics, and some nonunion employees taking an average 15 percent cut in wages for six years in exchange for a 55 percent stake in the holding company. The deal enabled UAL to stave off bankruptcy and expand at a time when other major carriers were saddled with higher costs. The deal worked reasonably well until the wage snapback approached. Then it became clear that as owners of the airline, pilots and mechanics felt they could set their pay as high as they wanted. They demonstrated little concern for other shareholders. The results were disastrous. When senior management didn't immediately accede to their wage demands, the pilots staged a disruptive, but effective, work slowdown in the summer of 2000. Management caved and the pilots received significant pay increases just as the industry went into a cyclical downturn. With higher costs, customers annoyed by the job actions, and less revenue, UAL filed for bankruptcy protection in 2002. It was a tragedy not only for the independent shareholders but also for the pilots and mechanics, who saw the value of their stock wiped out.

There's another flaw in employee stock ownership plans:

Reward people with stock, and you'll hurt long-term productivity.

This may seem counterintuitive; after all, stock ownership would seem to give employees a reason to work harder and better than ever before, but it has other effects that negate this owner mentality. When employees have much of their net worth tied up in a company's stock price, it's often detrimental to the long-term interests of outside investors. Many option-heavy Silicon Valley firms see significant brain drains when their stocks do well; their employees can afford to retire. The problem becomes even worse when a company's stock stops rising (as all stocks inevitably do, because eventually a company's growth prospects get priced in). Intel, the premier semiconductor maker, experienced a 17 percent increase in employee turnover in 2004, when its stock stagnated after almost doubling in 2003. It's no coincidence that after this brain drain the company struggled and two years later had to lay off 10 percent of its employees as its results sagged.

I'm not arguing that you shouldn't reward people for good performance, but you should:

Pay your people, whenever possible, with cash.

Though some professional investors talk a good game about stock being the best reward, most will admit that to really motivate people, cash is king. I remember speaking with a top equity analyst who told me that one of the most important things he looked for in potential investments was shareholdings by employees. Yet minutes later, he lauded the advantages of working for a hedge fund versus a bank-affiliated money manager because hedge funds pay bonuses in cash whereas banks pay in stock. On a personal level, he was acknowledging that he much preferred receiving cash rather than stock. Your employees will feel the same. A dollar is always worth a dollar (more or less), while a stock's value can plummet through no fault of one's own.

On a company level, too, I have seen greater long-term success in companies that pay their people with cash. Jefferies, a midsize brokerage firm, has succeeded in a field dominated by much larger players because it has tapped into the motivating effects of cash. Unlike other big brokerage houses, where much of employees' compensation is in restricted stock or options paid out over three-year vesting periods, Jefferies pays its employees their commissions monthly and in cash. Traders and salespeople see a direct connection between their efforts and their spendable paychecks. This compensation system has worked for Jefferies; its stock price almost doubled from the end of 2003 to the end of 2006, and it avoided most of the problems other brokerages faced in 2007–08. Moreover, even though it does not lock employees in with restricted stock, the company's turnover is lower than at other brokerage firms; Jefferies' employees stay because they like working in an environment where they see concrete rewards for their efforts.

When awarding cash bonuses, you need to calibrate reward cycles based on the time required to judge success, given your employees' tasks, as well as your business's sales or product cycle. In brokerage firms, employees oversee dozens of profit-generating transactions daily, so monthly rewards are appropriate. In longer-lead-time businesses, annual bonuses may be more appropriate.

The primary exception to the rule against paying in stock is start-ups; here, paying in stock makes more sense. Start-ups rarely have the cash to pay employees, so stock is often the only option. The firms are small, so interests are more readily aligned through personal contact. Plus, the upside is much greater if a company survives, so the motivational impact of the stock is more powerful. At the same time, paying in stock creates sanctions for failure. If a company doesn't survive, the stock is worthless; naturally, stock compensation results in high turnover in start-ups. But this unfortunate repercussion is tolerable given the constraints. Leaders of start-ups also need to remain aware that they can't stick with stock compensation for too long. As a company gets bigger and more established, the potential upside in the stock value will decline and the negative impact of stock's inherent disconnect between pay and performance will overwhelm the benefits.

Inside Information

- Never forget that cash is king. Payments in stock and options divorce pay from performance.

(*continued*)

- Pay rewards based on your business cycle. They should be frequent but still allow you enough time to assess the effectiveness of employees' efforts.

- Use stock as compensation in a start-up, if necessary, but transition to cash rewards once your business gets on its feet.

SYNTHESIZING SYNERGIES

Cross-department and cross-territory collaboration through group metrics and shared stock prices has failed to deliver so often that my investing colleagues and I consider "synergy" to be a four-letter word. But you shouldn't. In many operations, opportunities exist to earn significant profits by having different divisions or functions work together. The difficulty is that systematic solutions almost never create reliable cooperation across boundaries.

Synergies cannot be mass-produced; they need to be individually crafted. Moneymakers use their influence over their employees to encourage, cajole, and even bribe different groups to work together. By spending time in the trenches, learning the details, and asking seemingly simple questions even when you know the answers, you can encourage your frontline workers to be open about the challenges they face. This knowledge will enable you to hear about and identify opportunities across operations. When you foster a transparent, participatory culture, you encourage your employees to share their ideas, information, and requests for assistance, overcoming the mistrust that often stands in the way of synergistic efforts. Finally, if you compensate people for their individual contributions, including those on shared projects (even compensating two people for the same results on a narrow basis), you prevent the infighting for rewards and recognition that often occurs when there is a "shared pie."

Steve Ross, who grew a chain of funeral homes into Time Warner, the world's largest entertainment company, was a master at exploiting these forms of synergy. After he acquired Warner Bros. and merged it with Time Inc. in 1990, the divisions at the new Time Warner were run separately, with each one charged to excel in its field and paid according to its own successes or failures. In some instances, though, opportunities arose that required collaboration across divisions. Generally, these opportunities involved one group needing a resource from another. Ross would take the two division heads to dinner, where the one needing the cooperation would request it of the one needing to supply it. They would stay at dinner until the two divisions had worked out the outlines of a deal, even though the division providing the favor often did not benefit and the favor would distract that team from achieving its own performance targets. However, once a deal was worked out, Ross would turn to the division head making the sacrifice and ask him what favors he needed. The division head would then be able to gain something of value to his team from elsewhere within the corporation. In this informal, management-intensive way, Ross achieved synergies while maintaining a culture in which each unit strove to be the best in its field.

I can't stress enough that this approach to synergy requires enormous care, time, and attention on your part. Indeed, after Steve Ross's untimely death, Time Warner devolved into a corporation of warring factions, because no one was brokering cooperation among the divisions. Borrowing from Winston Churchill's quote about democracy, brokered synergies are the worst system of management—except for all the other ones.

●   ●   ●

JAMIE DIMON, THE CEO of JPMorgan Chase, similarly brokers cooperation across his divisions. After the merger of Bank One and JPMorgan Chase in 2004, the firm moved to put all its bank branches on the same technology platform. A branch in Louisiana was selected as the first to cut over to the new system. Dimon flew to the branch to facilitate the preparation necessary for the switch. While at the bank, he told the bank manager that he was holding him personally responsible for the success of the cutover. Later, back in Ohio with the bank's technology department, the head of the systems consolidation project expressed his annoyance that the Louisiana bank manager had, in his opinion, been put in charge of the project. He felt his turf had been invaded. Dimon let the technology project leader know that he, Dimon, was also holding the tech leader personally responsible for the project. With both the bank manager and the tech manager being charged with success in this crucial project, the cutover proceeded smoothly, setting the stage for rolling out the new technology across the Bank One branches. This systems consolidation, eventually rolled out across all the branches, contributed substantially to the $1.5 billion in merger savings that JPMorgan achieved in 2005 and to the 30 percent rise in the stock in the three years after the merger was announced.

Given what Dimon and Ross accomplished in the synergies department, you should ask yourself the following questions:

- How often do you use your power and influence to "broker deals" between different groups in your organization?

- Are you willing and able to use your resources to compensate someone who feels she is "losing out" when helping another group?

- Do you play hardball with your employees to get
  diverse teams or other units to work together on an
  opportunity? Will you hold their feet to the fire even if
  it makes them angry or resentful?

No doubt, some opportunities will slip through the cracks
when you individually broker synergies. You might be tempted
to create a matrix organization wherein your people report to
two bosses, most commonly a head of a geographic region and
a head of a functional or product category. That doesn't work
either. Though matrix organizations sound good on paper, they
diffuse responsibility on an ongoing basis—as opposed to the
focused situation that Dimon created. With often conflicting priorities on each side of the matrix, employees get pulled in too
many directions. Without a clear sense of what performance will
be rewarded, employees tend to lose focus and apathy sets in.

Don't fall for the theoretical attractiveness of synthesizing
synergies through overarching systems. You must handle this
task personally and with great focus.

The intense management required naturally limits the number of synergy opportunities that you can work on, and this is
an added benefit of this artisanal approach. Working on cross-
divisional synergies diverts people from performing their main
tasks. For this reason, synergy opportunities should be pursued
selectively. Because it requires a lot of time, the nonsystematic
process of attaining synergies requires you to prioritize which
synergies to pursue and limits the number that can be acted
upon.

On the surface, I'm describing a process that puts more pressure on you to use your powers of investigation and persuasion
to find and propel synergies. Ultimately, however, this way is
more fun because it is tremendously involving and it works.
It offers you a method to motivate your employees to cross

boundaries and work together effectively, without overly diluting their effectiveness in their main tasks.

Inside Information

- Don't be lulled into the illusion that cooperation among diverse groups can be "legislated" by structures or systems; you have to shepherd collaboration personally.

- Broker sharing between different profit centers on a case-by-case basis. Find rewards outside the project for those who give up more than they gain. Use the power of management recognition and other "soft" rewards.

- Prioritize and limit the number of cross-divisional projects. They distract from your core business and require substantial attention from you and all involved. Make sure such projects earn returns well above those of the core business, to warrant the additional effort.

NOT BY BREAD ALONE

By now I hope you appreciate that the "worst" companies are the best for certain employees. Yes, bosses sometimes micromanage; yes, cash is king, and yes, people are rewarded for individual rather than group production. Yet, in the best results-oriented cultures, a sense of shared purpose often exists:

Profit and purpose are not mutually exclusive.

Indeed, in the best organizations, the two goals reinforce each other. As you drive for great financial results, don't neglect to define and communicate your organization's purpose. A shared purpose can work wonders, but only if it is well suited to your organization. In particular, it has to incorporate and bolster whatever drives your organization's performance. Then cultural rewards can provide perspective as employees pursue their monetary goals, create an environment to promote honest communication about any problems, and serve as a powerful motivator.

For the biotech pioneer Genentech, monetary rewards were not enough to attract the caliber of scientists it needed to create Pulmozyme, Avastin, and other biotherapeutics. Founders Bob Swanson and Herb Boyer understood that to attract the best researchers from academia, they needed to create an environment with rewards that scientists valued, and none was more important than the ability to publish their findings promptly. Having their work judged worthy of publication by a panel of their peers is the gauge of success among scientists. Publication also enables them to solicit feedback from others in their field and thus advance their own thinking. However, profit-minded organizations tend to abhor publication, because it can give valuable information to competitors working on similar products. Most pharmaceutical companies have traditionally restricted their scientists' ability to publish. Aware of the importance of publishing, Genentech overcame its "publish and perish" fear and allowed its researchers to report on their findings at a time when most other corporations didn't. By making scientific achievement and recognition a key component of Genentech's shared purpose, it has been able to attract first-class scientists.

Good science is not the only shared goal at Genentech; it

also hires and cultivates people with a strong desire to bring products to market. This second shared purpose, which dovetails so well with its business goals, sets Genentech apart in an industry where many companies champion scientific excellence but don't achieve strong product and financial success. By combining the ability to attract great scientists with a drive to create useful products, Genentech has given its employees a reason beyond money to put extra effort into their jobs. This driving force has helped it bring more than a dozen products to market, while many biotech firms have failed to live up to their promise.

Even if your business does not involve life-or-death illnesses, you can develop a shared purpose that creates urgency and motivates your people to achieve their best results. Goldman Sachs, as I touched on earlier, does it by fostering a shared ideal of excellence. Employees are certainly motivated by their generous compensation, but the company also has a shared ideal of being the best, both individually and collectively.

For many, particularly those on the outside, Goldman Sachs seems a very tough place to work. Annual reviews are tough and honest, not the bureaucratic grade inflation exercises found in so many organizations. There's a strong "up-or-out" career track, which can seem heartless to people expecting long-term job security. Its up-or-out philosophy, though, serves the business well; the continuous turnover in leadership means the firm regularly reexamines problems. It also keeps Goldman from getting stuck in a rut. When a leader has had his initial career success in derivatives, for instance, it's human nature to try to solve all problems with derivatives. If you have a hammer, everything looks like a nail.

The regular turnover—Goldman had five CEOs (including joint tenures) in the sixteen years from 1992 to 2008—also helps balance the tension between its traditional profit centers: the brokerage/trading operation and the investment/merchant bank.

Top performers on both sides of the house know that the relatively frequent CEO changes mean that power regularly shifts from one side to the other, so everyone has an incentive to cooperate. It also keeps the internal competition healthy by fostering a shared vision of excellence. Goldman's employees recognize a larger purpose (the pursuit of excellence) that tempers the competitive atmosphere. Goldman's quest to be the best puts everything else in context.

CREATING A SHARED sense of purpose not only supports day-to-day activities but also can create rallying points for organizations to address threats before they become overwhelming. In 1994, when Netscape launched Navigator, the first commercially successful Internet browser, Microsoft's Bill Gates recognized the threat it posed to Microsoft's dominant position in desktop operating systems. His concerns culminated in a May 1995 memo to Microsoft's top executives entitled "The Internet Tidal Wave," in which he described how impactful the Internet was going to be and how Netscape's browsers, which effectively functioned as an operating system for the Internet, could commoditize Microsoft's mainstay, the Windows personal computer operating system. He implied that the Internet, though nascent, could obsolete Microsoft if the company did not respond to the threat forcefully and immediately. Given Microsoft's overwhelming size, it's remarkable that Gates's "call to arms" worked. Even in 1995, when Netscape had more than 90 percent share of the browser market, the company's total revenues were less than the interest Microsoft earned from the cash on its balance sheet.

A shared sense of purpose can rouse employees to make extra efforts at even the most successful organizations. Microsoft meant something to its employees; they took great pride in its success and leadership position in the market. Motivated by the risk that the Internet and Netscape could destroy Microsoft, employees throughout the organization took steps to fend off the threat. Historically known for rejecting anything "not invented here" and for long delays in software upgrades, Microsoft licensed code to get a leg up in building its own browser, Internet Explorer. Version 1.0 was released in August 1995 and was quickly followed by 2.0 and then version 3.0 within a year. Version 4.0, surpassing the equivalent Netscape product in features and usability, came out in September 1997. Microsoft also became much more flexible in collaborating with outsiders, doing a deal with America Online in which each party bundled the other's offering. Indeed, Microsoft went after its shared goal so aggressively and with all of its assets that the U.S. Department of Justice sued the company for antitrust behavior.

Though I'll leave it to the lawyers as to whether Microsoft crossed the line in its zeal, my point is that shared purpose has a powerful impact on employees. In this instance, it caused an entrenched behemoth like Microsoft to move with unprecedented speed and creativity. By 1998, Netscape had become a shadow of its former self and Internet Explorer was the dominant browser in the market.

Inside Information

- Inspire employees with both ideals and money. Find and promote a shared ideal for your company above and beyond making your numbers.

- Define a shared goal that supports achievement and value creation within your business. Overly abstract or politically correct goals can produce activity without returns (e.g., some biotech companies do great science but never seem to produce marketable products).

- Include the shared goal in your assessments, but tie it more to soft opportunities than to hard rewards such as cash bonuses. Soft opportunities include promotions or assignment to task forces that will gain high performers extra recognition.

How Much Is Too Much?

I would be remiss if I ignored a common complaint about the so-called worst corporate environments: excessive CEO pay. The media are fond of spotlighting companies where the CEO's pay seems exorbitant. They look at a handful of top executives making huge amounts of money and the relatively low pay the bottom third of employees receives and declare that these are not good places to work.

Too often there's a "heads I win, tails you lose" approach to CEO pay in which CEOs are well compensated regardless of a company's results or pay themselves on easily achieved metrics that have little bearing on profits and returns. The problem with this approach is that it seeps throughout the organization. For any leader, it's hard to tie your employees' pay to performance when you don't. I know that leadership in this day and age is challenging and that you must work harder than ever before to be successful. For this hard work, you should be paid well, but the same is true for your employees as well.

Employees' motivation can suffer if they believe their leaders are receiving pay that far exceeds their contributions to the organization's success. To counteract this problem, the best companies pay their stellar performers more than their CEOs. Goldman Sachs rewards its CEOs with headline-making compensation, but morale doesn't suffer because employees throughout the firm are well paid and in most years there are a few traders who make more than the CEO does.

On the opposite end of the spectrum, Costco CEO James Sinegal takes a salary of only $350,000 and with bonus, options, and stock earns less than $3 million a year. This compensation is quite modest by large-company CEO standards. Also, unlike at most large corporations, Sinegal's compensation is not significantly more than that of his direct reports; the top six earn in the $2 million to $3 million range. Keeping pay relatively low and evenly distributed certainly helps morale in a retail organization that relies on thousands of modestly paid workers (though Costco pays better than its rivals for comparable positions, retail workers are among the lowest-paid in the country). Now, I'm not arguing for a specific ratio of CEO pay to that of the median worker; it depends on the size and skill level of the organization, the ownership and tenure of the CEO, and other factors. I merely note that senior managers—at a minimum the ones whose compensation is in the proxy and therefore available for all to see—should consider the impact on their employees' willingness to take responsible risk and strive for returns when the senior managers themselves receive mammoth salaries and huge bonuses despite mediocre or poor organizational performance.

The CEOs of both Delta Air Lines and AMR Corporation, which owns American Airlines, learned firsthand the destructive impact of disproportionate pay for senior executives in 2003. In the wake of an air travel downturn early in the decade, both companies were teetering on the verge of bankruptcy. Despite the poor performance, both Delta's Leo Mullin and AMR's Don Carty paid their executives retention bonuses and attempted to put their pension assets into bankruptcy-protected vehicles. These moves were made at a time when both companies were negotiating with their unions for wage concessions. When the moves to protect executives' compensation and pensions became public, infuriated employees and their unions saw little reason to grant concessions if management wasn't sharing the pain. Mullin and Carty both resigned shortly thereafter to clear the way for their companies to negotiate the wage reductions they needed. (AMR managed to avoid bankruptcy; Delta didn't.)

The contrast between how AMR and Delta paid their CEOs and how Southwest Airlines compensated its chief is as striking as the difference in their results. From 2001 through 2003, Delta's Leo Mullin earned $8.2 million, excluding stock options (investors very much consider stock options to be compensation; I exclude them only because there is insufficient disclosure on their value). AMR's Don Carty resigned in April 2003; during his last three full years (2000–02) he received compensation of $6.2 million. In contrast, Southwest's chief executive—Doug Parker at the time—received nonoption compensation of $1.7 million from 2001 through 2003. Even if you add the $2 million paid to Herb Kelleher as executive chairman of the board, the Southwest team is quite a bargain, and even more so when compared against their results. From the beginning of 2000 to the end of 2003, Southwest's stock price rose by 50 percent whereas AMR's fell 80 percent and Delta's went to zero when the company declared bankruptcy in 2005. Part of Southwest's success comes from the far better relations among employees, the unions, and management at the company—relations that were helped by its more aligned CEO salaries.

Inside Information

- Make sure senior managers' pay is tied to performance. High pay makes sense in good years, especially when top executives have made meaningful contributions to the organization's success.

- Reduce pay for senior management dramatically in poor years; the percentage declines should be meaningfully greater than wage cuts for the rank and file.

- Consider the impact of high pay on morale. If business leaders are extracting every penny they can from the business, you can hardly expect other workers to sacrifice for the organization.

• • •

HAPPY EMPLOYEES

The best companies to invest in are the worst to work for only when you're viewing them as an outsider. Most people who work in these companies relish environments that demand and reward high performance. The companies look difficult only for those who are interested in a more leisurely pace of work and want to avoid the pressure of having to perform. Just as running a marathon is torture for a couch potato and satisfying for a trained marathoner, your view depends on your background and perspective. High-performance organizations are not for everyone. The right people generally self-select for them, and many of these organizations have rigorous processes to cull out people who do not fit the culture. In the end, they are left with people who really enjoy the environment. This is why many of the organizations mentioned here, such as Goldman Sachs and Genentech, regularly find themselves topping surveys such as *Fortune*'s "100 Best Companies to Work For."

To determine if you have a workplace that will attract and retain high performers, here are some questions to consider:

- Is there a tight link between performance and rewards? Do the rewards ever decrease? If they're not variable, either the link is tenuous or the measure of performance is too easy.

- Do employees spend a lot of time explaining how exogenous factors keep them from reaching their goals? If so, reexamine how performance is judged so that it ties more directly to what employees can control.

- Are you paying rewards in cash? As long as it is economically feasible (i.e., you have enough cash flow), cash is the best motivator.

- Do employees tell you about opportunities for synergies? Do you have a culture of openness that allows employees to identify opportunities without causing others to react defensively?

- Do you rely on a system of shared rewards to produce cooperation? Cooperation and synergies cannot be put on autopilot. As a manager, you need to manage them personally.

- When encouraging people or groups to work together to achieve synergies, do you provide separate favors or opportunities for the group/person who doesn't benefit from the work required in the cooperation?

- Do you have a shared ideal—above and beyond making money—that you communicate to your employees? Are they motivated by this ideal? If not, it's time to find a new ideal.

- Does your shared ideal reinforce your performance goals? If not, tweak it or find a new one.

- Do you reward employees' dedication to the ideal with "soft" rewards such as opportunities for recognition and advancement?

- Do you make sacrifices to advance your company's goals and fortunes? If not, you cannot expect your people to do so.

- Do you have an environment in which employees are performing and are happy, regardless of what outsiders may think?

CHAPTER 8

GOOD PERFORMANCE REQUIRES INEFFICIENCY AND DUPLICATION

W ASTE" AND "DUPLICATION" ARE DIRTY WORDS to most businesspeople. You are taught to maximize profitability, and what could be less productive than waste and redundancy? Nonetheless, I've seen firsthand that:

A single-minded focus on squeezing every penny from your operation hinders optimal profitability.

Though I'm not advocating creating sloppy, inefficient organizations, the most profitable approaches lie between waste and extreme efficiency.

Over the years, I've encountered some enormously effective moneymakers who were masters at managing this efficiency balance. They knew not only when to maximize efficiency by cutting out waste and redundancies but also when to encourage inefficiency by allowing serendipity and competition to catalyze superior long-term results. Generally, areas that involve creativity and individual initiative flourish in "looser" environments, while activities heavily involved with goods or capital equipment benefit from a more rigorous focus on efficiency. Here are some ways to strike the efficiency balance in your own business.

THE ENTICING ILLUSION OF CROSS-SELLING

Cross-selling, the practice of selling more of your products and services to your current customers, looks like the paragon of efficiency. Acquiring new customers is difficult and expensive; you should be able to enhance your sales force's efficiency by generating more revenue through preexisting relationships. Unfortunately, in practice it doesn't work unless you give your customers bundle discounts that devalue your product. Whenever I hear a company present a new growth strategy that relies on cross-selling, I assume that it has run out of more promising growth opportunities.

CBS Radio, formerly known as Infinity Radio, understood the perils of cross-selling (also referred to as bundling in some industries), while many of its competitors fell into this seductive trap. The modern era of radio companies began in 1996, when Congress passed the Telecommunications Act, which deregulated ownership and allowed companies to own up to eight radio stations in one market or metropolitan area. A wave of consolidation ensued, and a handful of large companies emerged that owned numerous stations (often the legal maximum) in multiple markets. Many of these operators adopted a marketwide sales approach and consolidated sales for all of a market's radio stations into one unified sales force. In some cases they even developed regionwide sales teams to sell across nearby metropolitan areas.

CBS/Infinity Radio, however, took a different tack, maintaining a dedicated sales team for each of its 150-plus radio stations.

By focusing each salesperson on a specific station, CBS required its people to sell the virtues of their specific radio offering. They couldn't gravitate toward the easiest sell—the station with the highest ratings—and throw the weak ones into a bundled sale for a nominal extra amount. Moreover, the sales pitch to advertisers wasn't diluted by salespeople shifting their pitch between different properties. ("I have the best station in the market to deliver young eighteen- to thirty-four-year-old listeners...oh, you're targeting older women with your ads...I have the best station in the market for them too.") With dedicated salespeople committed to selling every station, even the weaker ones, CBS required them to find the value in every property and to use their ingenuity to make sales for even the weakest stations.

If you're efficiency-minded, you might raise two objections to having related sales teams competing for the same ad dollars. First, the competition will become destructive; your salespeople will underprice one another to gain business. Though this fear is real, it can be managed by limiting salespeople's ability to set pricing and having higher-level managers monitoring the pricing trends in your markets.

The second objection—that you won't leverage your market power if you don't amass all your heft to dictate terms to advertisers—is more of an illusion. In the short term, you may be able to generate more revenue by taking advantage of your broad market power. But creating a monopolistic mentality will backfire in the long term. If you lean too heavily on your market power to drive sales, you will alienate customers. Moreover, market-dominating companies tend to get lazy. When competitors to their dominance emerge—and they always do—they generally respond slowly or ineffectively, while customers welcome the new provider.

Of course, you have to apply common sense when heeding this advice. If CBS were to take the logic too far, it would make each salesperson's products even more narrow—e.g., making one responsible for morning drive time (radio's prime time), another for midday, another for evening drive time. In practice, however, slicing the business this thin would be untenable for salespeople and overwhelming for clients—they would have a radio rep knocking on their door every ten seconds.

If you keep your business appropriately balanced, allowing some inefficiency to ensure maximum focus on generating returns from all your assets, you will win. Certainly the results at CBS Radio supported its strategy of allowing inefficiency in the sales force to drive results. By 1999, CBS's radio division was generating $11.3 million in revenue and $5.7 million in operating profit plus depreciation and amortization (OPPDA, formerly known as EBITDA) per station, whereas the radio stations of its primary competitor, Clear Channel Communications, which had organized around more market-based selling, produced $5.7 million in revenue and $2.5 million in OPPDA. Investors in CBS's stock noticed too, with the stock price rising more than threefold from the end of 1996 to the end of 1999, when Viacom agreed to buy the company for $37.3 billion.

NOW LET'S EXAMINE a cautionary tale about the dangers of cross-selling. Interpublic Group, a conglomerate of advertising agencies, public relations firms, direct marketing experts, and other marketing/communications advisers, grew to $5.6 billion in revenue through successive acquisitions throughout the 1990s. In 2002, the company entered a tough period when it disclosed profit overstatements and other accounting irregularities, prompting the government to open an investigation. In February 2003, after more bad news surfaced, then-CEO John Dooner stepped down and David Bell, who headed a publicly traded firm that Interpublic had acquired in 2001, took over as

CEO. He quickly addressed the company's pressing financial obligations by issuing more than $1.5 billion in convertible debt, and the stock price rose by 50 percent from its low as investors became more confident that Interpublic would resolve its problems and resume its historic growth rate.

To fuel the company's growth, the well-intentioned Bell focused on a cross-selling plan that he named the Organic Growth Initiative (OGI). He announced that his goal was "to change the culture at Interpublic and to drive increased collaboration." He hired a chief growth officer to oversee the initiative, and the team built tools and developed incentives to encourage Interpublic's various agencies to refer work to one another. The concept of having an advertising agency refer its client to an Interpublic public relations or direct marketing firm certainly made sense, and the program recorded some early wins.

However, the OGI program did not lead to growth for the company overall. Part of the problem was that OGI, despite its "organic" name, was imposed rather than evolving naturally from mutual business interests. No doubt the heads of Interpublic agencies felt as if they were being forced to make referrals. Rather than doing so when they perceived clients would benefit, they were being asked to do so regardless of the fit. In addition, business heads complained that the cross-selling initiative was taking time away from their core operations. As a result, revenues grew modestly in 2004 but fell again in 2005. Operating profits fell in both 2004 and 2005. The agencies were pricing aggressively to bring in the "organic" growth, and it wasn't helping the returns. Interpublic's stock price reacted negatively, falling 13 percent from August 2003, when the OGI program was announced, until early 2005, a period during which the broader market gained more than 10 percent. In January 2005, Interpublic's Board announced that David Bell would step down, and board member Michael Roth took the reins as CEO. Roth retained the chief growth officer role and emphasis on cross-selling, with equally disappointing results. Revenues fell yet again in 2006, and the operating profitability of 2.7 percent was a quarter the rate it should have been. The company has continued to struggle since.

CITIGROUP PURSUED A similar cross-selling strategy on an even larger scale. In 1998, when Sandy Weill and John Reed merged Travelers Group with Citibank, the rationale was to create a supermarket that could sell retail and corporate clients every financial product conceivable, from insurance to banking to brokerage. Weill was so convinced of the power of the combination that he proceeded despite a statute, the Glass-Steagall Act, that prohibited banks and insurance underwriters from being part of the same firm. He made the acquisition anyway and then set about lobbying to have the Depression-era law changed, which he and the rest of the banking industry achieved in 1999.

Though regulations didn't stand in the way of the newly minted Citigroup, the difficulties of cross-selling did. Almost from the time the merger was completed in late 1998, it had difficulties. Earnings were disappointing, and major management shake-ups and reorganizations seemed to occur every year. In an effort to achieve some of the benefits of its multiple business units, Citigroup pressured analysts such as Jack Grubman to change their outlook on corporate clients' stocks, which landed it in well-known trouble. Even when it was able to cross-sell without skirting regulations, it was unsuccessful. In late 2001, Citigroup announced that it would spin off its Travelers Property Casualty business because customers who were cross-sold insurance turned out to be very poor risks; the more successful it was in cross-selling, the more money it was losing. Still the firm struggled, and in mid-2007 Weill's successor, Chuck Prince, retired from the CEO role. It remains to be seen if the new CEO, Vikram Pandit, can succeed where the others failed; he is certainly moving in the right direction by continuing to sell off operations and shrink the bank, thus reducing the cross-selling temptations.

So how can you take advantage of cross-selling opportunities among your product lines? David Bell had the right idea, if the wrong execution. Forcing the process on people may seem to create efficiencies, but if they emerge, they will be fleeting. A more natural process, however, makes cross-selling feasible in both the short and long term:

The best way to cross-sell is not to.

This paradox makes sense when you observe how money-makers operate. They focus on making each of their businesses' products or services the best in its field. In this way, if a client notes the need for a product or service that falls within your organization's capabilities, your people will make an introduction to the appropriate corporate sibling without prompting. If the product or service is high quality, it's in your employees' interest to make the introduction and earn kudos from their clients. At the same time, your clients will trust the recommendations more because they are motivated by sound business practice rather than an internal cross-selling mandate. Omnicom, a marketing/communications holding company similar to Interpublic, has been far more successful in selling multiple products to its clients by taking this "best of breed" approach. Indeed, it will often buy small agencies that its clients are happy with, rather than try to usurp that role with one of its own offerings. This approach has served it well. Over the decade from 1998 to 2007, its top-line growth compounded at 11 percent a year and earnings per share at 14 percent; the stock price more than doubled.

Inside Information

- Don't build your strategy around cross-selling. Though it looks very efficient on paper, it rarely works.

- Allow cross-selling to develop naturally; create high-quality products and services, and trust that this quality will prompt referrals of customers to other groups under your umbrella.

- Resist salespeople's inclinations to have a broad product set to sell from. Use common sense to make sure they don't have too little to sell, but if in doubt, narrow the focus.

YOU CAN'T CONTROL CREATIVITY

Creativity is messy, but it is also the engine of many of the most profitable products. Every endeavor needs some inefficiency and duplication to foster creativity. When all your processes are buttoned down and people believe they must follow procedures to the letter, no room exists for innovation. If you maximize efficiency, you and your people can't test new ideas or suggest concepts that go against the conventional wisdom.

Consider how extreme efficiency damages the new-product development process. Many newly appointed executives look to streamline their organizations by making product development more efficient; they want to develop only the products that work. They want to map out a smooth process that moves successful products through each stage of development logically, quickly, and cost-effectively. Breakthrough products and services, however, tend to emerge out of conflict, uncertainty, and risk taking.

New-product development is as much art as science, and when you build a certain amount of laxity into the process, you provide your people with opportunities to try new approaches and give dark-horse products a chance.

3M has traditionally harnessed the serendipity and inefficiency needed for a vibrant new-product culture to flourish, because it understood the importance of building inefficiency into its management system. Consider the classic story of how Post-it notes were invented. A determined scientist, Art Fry, championed what looked like a failed adhesive—it stuck but not permanently. Fascinated by the science, Fry struggled to find a use for the adhesive—it was pure serendipity that he came up with the note format. He then drove the product through skeptical engineering/manufacturing and marketing organizations to develop a $1 billion product. It was only because 3M allows its people to "waste" 15 percent of their time on independent projects that Fry was able to make the breakthrough.

Yet even 3M was susceptible to the siren song of efficiency. When James McNerney took over as 3M CEO in 2000, after a long, successful career at GE, he brought with him GE's emphasis on Six Sigma and its relentless drive for efficiency. Initially his impact was very positive; after years of success 3M had become bloated, and introducing Six Sigma efficiency metrics improved its manufacturing operations. After this initial success, McNerney broadened his efficiency drive to areas that depend on creativity. He required the research organization to do more reporting on the end uses of its research and to conform its processes to a Six Sigma methodology. Convinced he could make new-product development more efficient, McNerney also throttled back spending on R&D. In 1999, the year before he became CEO, 3M spent 6.7 percent of revenue on research and development. By 2004, his last full year with 3M, the ratio dropped to 5.7 percent. The impact on the business was noticeable. Prior to

McNerney's arrival, a centerpiece of 3M's strategy was that 30 percent of sales came from products less than four years old. In 2007—since innovation has a long tail—only a quarter of the company's revenues came from new products.

Many lay the blame for overzealous efficiency drives like McNerney's at the feet of shareholders, but investors evaluate stocks and companies based on their future earnings generation. At 3M, McNerney's approach resulted in early stock price gains as his approach saved money. But by 2004, shareholders grasped the downside of McNerney's methods; the improved productivity was damaging 3M's product pipeline, which was the source of its future profitability. The stock price stagnated throughout 2004 and started to fall in early 2005. With a poor outlook, McNerney jumped ship from 3M to Boeing on June 30, 2005. It's been up to his successor, George Buckley, to make the company less efficient. Buckley has eased the Six Sigma requirements for the research organization, and in his first full year, 2006, he increased R&D spending by 20 percent, returning it to its historic 6.6 percent of sales. Though it will take time and serendipity for the extra spending to produce marketable products, investors have cheered the increased spending, driving the stock price up 20 percent over the two years after McNerney left. To keep the momentum, Buckley will have to continue to advance 3M's value edge with consistent research spending.

THE INTERNET GIANT Google understands the importance of inefficiency in its new-product development. Doing 3M one better, it requires its engineers to spend 20 percent of their time working on whatever interests them. As the founders of the mathematically inclined organization, Larry Page and Sergey Brin have even developed a proof for why 20 percent is the proportion of time that optimizes inefficiency and risk with the serendipity required to find unexpected opportunities (not being a mathe-matician, I cannot explain it; I rely instead on the outcomes I see at companies).

To be clear, I'm not advocating that you allow your people to goof off during a fifth of their workday. Google's inefficiency works, as I noted in chapter 5, because it's not completely loosey-goosey; there is a method to the madness. All employees have to report on what they are working on, and success in "20 per-cent time" projects is part of one's annual evaluation. Moreover, success in these projects earns workers the respect of their peers, a strong motivator for this competitive organization. Sen-ior management have also developed additional bonuses, called Founders Awards, to provide economic rewards for work that is particularly impactful.

Engineers working on their "20 percent time" have pro-duced some duds, as in any product development or creative processes, but they have also produced fantastic winners. Thus far the most successful of these efforts has been AdSense for content, which puts relevant search listings on content sites that have partnered with Google. When crawling these partners' sites, Google's algorithms analyze the content on the partners' pages. They then select ads based on that content's primary topic from Google's database of ads. AdSense for content has created significantly more places for Google to place ads and makes up a third of Google's sales. Revenue from partner sites grew by 560 percent in the product's first three years, from 2003 to 2006.

On a smaller scale, Chase Card Services, the credit card arm of JPMorgan Chase, implements the same controlled ineffi-ciency principles in its advertising programs. To solicit new cardholders, the program has relied primarily on direct mail solicitations, an especially quantifiable form of advertising. The division's marketers can predict with great accuracy the new customers and economic returns they will generate on the millions of pieces of mail they "drop" (i.e., send) each year. Yet even with—or perhaps because of—the great quantification within their business, these marketers understand the importance of serendipity in their new-client programs. In the last decade the Internet and other new technologies have multiplied and fractured the ways for marketers to grab the attention of potential customers. Tried-and-true methods have become less effective, so marketers have had to become far more creative in their use of media.

To address this challenge, Chase Card Services allocates 10 percent of its advertising budget each year to new, unproven forms of advertising with an expectation of zero-percent return on the investment. To spend money with such a dismal expected return requires faith in the power of inefficiency. In many companies, efficiency gurus would successfully argue that the company should redirect all its spending to established channels where the ROI is strong and known. However, doing so is shortsighted, as these returns will gradually diminish as these channels reach the end of their life cycle and become less effective. Chase's inefficient approach enables it to identify effective new channels before its current methods lose their efficacy. Moving into new channels early on also allows Chase to secure more advantageous pricing, terms that will last even when a channel becomes proven. As a result of this inefficient philosophy, Chase jumped fast when online television shows first took ads in 2006. This move proved the value of experimentation, producing abundant new card sign-ups and returns well above the anticipated zero.

Inside Information

- Allow for serendipity in areas where creativity or fresh thinking is required; be willing to tolerate some redundancy, lack of control, and unscheduled time so that innovation "magic" can happen.

- Trade more experimentation for less efficiency in creative processes.

- Allocate a portion of your budget (both time and money) to give your people unstructured time, even if it results in duplication and inefficiency (it probably will). The amount of unstructured time you allow should depend on how important creativity is to your endeavor, the pace of change in your markets, and the overall health of the business (in particularly high return businesses, more should be allocated; even in lower-return efforts, allow a small amount).

- Ask how your employees spend their free time, but do so unobtrusively. Require quick reporting on what's being done, but make sure it does not quash the effort or demand tangible results or even a specific goal too early in the process.

- Examine what didn't work in order to advance the learning of the entire organization; be sure to praise experimenters for their risk taking instead of tagging them as failures.

TRAINING: WORTH THE TIME

Like many professionals who work in larger organizations, I generally dreaded having to spend time in training classes or departmental off-site meetings. I would prefer to be picking stocks, visiting with company managements, reading SEC filings, or forecasting corporate earnings. Though I moaned about my own training sessions, I came to learn from studying moneymakers that the most effective companies devote significant resources to internal training. Though everything from executive development programs to specialized training courses may seem like exercises in inefficiency—they divert considerable attention and resources from core business activities—I have seen training improve businesses' competitive position, enable them to move up the value chain, foster cross-divisional cooperation, and generally help employees to understand the economic imperatives of their businesses and how they can contribute to advancing the ball.

Infosys Technologies, an India-based information technology services and consulting company, has used training to improve its positioning and move into higher-value offerings. Founded in Pune, India, in 1981 by N. R. Narayana Murthy, Nandan Nilekani, and five others, the company landed its first international client in 1987, when its value edge was low-cost labor. Business grew steadily until the late 1990s, when demand for COBOL programmers to update legacy systems for the Y2K conversion caused the demand for Indian programmers to balloon. Few programmers in the developed world wanted to learn COBOL since it was an outdated programming language. India's universities, however, still taught the language as part of their curriculum, so Infosys had the necessary skills and won many contracts to remediate systems. Offering low-cost labor to do mundane, low-skill programming enabled Infosys to achieve Rs 882 crore (U.S. $203 million) in revenue in the year ending March 31, 2000. Infosys was not alone in capitalizing on this opportunity; many Indian outsourcers thrived during this time. However, by investing some of those profits in inefficient training programs, Infosys set itself apart.

Infosys had established its edge through a cost advantage, and any company that owes its competitive edge to cost is tempted to squeeze out every penny (or rupee) to maximize its lead as a low-cost provider; efficiency becomes the mantra. Infosys, though, resisted this temptation. It devoted considerable resources to training, and the percentage of time its employees spend on billable work (i.e., utilization) suffered; the company's utilization runs at a much lower level than that of its technology-consulting counterparts (such as Accenture) in the United States.

This inefficiency, however, has served Infosys well in the long run. Extensive training allowed employees to acquire more sophisticated skills and knowledge of newer programming languages and software packages. Then Infosys could bid on and win higher-value-added work. The firm leveraged the relationships it forged with large U.S. and European multinationals when doing the Y2K work to win contracts for installations of enterprise resource planning software, application development, and consulting. Despite a dramatic dropoff in Y2K assignments in fiscal 2001, Infosys's revenues and profits didn't skip a beat; they more than doubled over 2000.

Again, I'm not suggesting that all efficiency-minded efforts are bad. Infosys avoids wasting money in many different ways. For instance, employees fly coach class on international flights and stay in nonluxury hotels. But management, led by Nandan Nilekani, who served as CEO from 2002 to 2007, understood where to build long-term value by being less efficient in the short term. The strategy has paid off handsomely. In Nilekani's last year, fiscal 2007, the company generated Rs3,149 crore (U.S. $3.1 billion) in revenue and Rs3,777 crore (U.S. $850 million) in net income, with a 32 percent operating margin and a 42 percent average return on net worth.

The investment in training has had other benefits as well. By giving its employees the opportunity to learn and improve their skill sets, Infosys has improved retention in the notoriously high turnover market for programmers in Bangalore (India's Silicon Valley). The shared training experience has also helped build cohesiveness among employees based in India and around the globe. These connections have yielded another value edge for Infosys: faster delivery of projects through the ability to work on projects twenty-four hours a day by moving them around the globe. Shareholders have noticed the benefits of Infosys's model, with its stock rising more than threefold in the five years after the Y2K growth spurt (2001 to 2006).

Omnicom Group has also invested in training to foster synergies among its employees and improve their skills. A holding company of advertising agencies and other marketing consultancies, Omnicom was formed in 1986 when three midsize advertising agencies—BBDO, Doyle Dane Bernbach, and Needham Harper Worldwide—merged in a "big bang" to compete with the larger agency holding companies that Interpublic and others were forming. Dozens of other agencies in a variety of marketing and communications disciplines have merged with Omnicom since. For most of these business units, revenues are generated primarily through time-and-materials contracts, so any time spent on nonclient work drags down an agency's profitability. Leaders of its 1,500 offices spread around the globe are strictly compensated on the operating profit that their offices generate (even receiving large bonuses in years when the overall firm's performance is subpar).

Given this profit-centric approach, you would think that each office would bend over backward to bill as many hours as possible. What you wouldn't expect is that Omnicom has one of the strongest corporate education programs around, one that it supports even though cutting it would improve the numbers that it delivers to Wall Street in the short term. How does it justify all the time its employees spend in classes when billable hours are so important to its revenue generation? Employee education has been crucial to achieving synergies while maintaining CEO John Wren's "best of breed" strategy, in which each Omnicom agency has to stand on its own and excel within its particular discipline.

The centerpiece of Omnicom's training efforts is Omnicom University, an invitation-only program for fifty senior Omnicom managers at a time. With undergraduate, graduate, and post-graduate levels, the program is taught by leading business school professors and uses a case study method to engage manager-students in examining the best operating practices for professional services firms. Omnicom also has a Business Learning Program for less senior managers and an MBA residency program, which brings new business school graduates into the company and rotates them through six assignments.

These programs not only give managers the know-how to run their individual businesses better but also help forge relationships across the organization. If an executive at Goodby, Silverstein & Partners, an Omnicom-owned ad agency, has a client who says it needs a new public relations firm, that manager has an incentive to refer the client to a senior leader from Ketchum, whom he met at Omnicom University and who he knows is capable because he has seen her in action. This approach is far superior to headquarters-driven forced-collaboration initiatives, which tend to raise clients' suspicions about the motivation behind referrals. Instead, at Omnicom, referrals come from personal experience with individuals from sister agencies. The referrer knows the quality of the person he is introducing and makes the introduction to improve his standing with his client. The clients also know the referral is more credible. It's telling that the founder of Omnicom University was Tom Watson, a vice chairman of Omnicom until his retirement at the end of 2004. His primary responsibility was to broker cooperation among the various Omnicom agencies.

Again, committing to seemingly inefficient education programs pays dividends. In 2006, Omnicom's top 100 clients had relationships with, on average, more than forty of its agencies. The natural collaborative mentality drove the double-digit growth in financial results that I mentioned earlier.

Southwest Airlines, too, has embraced training despite the short-term hit to its earnings. It has used training for a higher long-term purpose: to align the actions of its employees with the goals of the corporation. Southwest has a philosophy of "Hire for attitude, train for skills," so it does a lot of functional training at its University for People as well as introductory sessions for new employees and managerial programs.

In recent years, however, it has taken its training programs one step further and developed an educational program that explains and simplifies the drivers of profitability in the business. Top managers selected the four metrics most important to Southwest's results: net income, net income margin, return on invested capital, and cost per available seat mile (the standard unit of capacity in the airline industry). They called them the Magic Numbers and created a video that entertainingly conveyed the role of each metric in Southwest's overall strategy and employees' profit sharing, and how individuals' actions can impact the numbers. In training sessions, employees watch the video and then discuss how their groups can impact the four numbers. Southwest's CFO, Laura Wright, credits the training with enabling the company to keep head count flat while growing the business by 30 percent from 2003 to 2006. In the longer term, this business training will help facilitate negotiations when Southwest's current union contracts expire. Successful hedging of fuel costs has contributed significantly to Southwest's profitability in recent years, and Southwest doesn't want to fall into the same trap that Delta did and pay operating employees long term with financial engineering results which are shorter term. Business training should enable Southwest and its employees to understand how financial decisions can affect its underlying profitability.

Inside Information

- Overcome antipathy toward "wasteful" employee training programs. Look beyond the short-term hit to productivity to find the long-term benefits.

- Make your training program about something concrete that employees can use. Employees view soft, culture-focused programs as a waste of their time. Ensure that your program offers something that will make the trainees' jobs easier or enable them to advance.

- Don't underestimate the soft impacts of your training efforts. Though the program should not be about soft culture issues, these values can be imparted indirectly through the program. Employees know that what you spend resources on is what you value.

- Run programs with small groups (no more than fifty people) drawn from all over your organization to improve synergy and communication.

• • •

TO BE OR NOT TO BE ... EFFICIENT

Allowing a certain amount of inefficiency to creep into your systems seems heretical, especially at a time when there's tremendous pressure to cut costs, streamline processes, and maximize every employee's productivity. The counterintuitive nature of inefficiency may cause you to hesitate about implementing the advice in this chapter. If so, let me remind you of another investing paradox:

Long-term ROI gain often necessitates short-term ROI pain.

There are times when it pays to be efficient—and times when it pays to be inefficient. To determine where to maintain tight control for maximum efficiency and where to be looser, consider the following questions:

- How much are things involved? The more physical goods (e.g., inventory) and capital equipment are involved, the greater the push for maximum efficiency should be.

- How much creativity is required? How unpredictable are your results? The more creativity and serendipity involved in your success, the more inefficiency and duplication you should encourage. New-product development is not an area in which to push for maximum efficiency.

- How much investment is required, and how far has that investment spending gone? The less the spending and the earlier in the spending cycle, the more inefficiency you can allow.

- How rapid is the pace of change in your business? The faster the pace of change, the more experimentation is required to catch the next wave of innovation. Experimentation is, by definition, inefficient.

- How big a factor are people? The standardization and centralization required for maximum efficiency can often be demotivating. The more important energized people are to your operation (especially in service businesses), the more tolerance you should have for inefficiency.

- How important are synergies to the success of your business? The more cross-functional cooperation is required, the less standardized and less efficient your business model can be, because training programs, brokering of cooperation by individual leaders, and other "soft" techniques are required to achieve cooperation reliably.

- How much experimentation is built into your systems? In every operation, some experimental inefficiency should exist. Size experimentation budgets proportionally to the cost of the experiments and to the payback periods (all else being equal, the longer the payback, the less experimentation, because you want a given approach or spending to earn a decent return before overhauling it).

- What are your plans for moving your company up the value chain to higher-margin efforts? Breaking into new areas and improving your company's profitability will require investment and experimentation.

CHAPTER 9

MEGATRENDS START AS RIPPLES

A T LEAST ONCE A MONTH, AND MORE OFTEN DURING earnings season, I see on CNBC or in *The Wall Street Journal* a CEO or CFO complaining about how Wall Street won't let him invest for the future. I'm always bemused because no one cares more about the future than shareholders. A company can announce the most awful quarterly results with huge losses and writedowns, but if management credibly raises future earnings expectations, the stock price will go up. Stock prices are based entirely on expected future earnings, so shareholders want you to take the steps necessary today to generate those profits.

However, it's not necessary to pour huge amounts of money into long-shot ventures that won't bear fruit for years in order to grow. Moneymakers have shown repeatedly that if you identify megatrends while they are still ripples and position yourself early and flexibly, you can grow easily and cheaply.

CATCH THE WAVE

Easy growth is based on a seeming paradox:

It is easier to predict the future ten years out than two.

The trends that will shape the world a decade from now are large, massive waves that start small and build force over time; because of their size, they are relatively easy to predict. Projecting when they will gain enough momentum to transform from a ripple moving across the ocean into a tsunami, however, is very difficult. You can make a reasonable prediction a decade out by merely identifying the large trends. If you are asked to make a good two-year forecast, you have to identify how far along a trend will be and what form it will take, the latter task being the most challenging. In fact, it's daunting to predict how a general trend will develop into specific manifestations and events.

When NAFTA was signed in 1992, it was easy to predict that the world was going to become more global and manufacturing would move out of the more expensive, higher-skilled United States. However, few people at the time foresaw that China, not Mexico, would produce much of the United States' imports fifteen years later. Similarly, when Warner Amex Cable Communications (a predecessor of Time Warner Cable) was experimenting with interactive television through its Qube system in Columbus, Ohio, in the 1970s, many predicted the evolution of two-way electronic communication. But who would have forecast that twenty-five years later most interactive video would be viewed on computer screens in short amateur clips?

What astute moneymakers grasp is that, in the words of Bob

Dylan, "you don't need a weatherman to know which way the wind blows." Megatrends move slowly. By looking regularly to the horizon, you can see the waves that are coming while they are still ripples on the surface. By thinking about the long-term implications of current business developments, you can identify the primary trends—they've usually been occurring in successive waves over decades—for your industry. Then, by evangelizing the coming trends among your people, you can get them to look for ways to prepare for these trends. You can then invest early and easily. It's important not to seek to predict the exact form a trend will take but rather to build interim products that work for customers today and provide you with the real-world experience necessary to capitalize on the megatrend when it hits in full force. If you follow this strategy, you will quickly gain a reputation for uncanny foresight.

WHEN BOB IGER took over as CEO of the Walt Disney Company in 2005, he immediately identified three trends that he wanted his employees to focus on: (1) creativity, the engine of product creation in the entertainment business, (2) globalization, to transform this U.S.-centric company into one that capitalized on less penetrated markets internationally, and (3) technology, which was changing the production and delivery of entertainment content. Iger spoke repeatedly about the trends and as a result got what had been a hidebound organization to embrace less conventional and riskier moves in pursuit of the three trends. Anne Sweeney, the head of Disney's television division, once joked that Iger had them sew the three themes onto their underwear.

Due in large part to Iger's evangelizing, Disney's ABC television network became the first to sell television episodes online through Apple's iTunes and then to put ad-supported versions on its own ABC Web site. Disney became more aggressive

internationally, not only speeding the launch of its Disney network channels around the world, but also buying a TV channel
in India. On the creativity front, it solidified its dominance in
animated films by acquiring Pixar, and in the process hiring
Pixar's creative chief, John Lasseter, whom many consider the
Walt Disney of computer-animated film. Investors have responded positively to Iger's moves to capitalize on these three
trends; in the two years after he assumed the CEO role and
rolled them out, the stock climbed more than 40 percent.

You can adopt Bob Iger's approach and focus your people on
the trends sweeping toward your business. The first step is to
identify the megatrends that are impacting your business. Here
is a list of broad trends to consider:

- **Globalization.** How will competition from abroad and
  new markets impact your business? Who are the up-and-
  coming nondomestic competitors? How will they think
  about the world differently? Separately, what
  opportunities does the world offer for new customers?
  How are their needs different?

- **Technology.** How will the continuing evolution and
  declining cost of computing power, data storage,
  connectivity, and other technologies affect you? Where
  can you put more electronic intelligence into your
  products and production chain, and how will that change
  the way you conduct business? What will you be able to
  do in ten years, when costs are lower still? What new
  technologies can potentially disintermediate you from
  your clients?

- **Innovation.** What is the engine of improvement in your
  industry, and how are you positioned to capitalize on it?

What changes are there to speed up the process, make it more cost-efficient, or just do it differently? What new disciplines can you tap into to bring a fresh perspective?

- **Environmental and other causes.** Should you position your product to capitalize on customers' desires to feel good about their purchases? What philanthropic goals fit best with your organization and culture? How can you tap into them authentically? What causes, if taken up broadly, could pose a threat to your business? How do you prepare to address those threats?

- **Regulation.** Can you take advantage of increasingly unified regulation globally? What do converging accounting standards mean for your company? What would be the impact if the world moved to more stringent environmental, safety, privacy, or other relevant regulations? What products can you develop to meet these tougher regulations?

- **Customization.** Can you ride the trend toward specialized products and services for market niches? What would it take to make individually customized products? How close can you get today without sacrificing too much efficiency? If not very close, can you create an advantage of standardized product in customers' eyes?

- **Consumer power.** How can you take advantage of cheap one-to-one communication? How can you capitalize on the trend of increasingly smaller entities as less scale and infrastructure are needed in many industries? What are customers saying to one another about your product? Have you checked out the word of mouth about your products online? How can you make your value-added more tangible for customers?

These questions are not comprehensive or specific enough for any individual business. I'm sure you have other large trends relevant to your business. Use the above list to help start conversations with and among your employees and spark organizationwide thinking about long-term trends.

Next, select a few (preferably three) trends to focus on. All of the above megatrends plus other industry-specific trends are likely to impact your business in some way, but focusing on a few key trends will make your prognosticating more effective. Here is a step-by-step process to help narrow the focus.

1. Pick the factor that most underlies value creation in your business and where continuous change takes place, even if it is not a megatrend per se. For Disney, the foundation of its business is creativity. For a bank, it might be risk assessment; for a technology or biotech business, innovation; and for a consumer products operation, consumer insight. Ideally, there will be a discernible trend that drives this portion of your business, but if not, just select an area of continuous change.

2. Identify which megatrend represents your biggest greenfield opportunity for your second trend. You want a large, evolving area adjacent to your current business. For Disney, this trend was globalization; as emerging markets became wealthier and developed markets more unified, it had a huge upside if it could sell its products as extensively overseas as it did domestically. Greenfield opportunities do not have to be new geographical areas; they can be adjacent businesses. For Infosys, the outsourced technology com-

pany, its biggest opportunity trend was the increasing complexity and sophistication of software, which allowed it to sell higher-value services to its clients. For Procter & Gamble, a move into higher-margin beauty products allowed it to leverage its consumer marketing skills in a broad new category.

3. For your third trend, identify the area of major change that represents the biggest potential threat to your business. By tackling it early, you can turn a threat into an opportunity. For Disney, technology threatened to disrupt its traditional business models as the Internet provided new ways to access entertainment. On the other hand, technology also offered new channels to distribute its content and connect more directly with customers. By focusing his employees on the trend with an aim toward technology playing a larger role in Disney's businesses, Iger turned the trend into a benefit. You can do the same. Just look for the largest evolving risk to your business and embrace it to make it work for you rather than against you.

As you select your three key trends, avoid defining them narrowly; you want them to encompass numerous aspects of your business and allow your employees wide latitude in addressing them. Once you have selected the three areas to focus on, evangelize them among your people. In this way you will encourage employees throughout your business to identify long-term growth opportunities within those three areas. You can also reduce your growth preparation costs by gathering information and doing analysis in a continuous but ad hoc manner that best leverages the knowledge of your employees, customers, and suppliers.

Inside Information

- Pay attention to large, slow-moving trends, even if they do not impact you and your profitability today.

- Adopt a handful of the trends with the largest potential impact. Strike a careful balance between targeting areas for your employees to focus on and reflecting the diversity of trends affecting your organization.

- Proselytize about your selected trends repeatedly; keep in mind that your employees can easily lose sight of the larger trends in the face of pressing daily tasks. So it's important to repeat, repeat, repeat.

THINK LONG TERM, ACT TODAY

Evangelizing is not enough. After selecting your three trends, find ways to prepare for them while they are still in their formative stages. Remember, this is the time when you can deal with them relatively cheaply. When Cisco invested in The Network Is the Platform, CEO John Chambers was not only thinking ahead of his customers but also preparing for a megatrend in the industry: lower connectivity costs that allowed for more distributed computing. When customers were telling him that the product had no appeal, he was directing his team to invest its no-return-expected funds to innovate in the area. The cost was relatively low because the expense was spread over years and no deadline pressures existed. By thinking ahead, Chambers was able to invest slowly and cheaply to develop products. When clients were ready to embrace distributed computing, Cisco looked prescient for having products ready to go.

In the automotive industry, General Motors, Ford, and Chrysler responded quite differently to their most impactful megatrend: the rising consciousness of global warming and the role of auto emissions. With an overwhelming scientific consensus, increasing political and popular awareness, and the drafting of the Kyoto Accord in December 1997, auto manufacturers have known for more than a decade that tailpipe emissions, a major producer of greenhouse gases, were a problem. Though the trend has been apparent, it's also been easy to ignore. Few hard mandates have required the auto manufacturers to make changes. Most have ignored the underlying trend, but not Toyota (and Honda, though less effectively). Starting in 1993, Toyota's top management began an initiative called G21 (for Global 21st Century) to consider the future of the automobile and specifically how to lower fuel usage and emissions. The company funded an R&D effort whose results determined that a hybrid power system (a combination of a battery-powered electric motor and a smaller but conventional gasoline-fueled engine) would move it toward the trend while still being practical enough for consumers to accept today; they wouldn't have to alter their behavior and no new fueling infrastructure would be required.

Here is another secret of how to capitalize on megatrends:

> **Do not seek to create the *solution; rather, develop*
> *something that moves toward the trend.***

By addressing a trend early, you can test, work out any kinks, and be well on your way toward creating the ideal product or service. This approach is far more effective than getting so enamored with your trend spotting that you pour huge amounts of money into developing the breakthrough solution. Most often, taking a step toward the trend yields a more marketable product and costs significantly less but still generates valuable insights into how to meet the trend.

IN 1995, TOYOTA Motor Corporation announced that it would launch its hybrid vehicle, and in December 1997 the cars were available for sale in Japan. Three years later, it introduced the Prius in the United States. The development timetable was compressed because Toyota wanted to get the car to market quickly so it could gather real-world consumer feedback as soon as possible. Sales were slow initially, as Toyota had little idea how to market the vehicle; focus groups had given it a thumbs-down. Nonetheless, Toyota pressed ahead, looking to move forward on the environmental megatrend. In time, celebrities and others concerned about global warming discovered the benefits of the vehicle, and sales took off. In 2004, Toyota introduced the second-generation Prius, in which it improved upon the compromises made during the initial rush to develop the car. In 2007, seven years after the initial introduction, the environmental movement reached a tipping point with help from rising gas prices and Al Gore's campaign on the dangers of global warming. The Prius quickly became Toyota's fourth-largest-selling model. Toyota sold 278,000 hybrids in the United States that year and has since sold more than a million Priuses globally.

It's estimated—Toyota doesn't share the number—that the Prius cost about $1 billion to develop, roughly equivalent to the cost of developing any new car. By acting on the trend early and investing some of its inefficiency funds, Toyota prepared for the future without spending inordinately. Because it set its sights on a highly achievable goal, brought the car out quickly to garner fast feedback, and made changes based on that feedback, Toyota now dominates a trend that offers growth for years to come.

Let's contrast Toyota's approach with that of General Motors. GM also made a big splash in developing a low-emission car when it developed its EV1, which it made available for lease in California and Arizona in 1997. Rather than seeking to capitalize on a slow-moving but inevitable trend, GM developed the EV1 in response to a specific pressure point. In 1990, the California Air Resources Board (CARB) mandated that 2 percent of new cars sold in the state must be "zero-emission vehicles" by 1998, rising to 10 percent by 2003. Most automakers, including Toyota, adapted an existing model to create a battery-powered car. GM, however, set out to create a whole new car, the only one that it has branded with the General Motors nameplate. The company spent around $1.5 billion (partially offset by some tax abatements) to develop the EV1, which was widely acknowledged as an engineering marvel. But with a maximum 100-mile range, the car had severe usage limitations and required consumers to remember to charge their batteries. Given the required changes in consumer behavior, the EV1 would need years and years before it could become a mass-market seller.

Once the CARB backtracked on the zero-emission mandate, GM quickly scrapped the EV1 program and its efforts to address the global warming trend. It had spent so much that it was impossible to justify further support for the project when it wasn't an immediate success. In recent years, as high gas prices and concern about global warming have reached a tipping point, CEO Rick Wagoner has said that axing the EV1 and not putting more resources into developing hybrids were the worst decisions of his tenure. Now GM is scrambling to catch up on a trend that it was well aware of more than a decade ago. Meanwhile, Toyota is selling hybrids at a fast clip, is considered the most environmentally progressive auto company, and is making money from licensing its technology to others such as Nissan that want to catch up. Moreover, because it has garnered so much real-world experience with automobile batteries, Toyota will be far ahead in developing a profitable electric car when battery technology and consumer attitudes are ready for the next step.

Here's another paradox to keep in mind:

To succeed in long-term trends, you must remain acutely aware of current realities.

Executives who fall blindly in love with their vision of the future may well lose sight of what their customers will accept today. You want to lead your customers, but you cannot push them too far ahead of what they are comfortable with now. Toyota's hybrid cars were more readily adopted by consumers than GM's EV1 because they didn't require planning around the cars' limited range or remembering to recharge them.

Similarly, when Cisco determined in 2002 that video transmission was the next frontier in connectivity, CEO John Chambers and his team began studying the market. In 2006, they acquired Scientific Atlanta, a designer and manufacturer of set-top boxes and related products for cable system operators. Many observers found the acquisition puzzling, because the clear long-term trend is that video will be delivered using Internet technologies, a domain where Cisco has dominant products and that Scientific Atlanta's products don't serve. Chambers and his team, however, understood that while the trend is clear, the timing is not. Internet capacity constraints mean that much video, particularly television, will continue to be broadcast over dedicated bandwidth rather than cut into packets and transmitted over shared lines, as happens on the Internet. Even among the telcos that are starting to offer video, much of the programming is broadcast on dedicated sections of their fiber-optic cables.

While waiting for the Internet future to arrive, Cisco realized that the acquisition of Scientific Atlanta gave it the opportunity to learn the art of video compression, delivery (which usually starts with satellite transmission to local areas and then wired transmission to individual homes), and other quirks of complex, data-heavy video. An added bonus was the strong relationships that Scientific Atlanta had with its cable systems customers, which will be major players in the evolution of video (either through traditional broadcast video distribution or as providers of high-speed Internet connectivity). Scientific Atlanta, meanwhile, can tap into Cisco's Internet expertise and strong relationships with the telcom companies that are entering the video market. Certainly the acquisition has been a success in terms of performance; in the fiscal year after the merger, Cisco's revenues jumped by 23 percent and its net income by 31 percent. Cisco attributed much of the growth to the beneficial impact of online video across its businesses. And even more important—just as Toyota's wealth of real-world battery experience will benefit it when true electric vehicles are viable—Cisco will have the video expertise necessary when Internet delivery of video is ready for prime time.

Inside Information

- Devote your experimentation funds to capitalizing on emerging trends. You can keep costs down if you start when trends are young.

- Look for implementations that move you in the direction of the trend but are still practical today and don't require the development of a whole new ecosystem to support them.

(continued)

- Use "partway" tactics to gain real-world knowledge about the larger trends; view the knowledge gained from testing less-than-ideal products and services as a small price to pay for insights into big trends.

EVERY STRATEGY HAS A SEASON

You can ride the right megatrends for years. As an investor I am reassured when business leaders talk year after year about the same two or three trends driving their businesses. It means they positioned themselves early to capitalize on them.

Though trends last for years or even decades, the strategies you use to address the trends need to be far more nimble. A trend will morph and evolve over the years, and your strategy needs to do the same. Moreover, most strategies have a life cycle. Don't be lulled into thinking that, because you have the long-term trend right, you can ride your strategy for the long term as well. Every strategy has a season, and you need to be prepared for when your statregy's season is ending.

Many businesses stick with strategies long past their prime. Pharmaceutical companies such as Pfizer have struggled throughout most of the current decade as new innovations in small-molecule drugs, their specialty, have dried up. For the last decade, the best drug innovations have, for the most part, come from biotech firms, which produce large-molecule drugs. Pharmaceutical companies are moving into biotechnology but have been far too slow to recognize the decreasing effectiveness of their primary research strategies. This lethargic response has been costly to the careers of many pharmaceutical company executives, most notably former Pfizer CEO Hank McKinnell, who was ousted by his board when shareholders tired of his high pay and poor results.

Though all strategies, including small-molecule drug research, eventually become less effective, some strategies are inherently short-lived. It's particularly surprising when leaders of these businesses fail to prepare for the inevitable decline of their strategy. Retailers whose growth relies on adding additional stores frequently fall into this trap. The department store Kohl's suffered this fate in 2003, when its new stores started to cannibalize its existing stores—a common pitfall of any chain that builds too many stores in too small an area. In 2003, as it surpassed five hundred stores, sales at its existing stores dropped. So did its stock price, which lost a third of its value from its high in mid-2002 to its low two years later. It took Kohl's more than four years to implement a strategy to reignite its growth, and even then the growth was tenuous.

The short-lived nature of roll-up strategies regularly trips up executives across industries. In their prime, roll-up strategies work brilliantly. Companies in fragmented industries buy competitors in adjacent geographical areas or even direct competitors in the same area (if enough competition exists to allay antitrust concerns). Because the acquisitions accelerate growth and the combined companies benefit from economies of scale, acquirers tend to trade at high stock prices and have access to cheap capital, which makes it all the easier to acquire more companies. The problem is that growth from acquiring other businesses masks the growth rate in the underlying business. Completing acquisitions is hard work, and once it's done, executives may rest on their laurels. As a result, they don't bother with the even harder work of consolidating their acquisitions to extract the benefits of size. This leads to an inside tip about all strategies:

Even the most successful strategy eventually loses its power to impact your business's growth.

For Kohl's, adding seventy to ninety new stores a year had an increasingly smaller impact on the top line as it built a larger base of existing stores. In roll-ups, eventually the acquirer becomes big enough that the small, generally privately held (and therefore illiquid and cheap) acquisitions are not large enough to provide the growth they expect. At this point, acquirers often start going after ever-bigger—and therefore riskier and more expensive—targets. Occasionally roll-ups succeed with a few big deals, but that just raises the bar and makes acquiring the next growth component even more difficult. In the worst-case scenarios, companies "adjust" the numbers to deal with the shortfall in their acquisition strategies. Tyco and WorldCom are two well-known roll-ups that fell into that trap.

KFORCE, A ROLL-UP of staffing companies, experienced how quickly a strategy can fail to achieve long-term growth objectives. Starting life as Romac & Associates, Kforce helps clients find part-time and full-time employees. In 1995, it sold shares to the public at a split-adjusted price of $3.13. Armed with its public equity currency, it embarked on a massive buying binge, acquiring other staffing agencies as well as consulting and training firms. In the beginning the acquisitions worked well. The sellers were generally mom-and-pop operations whose proprietors wanted to cash out after years of building a business. Generally too small to go public themselves, they had few options to monetize the equity they had built up in their businesses. These owners were happy to sell at reasonable prices, and Kforce was delighted to buy. It acquired fourteen businesses from its IPO in August 1995 through the end of 1997. In these two years, revenue grew fourfold and earnings per share almost 2.5 times. Investors noticed, driving the stock price up to $24.44, 780 percent above the IPO price, by the end of 1997.

Then, in April 1998, needing ever-bigger deals to continue its growth, Kforce acquired Source Services Corporation. The combination quadrupled its revenues and doubled the company's net income. The stock price zoomed, peaking over $32.00 per share. But then the reality of running the larger entity set in. Top executives were not prepared to capitalize on the larger size or even organized to manage the bigger entity. Despite the company's being larger, its earnings per share fell 25 percent in 1998; its returns were even worse since the earnings were on a larger capital base. With its stock falling precipitously, Kforce was unable to make additional acquisitions, which hurt its growth rate, in turn causing the stock price to drop further. For the next few years, the company had to repeatedly ratchet down its growth and earnings expectations as it struggled to find a new strategy for growth. In 2001–02, recession and industry headwinds exacerbated management's challenges. Kforce's stock price hit a low of $1.63 in October 2002, roughly half its IPO price seven years earlier.

My colleagues and I were disappointed that management had not prepared for the inevitable decline of Kforce's growth-through-acquisition strategy. While growth was really strong, CEO David Dunkel and his management team could easily have afforded to deploy no-return-expected funds to prepare the next leg of growth. Instead they waited until 1999–2000 to devote considerable resources to building an Internet business. But trying to fashion a new strategy while the wheels are coming off is virtually impossible. Thus, another moneymaker secret:

Prepare for your current strategy's demise while it is still working.

The marketing and communications firm Omnicom has rolled up dozens of advertising and marketing services agencies since its founding in 1986. Unlike others entranced by the power of roll up strategies, CEO John Wren and his team understood the limitations of acquisition-fueled growth and laid the groundwork to continue growth when acquisitions could no longer propel it.

In the late 1990s, Omnicom developed a strategy of focusing intently on its 250 largest clients, understanding their needs intimately and working to provide solutions for them. Its managers reasoned that their largest clients were their most sophisticated. If they could provide solutions for them, thousands of other clients would buy similar offerings. The team also let its large clients' actions drive its acquisition strategy. If a large client was using a small independent agency with good results, Omnicom figured that the agency must be highly capable. It would seek to acquire the independent, usually with encouragement from the large client. If successful, Omnicom would work with the newly acquired agency to identify other clients that might be interested in its services. Unlike forced cross-selling, this effort built awareness internally about a valuable service validated by a sophisticated client. Moreover, Omnicom structured deals with earnouts, in which sale prices were determined based on a fixed multiple of the acquired business's earnings in the three years *after* a merger. Leaders of the acquired agencies had a powerful incentive to integrate their businesses with other Omnicom clients: the bigger the acquirees built their businesses using Omnicom's connections, the more money they received for selling their firms.

The strategy of remaining close to the needs of the largest

clients built upon and supplemented the growth that Omnicom generated through its active acquisition program. It also enabled Omnicom to identify trends quickly; it was, for example, an early acquirer of Internet advertising agencies.

Moreover, Omnicom's top-client focus enabled it to continue to grow even when its stock price fell dramatically in June 2002. Though eventually cleared, it was accused of inappropriate accounting and had to respond to an SEC investigation and shareholder lawsuits. These distractions put an abrupt halt to its acquisition activity. While almost no acquisitions were done in the twelve months following the stock decline, the strategy of staying close to large customers enabled it to grow revenues by 9 percent and operating income by 14 percent in 2002. The subsequent two years saw some impact from the slow pace of acquisitions as well as softness in advertising spending industrywide; revenues grew by double digits but operating profits averaged 5 percent increases. However, the wheels did not fall off as they had at Kforce, and by 2005 the company returned to 10 percent operating income growth. The stock price recovered before then, returning to pre–June 2002 levels by the end of 2003. Since you can never predict when your strategy will hit a rough spot, you need to be developing your next strategy while things are running smoothly.

EXPANSION STRATEGIES AREN'T the only ones that lose their effectiveness over time. Every profitable business strategy will attract competition that will diminish its results. Consolidation of customers, regulatory changes, and other factors can also hasten the demise of a strategy. Yet you don't have to be victimized by these factors; they generally occur with sufficient warning signs that you can adapt your strategy.

Goldman Sachs faced such a challenge in the early 2000s, when profitability in its historic powerhouses, the brokerage and investment banking businesses, eroded due to a confluence of factors. New entrants—from aggressive boutiques to commercial banks to electronic crossing networks—drove down commission rates on trades, a trend that had been developing since May 1975, when the Securities and Exchange Commission (SEC) had disallowed fixed commission rates. Other trends, including technology advances, and commercial banks' encroaching on the territory of investment banks, exacerbated the decline in its profitability.

Goldman's leadership recognized these trends early and gradually changed its business model. In the last decade, it has moved from making money by charging others for brokerage and investment banking services to making money by investing its own capital. In essence, it has become one of the world's largest hedge funds. To adjust its strategy, Goldman devoted more capital and resources to its own investing activities, hiring more aggressively in these areas and committing capital sensibly but in increasing size. At the same time, it shifted resources out of the brokerage businesses, downsizing its sales force and hiring less experienced and less expensive analysts for its research operation. However, it did not abandon brokerage entirely. Its sales and trading operations provide great insight into how other investors are positioning themselves. This valuable knowledge helps Goldman when trading for its own account. Being in the flow of trading and underwriting has enabled Goldman to remain standing as the global credit crisis waylaid other investment banks in 2008.

Infosys has also evolved its business strategy. Nandan Nilekani and the rest of Infosys's leadership understood the long-term trend of continued competitive pressures and increasingly sophisticated software. Though its labor-cost advantage relative to North America and Europe was durable for the foreseeable future, Infosys invested in training to move its employees' skills up the value chain and then offered higher-value-added services such as application development and consulting.

Though cheaper competitors to Infosys emerged not only in India but in Vietnam, Thailand, Croatia, Russia, and elsewhere, Infosys continued to prosper because it had evolved beyond its initial successful strategy.

I mention Infosys and Goldman Sachs because one obstacle to strategic evolution is an unwillingness to discard the one "who brung you to the dance." A misplaced loyalty to successful strategies exists in many organizations. But if you view this process as a natural evolution rather than as a heretical revolution, it will come more easily.

Inside Information

- Pay attention to the impact of slow-moving trends on your business strategy. Remember that no strategy lasts forever; in particular, financially driven strategies (including debt-financed asset growth, roll-ups, and lower costs through hedging) can come to very abrupt halts.

- Start developing additional growth drivers early so they're ready when your current strategy becomes less effective.

- Look for ways to leverage your existing strengths into other profitable areas as conditions change. Ask yourself what differentiated information your business possesses and how you can evolve your strategy by leveraging that information advantage.

- Challenge yourself to move up the value chain into higher-return, generally more intellectual property–based pursuits.

• • •

WAVES START AS RIPPLES

To earn a reputation as a visionary business leader, you do not need to be able to see around corners that others can't, but you do need to have the fortitude to stick with evolving trends. Most megatrends take so long to reach critical mass that people lose interest and then are surprised when a trend "sneaks up" on them. For instance, in 1999–2000, when everyone was panicking about the Internet, creating separate divisions and throwing tens and even hundreds of millions of dollars after the "revolution," the commercially viable browser had been around for five years and the Internet for far longer. If you identify trends early but invest slowly, you can stay with them as they develop, thus positioning your business for the future and earning a reputation as a visionary. To do so, consider the following questions:

• How much time do you devote to the long-term trends that will affect your business? Have you set aside some time every month to think about the forces that may impact your company five or ten years down the road?

• Do you remain intellectually curious, learning about broader trends in international relations, technology, and other realms that may spark ideas that impact your business? Do you converse with your employees about their views on the long-term ripples that might turn into waves? Do you remain open-minded about ripples that are constantly on the horizon but have not (yet) turned into tidal waves? Have you dismissed certain trends simply because they move too slowly and seem irrelevant now? You'd be surprised how quickly they can become extremely relevant.

- Have you selected a limited number of trends for your employees to focus on? Do you encourage them to help find ways to meet the challenges these key trends will pose? Are you disciplined enough to focus on the three most meaningful over the next five years, despite the hundreds of potential trends? Can your employees, unprompted, name the trends most affecting your organization's future?

- Do you keep your new-product development efforts grounded? Do you get so excited about the long-term trend that you push to develop the ultimate product or service that will fully embrace the trend (and most likely be rejected by customers)? Or do you identify the areas where you need to build your competencies to prepare for the trend and then build "partway" solutions that will enable you to test, learn, and grow so that when your customers are ready, you are too?

- Do you keep in mind the continuing effort to move your business into higher-value-added and more profitable areas over time? Do you understand that this pursuit cannot always be a straight line but has to remain ongoing?

CHAPTER 10

WE'RE ALL DEAD IN THE
LONG RUN

Y OU CAN TORPEDO YOUR CAREER AND YOUR BUSINESS preparing for a future that doesn't play out as you expected or in the time frame you planned for. Whenever a CEO waxes eloquently about a project that requires major capital commitments but that will offer unimaginable returns in the future, I remind him of the common investor saying, "We're all dead in the long run." No matter how great the rewards, if the long run is too far off, it's not worth it. As a professional prognosticator, I decide whether to buy a stock based on my estimates of its future earnings and returns. I use my experience and knowledge, but my predictions are often off. Indeed, the best investors are right 60 percent of the time, which means we spend a lot of time being wrong. My professional investor colleagues and I know how difficult it is to predict the future with precision. That's why we adhere to this truth:

Overestimating your ability to predict the long term is more deadly than failing to prepare for it.

For this reason, you should start early and remain flexible (as the previous chapter emphasized).

Perhaps even more important: you need to move incrementally. Trying to get a jump on the future by shooting your wad today is almost always a mistake. Even if you predict accurately, the wait for your prediction to come true can cost you dearly. In 1998, AT&T CEO Michael Armstrong announced a $31.8 billion deal to buy TCI, then the largest cable system operator. He had a vision of bundling pay-TV and telephone services. He was right on the trend but about ten years too early. By the time consumers were ready, AT&T had been broken up and sold in pieces. It couldn't support the debt it had incurred while waiting for the market to develop, so AT&T was dead by the time the long run arrived. To reach the long term, you have to balance the needs of the short term against your aims for the long term.

Though incremental approaches to growth trends and other business changes work best, I know that moving slowly is not as exciting as implementing a sweeping change in response to a grand vision of the future. It's more satisfying to make a bold move, but it's also riskier. When you change radically in response to long-term trends, you make yourself vulnerable to unpleasant and costly surprises. And as anyone who deals with professional investors knows:

Investors hate surprises.

We hate them for good reason, and it's not just because surprises often cost us money. Our antipathy has more to do with what they suggest about a company's management. Earnings that deviate meaningfully from expectations, dramatic changes in strategy, and transformative acquisitions are often signs that executives have not adequately prepared for long-term trends. The risk profiles of companies making big changes are also considerably higher than those of companies taking more measured steps.

My favorite way to learn about a company's management quickly is to read the letters to shareholders from the last seven to ten annual reports. If the letters are relatively boring, repeating the same themes consistently with incremental progress, I rest easy. When I read about a major new initiative or acquisition announced with great fanfare and then a few years later read that it is being discontinued or spun off or it simply stops being mentioned, I worry about the quality of the management team.

Though conventional wisdom argues for bold measures to prepare for the future, moneymakers make incremental moves to position their business for the long haul. Let's look at how some of the best prepare for the future incrementally and effectively.

ONE BITE AT A TIME

The value of domain expertise is often underestimated. Many business schools teach that management is an inherent skill, that the best and the brightest leaders can be dropped into any business situation and do well. As a result, business knowledge often takes a backseat to management skill. Companies regularly embark on major new business initiatives without fully understanding what they're getting into. They bank on the brilliance of their highly successful CEOs or other executives to win the day.

Yet hard-won knowledge trumps management wizardry nine times out of ten. The most successful companies build their expertise one step at a time, moving incrementally into new areas. I've described how Goldman Sachs moved gradually into principal trading, maintaining its agency businesses to support the now-primary principal business, and how IBM grew its consulting business from a thrown-in extra to support hardware sales into a central role within the company.

If you move too quickly, you are likely to stumble, even if you have correctly identified long-term trends. Duke Energy Corporation learned this lesson in the mid-1990s as electricity markets were being deregulated. CEO Richard Priory wanted to leapfrog his competitors by moving his North Carolina utility rapidly into the brave new world. In two years he doubled capital expenditures, spending more than $5 billion in 2000. Duke aggressively built and acquired power plants outside its service area, so it could lead the market in selling power as states deregulated. It had plans by 2002 to more than double the already accelerated increase in capacity. At the same time, it was constructing numerous facilities outside the United States. To support and further expand its energy sales business, Duke built a large operation to trade electricity supply contracts.

For a time Duke's aggressiveness seemed to be working. In 2000, operating profits from its North America Wholesale Energy group, which included the plants outside its traditional service area and its trading and marketing operations, more than tripled over 1998 levels and its International Energy group's profits were twenty-five times greater than two years earlier.

Duke, though, had entered areas that required expertise beyond what it possessed as a regulated utility. Building long-lived capacity without a regulatorily guaranteed return on investment demands skills in determining long-term supply and demand characteristics and assessing investment risk. Duke's marketing and trading operations brought it into competition with Wall Street firms with decades of experience in trading operations. In 2001, the limits of its experience became apparent. Duke had underestimated how much supply was being added to the market as many independents and well-known players sought to cash in on the energy deregulation gold rush.

At the same time, demand was not growing as quickly as forecast. States got cold feet about freewheeling energy markets and slowed or even reversed deregulation.

The results were disastrous. Duke found itself locked into unprofitable long-term electricity supply contracts and plants that wouldn't earn returns on their investment. It took more than $4 billion in impairment charges, primarily for its North America Wholesale Energy and International Energy businesses, in 2002 and 2003. After years of losses, in 2006 it sold off all the NAWE assets to a financial buyer. In 2003, CEO Priory lost his job, along with two thousand others. The stock lost two thirds of its value from its 2001 peak to the depth in 2003.

Duke's expansion into these new areas made sense. Preparing for trends that could massively disrupt its traditional businesses was a logical move, especially because these areas were tangential to its operations and it brought expertise in operating power plants. The big mistake was how aggressively it expanded into these new areas. In effect Duke banked on a smooth and rapid evolution of deregulated markets and underestimated what it needed to learn to succeed in these new businesses. Priory's successor as CEO, Paul Anderson, summed it up well when he said, "To eat an elephant, you have to take one bite at a time."

BY USING A more incremental approach, J.B. Hunt Transport Services successfully transformed itself from an asset-intensive truckload carrier into a higher-return, asset-light business. The incremental approach helped it overcome the inevitable obstacles and setbacks that come with any type of transformation. Today the company generates more than 75 percent of its operating income from intermodal (train/truck combination) operations that leverage railroads' assets, and dedicated contract services where customers hire dedicated trucking capacity on long-term contracts that dramatically increase the utilization of Hunt's assets.

Recognizing the trend early was one advantage that enabled Johnnie Bryan Hunt and his team to move incrementally. J.B. Hunt started small intermodal experiments in the late 1980s, before others felt the urgency to capitalize on this long-term trend. The Hunt team pursued the intermodal strategy because they knew success in freight transportation depends on being the low-cost provider. Rail service, though slow and inconsistent, is significantly cheaper than trucks due to lower labor costs (only two people are needed to move a 100-plus-car train compared to one person per one to two trailers in a truck, and less fuel is required per load of freight moved). In a typical intermodal trip, Hunt drivers and trucks pick up freight from customer locations, which they take to a railhead for loading onto trains; the railroad moves the freight to the railhead nearest the delivery point on the other end, where other Hunt drivers and equipment pick up the containers and deliver them to their destinations. In contrast, a typical truckload trip requires a Hunt driver and rig to pick up a trailer at the customer's location and drive it (usually with one to two overnights) to the destination.

In late 1989, Hunt signed a contract with the Santa Fe Railroad (now part of the Burlington Northern Santa Fe Railway Company). At the time most truckers dismissed intermodal transportation as too unreliable and time-consuming, since transferring containers from trains to trucks added significantly to the transport time. Seeing the potential in intermodal operations but also understanding that it required a different expertise than the truckload business did, Hunt and his leadership team worked incrementally to master the new challenges and optimize their offering. They doubled the business over a decade (not two years, as Duke tried to do), going from around 300,000 loads in 1995 to 600,000 in 2006. This steady pace allowed them to make course corrections. For instance, they moved to larger fifty-three-foot containers, which became the industry standard over the course of the 1990s. The team also invested steadily in building the information technology systems to support the coordination the business required.

Keeping the intermodal division within its larger Van (truck-load) division allowed Hunt to nurture it. The incremental approach also enabled it to withstand blows, such as the slow pace with which the low-cost advantage of intermodal transportation manifested itself. The years 1998 and 1999 were particularly difficult because the western U.S. rail system, including the Burlington Northern Santa Fe lines, became gridlocked following poor merger execution by another railroad. Hunt's intermodal loads and revenues fell as shippers diverted their freight off the clogged rails and onto trucks. Because it had moved in such small increments, Hunt did not have to discontinue its intermodal operations or even radically scale back when it hit this speed bump, since its standard truckload operation benefited from the railroad congestion. The difficulties were temporary, and soon Hunt was able to resume growing its intermodal operations.

Ten years after it started, the intermodal operation became large enough to stand on its own. At this point, conventional wisdom would argue that Hunt should have jettisoned its truckload operations in favor of its higher-return intermodal operations. However, management took a more measured approach. With the profitability and returns of the truckload operations challenged, Hunt's managers separated intermodal from the truckload operations in its financial statements, to give themselves and investors more insight into diagnosing the underperformance in the truckload segment. In the meantime, company leaders Wayne Garrison and Kirk Thompson, in their 2000 letter to shareholders, stated, "No growth in capacity is planned for the Truck segment until margins reflect the risk inherent in operating this random over-the-road business." With the more attractive returns in intermodal and dedicated contract services, these components grew to 70 percent of revenues in 2006 and 77 percent of operating profits (while using less than two thirds of the assets).

Maintaining a presence in the truckload sector provides Hunt with market intelligence and additional capacity to meet the needs of its intermodal and dedicated contract customers. Results have certainly borne out this incremental approach. In the ten years from 1996 to 2006, the revenues of the entire company grew by 124 percent but operating income grew by 500 percent, net income by 900 percent, and earnings per share by 860 percent, as the higher-return profile of the new businesses produced better profitability.

THE E.W. SCRIPPS Company has repeatedly and effectively used incrementalism to transform itself. Started in 1878 with a single newspaper, Scripps has successfully expanded into radio, television stations, and cable systems; a willingness to embrace new media is part of its culture. In the early 1990s, as it looked to position itself for the next wave in media, Scripps invested in the vision of one of its television executives, Ken Lowe. Seeing the popularity of home- and cooking-related shows, he wanted to create a cable network of lifestyle programming around home decorating, gardening, and remodeling. Home & Garden Television was born of Lowe's vision and Scripps's investment. Over the five years starting in 1994, Scripps funded about $67 million in operating losses plus additional funds for the acquisition of Cinetel Productions, a production company. In 1997, it also acquired a majority stake in a near-bankrupt lifestyle cable network, TV Food Network, on the cheap.

Scripps did not rush to get into this next wave of media immediately; instead, it worked methodically to learn the business while investing in losses over five years. In each year the start-up division had to show progress to continue to receive funding. As the profitability at the cable networks became more visible, Scripps invested more. Its investment never exceeded more than 10 percent of its operating income, preventing the networks from becoming a "bet the company" proposition. Scripps even passed on the TV Food Network when first offered it. It made the acquisition only years later, when Lowe and his team had proven they knew enough about cable networks to succeed with a second property.

Going slowly also enabled the start-up cable network to leverage the resources of other divisions in the company, rather than invoke turf wars with them. The networks were first carried on cable systems owned by Scripps, enabling the network to easily jump one of the most difficult hurdles for a fledgling network. When Washington mandated that local television stations had the right to demand compensation from cable operators for carrying their broadcast signals, Scripps bartered the retransmission consent of its TV stations for carriage of its start-up networks.

The incremental approach paid off. Because Scripps's management stuck with the investment over time and learned the nuances of programming and selling a niche cable network, they built a valuable asset. Indeed, by 2004, the cable networks had surpassed all the other divisions in profit and generated half of the overall company's segment profit (operating profit plus depreciation and amortization). From 1994 to 2004, the stock price more than tripled, and in subsequent years, as Scripps became known as a cable network company, it vastly outperformed its newspaper peers. Only after fourteen years of development did the Scripps board of directors feel the cable networks were established enough to stand on their own; in 2008 the company was split in two, with one company housing the newspaper and TV assets and the other the cable networks (cable systems had been sold in 1995).

Inside Information

- Don't overestimate your knowledge of a new venture. Move into it gradually so you can learn as you go, without costing yourself too much in "tuition."

- Leverage your existing businesses to give the new venture the best shot at success; incremental strategies take advantage of existing resources rather than just bolting on new ones.

- Spread an investment out over time rather than making a big bet on one spin of the wheel.

SLOW MERGE

The advice offered by road signs is also highly applicable when transforming your business through mergers and acquisitions. An incremental approach works best because it tasks everyone in an organization with successfully identifying and integrating mergers. By going slowly, you can tap into knowledge across your organization and take advantage of the feedback that is so crucial in all parts of managing a business. Whether you are the CEO or part of a small division, your career will be affected by the mergers your business takes on. As with all management efforts (as discussed in chapter 2), on-the-ground feedback is crucial, so you should add your voice to those you work for as well as encouraging your employees to speak up. By moving incrementally when making acquisitions, you can achieve success where so many have failed.

The advertising/communications firm Omnicom acquires more slowly but more surely than many of its competitors. It lets its competitors do the large, headline-generating mergers, as when Interpublic Group bought True North Communications. Interpublic added 25 percent to its revenues but also took on struggling agencies and years of integration difficulties. Instead, Omnicom acquires a steady stream of smaller, cheaper agencies. To manage the volume of acquisitions, its leadership relies on employees in the field to identify acquisitions. From talking with clients and being active in their markets, the divisional folks can find agencies that offer marketing services that resonate with clients. They then go through an internal process to vet potential acquisitions, approaching target companies only after doing their homework. Effectiveness in identifying acquisitions is even part of managers' annual evaluations. By relying on this incremental approach, Omnicom has been able to meet its clients' evolving needs and stay ahead of its competitors by diversifying into public relations, customer relationship management, Internet marketing, and other non-ad-based marketing services. This prescience led it to become the leading firm in its field.

Unlike at Omnicom, the rush to make large acquisitions is irresistible to some companies. Executives have a vision of the future, they see how an acquisition of additional resources positions them "perfectly" for that future, and they act. Many believe that decisiveness is the most crucial attribute and that they must think big to be market leaders. They don't realize that an incremental approach is a more effective, albeit slower, approach to getting big and dominating a market.

Here are some rationales that I've heard managers use to justify moving quickly and with great cost to capitalize on a future trend; see how many of these rationales your company has relied on.

- If we don't act immediately, our competitors will steal our thunder—and our market.

- If we build into a trend organically or through small acquisitions, we'll be too late.
- We've seen this emerging trend before anyone else, and the faster we jump on it, the farther ahead of the curve we'll be.
- When it comes to our company's long-term growth and sustainability, we must act boldly.
- We don't want to be accused of sitting on our hands when an opportunity presents itself.
- While making the acquisition/merger is a gamble, it's a bigger gamble to do nothing.
- We've been wanting to acquire Company X for years, and now that it's in play, we need to act since we probably won't get this chance again.
- Our people are too set in their ways to embrace this new trend; we need new people.
- This acquisition is so strategic that it doesn't matter how much we pay.

To understand how powerful these rationales are, consider Time Warner's merger with AOL. It illustrates well the perils of moving too quickly and of not utilizing your internal resources. When CEO Gerry Levin negotiated to sell Time Warner to America Online, he was worried that technology was moving too quickly and that he needed to be bold. He decided to stake Time Warner's future on the Internet trend and the premier company in the space at the time, AOL. Unfortunately, though the trend was evident, how it would play out was not.

The problem for AOL was that its core business, online access through telephone lines, was becoming antiquated by faster-speed broadband offerings from cable and telecom companies. When Time Warner and AOL forged their merger agreement, this development was on the horizon, and many in the industry were concerned about its impact on AOL. At investor meetings I attended following the announcement of the merger, the first question usually asked of AOL's management was, "Did you do the merger to solve your broadband problem?" Informed industry observers were fully aware of AOL's Achilles' heel. However, Levin was so determined to complete the AOL deal in secrecy (he succeeded on this front; there were no leaks prior to the official announcement) that he did not gather sufficient input (or didn't pay sufficient attention to that input) from his own internal folks working in online businesses. They certainly could have warned him about the broadband risk and about how difficult it would be to cross-sell AOL on Time Warner's cable systems.

Instead, Levin and AOL CEO Steve Case pushed through the merger, and initially it was well received by Time Warner shareholders. But soon, the dot-com implosion and the rise of broadband took their toll on the AOL business. Due to the size of the deal, AOL's problems affected the whole company. The stock price cratered, falling from $64.75 on January 7, 2000, the day before the deal was announced, to a low of $8.70 in July 2002. In the three years following the merger, Time Warner had to sell its book and music divisions to shore up its balance sheet, lost key executives who never got over their anger about the loss of value of their stock, and was generally distracted from running its other businesses. Meanwhile, AOL's value edge eroded so much in the face of competitive broadband offerings that Time Warner transformed it into a free service in 2006, and by 2007, Time Warner's cable unit had a larger online access business.

Monsanto, on the other hand, succeeded in the transformation to a higher-return, higher-growth business that Time Warner was attempting because it took five years to do it and built up its internal expertise along the way. When Bob

Shapiro was named CEO of Monsanto in 1995, it was known as a specialty chemical company even though half its operating income came from its highly profitable agricultural products (the Roundup herbicide for controlling weeds, genetically engineered seeds resistant to the herbicide, and bovine hormones to increase cows' milk production). Impressed with the long-term trends for bioengineering, Shapiro, his successor as CEO, Hendrik Verfaillie, and their team moved methodically to reshape the company through divestitures, acquisitions, and internal investments. Shapiro started by divesting chemical assets, with the bulk spun off as a new company named Solutia in 1997. In 1999, the crown jewel of the food business, NutraSweet, was sold. The next year Monsanto merged with Pharmacia, which wanted to build scale with the addition of Monsanto's pharmaceutical business. Immediately after the merger, Monsanto began a process to spin the agricultural unit off from the new pharmaceutical company, an effort that was fully completed in 2002.

At the same time that it was divesting other operations, Monsanto was slowly growing its bioengineered seed portfolio through its own research and acquisitions. The acquisition of DeKalb Genetics Corporation, a leader in genetically modified corn and soybeans, illustrates the company's measured approach. In 1996, Monsanto signed a research and development deal with DeKalb, in which it acquired a 40 percent economic stake (10 percent voting) in exchange for $145 million. Two years later, with intimate knowledge of DeKalb's products, Monsanto bought the rest of the company for $2.3 billion. By 2002, when it completed its spin-off from Pharmacia, Monsanto dominated the genetically modified foods category, which was gaining legitimacy and growing fast. By having an aggressive vision but moving incrementally, Monsanto's leaders successfully remade the company. Its earnings and stock price increased more than sixfold in the five years after the Pharmacia spin-off.

Inside Information

- Use acquisitions to transform your company "delicately"; recognize that this powerful tool can just as easily blow up in your face.

- Build internal domain experience before acquiring companies. Leverage all of your internal knowledge to evaluate every acquisition. For every buyer there is a seller; make sure you understand why someone is selling (he or she likely knows the business better than you do).

- Use joint ventures and other collaborations to build experience with and knowledge of a potential acquisition when possible; this strategy will greatly reduce your risk should you decide to buy. Success in such a collaboration will likely increase the ultimate acquisition cost, but the risk reduction will more than compensate.

- Don't panic and act rashly in response to an emerging trend. Remember, your industry will continue to evolve, so there is always time to develop the domain expertise to position yourself for the next manifestation of a trend.

CANCEROUS GROWTH

Adapting the socialite's expression "You can never be too rich or too thin," many executives believe their companies can never be too profitable or have too much growth. While I've discussed the perils of hyperprofitability (in chapter 6), here I want to share a biological truth that applies just as readily to business:

Uncontrolled growth is cancer.

A company that grows too fast often has more problems than one that grows too slowly. Over the long run, you are far better off with incremental growth.

Growing too fast almost killed Quality Dining. Founded in 1967 with one Burger King franchise, it grew over the years by adding additional franchisee locations, ending fiscal year 1993 with forty-four Burger King and four Chili's units. In 1994, CEO Daniel Fitzpatrick and his team sought to accelerate the company's growth by moving it up the value chain and becoming a franchiser itself. To access the capital to fund this plan, they took the company public in March 1994 and followed with secondary offerings in each of the next two years. The team used these funds to buy the restaurant concepts Spageddies Italian Kitchen, Grady's American Grill, and Bruegger's Bagels in 1995 and 1996. They then set about supercharging the growth. They focused on the Bruegger's bagel shop concept, which had great potential but was facing stiff competition from Einstein Bros' Bagels. Within four months of acquiring Bruegger's in June 1996, Quality had added 28 percent more locations and had plans to double the number of locations by October 1997. The stock price soared to a high of $39.50 in May 1996, on investors' anticipation of the earnings from such an exciting and growing concept.

The plan didn't work out; a year later Quality Dining was selling Bruegger's back to its original owners after taking $200 million in charges. In its attempt to "seize the moment" and fend off the competition, it had forgotten about the basics of the business. It could open the shops but couldn't operate them profitably. New units were added without sufficient thought to the quality of the location or the cost paid. More important, it did not devote enough resources to ensure that franchisees maintained quality standards. The bagel shops quickly earned a reputation for poor customer service.

After selling Bruegger's, Quality Dining survived but never quite recovered. The Grady's concept died a slow death, shrinking from forty-two locations in 1996 to none ten years later. The stock drifted lower. Management successfully fended off a hostile takeover attempt at $5.00 a share in 2000. Shareholders were far less lucky, finally selling the company back to management at $3.20 per share in 2004. The whole experience makes one wonder where Quality Dining would be today had it been more measured in its growth, paying attention to the quality of the dining experience and modifying its concept over time.

DURING THE LATE-1990s Internet boom, many companies fell into the trap of growing too quickly, but Digitas, a Boston-based Internet advertising agency, had the savvy to avoid this mistake. CEO David Kenny and his team understood that their business had natural limits to its growth. Advertising requires skilled creative people, media planners, and account executives to develop custom campaigns for each client. Finding and training talent to create a high-quality, tailored product can't be done overnight. As a result, taking on a slew of new clients within a short time frame can easily result in substandard advertising. Since it wasn't willing to sacrifice quality to chase growth, Digitas found itself turning away business. Newly funded dot-coms and established companies were all rushing to develop their online presences, and were beating down Digitas's door requesting help. Kenny and his crew resisted the impulse to open the door to everyone; instead, they cherry-picked the clients they took on. They selected those such as GM and Delta Air Lines with the best prospects to be long-term advertisers. When the Internet bubble burst, Digitas's "go-slow" approach paid off in spades. In its worst year (2003), revenues declined by less than 10 percent from their 2001 peak, and it had positive operating profits from 2002 on. By 2004, revenues were above the prior peak and profits were strong. In 2006, Digitas sold itself to the ad agency holding company Publicis for $1.3 billion, earning a solid return for its shareholders.

Contrast Digitas's experience to that of Razorfish, another Internet advertising agency that came of age during the late 1990s. Razorfish subscribed to the "get big fast" mantra. With clients throwing money at the Internet, Razorfish took on new clients left and right. It grew its revenues from less than $4 million in 1997 to $268 million in 2000, an astounding 6,700 percent growth rate over three years. By taking business from every client that came its way, it left itself vulnerable to hypergrowth's downside:

What goes up quickly can come down just as quickly.

When the Internet mania subsided, Razorfish lost money as quickly as it had made it. In 2001, revenues were less than half those of the prior year. Bleeding money, Razorfish agreed the following year to be acquired for $1.70 per share, or a total of $8.2 million; three years earlier, the stock market had valued the company at $4.2 billion. Though Digitas's shareholders never enjoyed valuations as high as Razorfish's, in the long run the business and therefore the shareholders were better off with Digitas's more measured approach.

NIKE, THE ICONIC athletic footwear company, experienced a variation on this hypergrowth pitfall. Its focus wasn't so much on huge growth as grabbing too much market share too fast. Having outcompeted its archrival Reebok and built the company to a dominant position, founder and CEO Phil Knight in 1997 seemed to regard any shoe sold by another company as one too many. In an effort to push for 100 percent market share, Nike acquired warehouses around the world and filled them with Nike-brand shoes and clothing. However, having the product didn't mean customers would buy it. With excess inventory piling up, Nike became more promotional to move the merchandise. Lower profits and more investment meant that ROI dropped when Nike could not seize market share gains by sheer force of inventory investment.

Over the next few years, with a new head of strategy, Frits van Paasschen, and a new CFO, Don Blair, Nike came to terms with a more measured pace of growth and inventory stocking. The leadership also accepted that the Nike brand couldn't stretch to satisfy all consumers' preferences. It began pursuing a multibrand strategy more diligently, acquiring Converse and Starter to cover the more fashion-oriented and value-priced segments of the market. The measured approach worked; after stagnant growth from 1998 to 2002, Nike grew its operating income and earnings per share by more than 80 percent in the three years from 2002 to 2005. The stock price just about doubled, and today Nike is regarded as one of the best-managed companies around.

Inside Information

- Don't chase "first-mover" advantage. In the long run, the race goes not to the earliest but to the most effective.

- Respect the natural growth rate of your business and adapt your investments in people, equipment, and inventory around that pace. Driving growth or building market share through brute force is not sustainable over the long run.

- Remember quality control. Fast growth often works against maintaining quality standards. Yet quality will determine long-term success.

- Cherry-pick customers and products when demand is so strong that you lack the resources to keep pace. Demand will not always remain so strong. Moreover, improving the mix of your business often produces better returns than merely growing the business.

THE MORE THINGS CHANGE

Everyone embraces change, at least theoretically. Yet most successful corporations are naturally change-averse, gravitating toward the status quo because it's worked in the past. An incremental approach works in part because it reminds you and your people that you always need to be changing to achieve your long-term goals (which are always on the horizon). It dispels the fiction that after making a herculean effort to develop the product of the future or transform your business, you can then coast.

Early in my career I learned to be wary of organizations that locked into "formulas" and stuck with them through thick and thin. In my own mind, I refer to this failing as the "new equipment fallacy." I've discovered that factories filled with shiny new production equipment may look impressive, but they have also locked themselves into a specific way of doing business for a long period—often a decade or more if they expect to earn a decent return on their investment. At the same time, companies that tinker around the edges and find ways to make old equipment useful may not look as good but they generally perform better. By making incremental moves toward your goals and adapting as conditions change, you produce the strongest results.

Continuous change is important not only in products and strategy but also from an organizational perspective. You need to keep adapting in significant ways as the world evolves around you. When the packaged-goods giant Procter & Gamble undertook a dramatic reorganization plan in the late 1990s, the outcome showed both the benefits of periodic restructuring and the difficulty of transformation when you haven't built up your change muscles. In September 1998, as John Pepper was easing out as CEO and Durk Jager was easing in, the pair announced Organization 2005, a plan to reorient P&G from geographic-based business units to product-based units in response to how the world had changed.

When the Cincinnati-based company first expanded globally, organizing around countries was enormously helpful as it lacked expertise in consumer preferences in various parts of the world. However, by the mid-1990s, the world had changed. Differences in cultures were appreciated, and as the world globalized those differences were becoming less pronounced. Faster and cheaper communications, more openness to global trade, more unified regulations and regimes, and the efforts of multinationals such as P&G had raised and standardized consumer expectations globally. Geographic boundaries had become less significant, and competition had increased.

For Procter, reorganizing around product categories allowed it to reflect these changes. With each product group having its own R&D effort, it could sharpen the focus on producing innovations and rolling them out quickly without the delays endemic to the geographic-based organization. The initiative was well received by the investment community despite coming with an announcement to expect lower earnings in the near term.

The response of employees, however, was not as positive. The realignment caused dislocations for thousands in the 110,000-person organization. Reporting lines changed and alliances shifted. For an organization justifiably proud of its many successes and with a strong commitment to the "Procter & Gamble" way of doing things, Organization 2005 was a major shock. In addition, errors were made in the execution. The change was radical, rather than incremental. The business was already stressed by a slowdown in earnings growth and by competitors taking share from the company. CEO Jager set overly optimistic targets for growth; he had to lower expectations repeatedly and announce additional restructuring charges. Moreover, he attempted to transform the organization into a higher-return business with acquisitions of pharmaceutical businesses. These attempts failed because investors reacted negatively to Procter branching into pharmaceuticals, an area with vastly different dynamics from the consumer-marketing-driven businesses where its expertise lay. After seventeen months, with employees in revolt and disappointing operating results, Jager was forced out.

A. G. Lafley, a longtime veteran of P&G, took over as CEO in 2000. Despite calls to return to the old geographic structure, he stuck with the product-oriented strategy. However, Lafley took a more measured approach and introduced changes more gradually. He too sought to move into higher profit areas, but ones better aligned with Procter's expertise. His big push was into beauty care, which played more effectively to P&G's historic strength in branding and was an area where the company was already generating a quarter of its operating income with Pantene and Cover Girl. Lafley understood the need to prune as well. He wrote off the company's big investment in Olean, an artificial fat substitute, and sold off most of the food brands and other low-growth products such as Comet cleanser. He also set much more achievable growth goals. The strategy worked, though it took far longer than expected. By 2006, the stock price had more than doubled, and numerous organizations, including *Chief Executive* magazine and the John F. Kennedy School of Government at Harvard, were naming Lafley CEO of the Year.

Perhaps the biggest accomplishment of Organization 2005 was that P&G became much more adaptable. When it acquired the hair products firm Clairol in 2001; Wella, a German beauty care business, in 2003; and the biggest deal of all, the razor and battery company Gillette in 2005, the acquisitions were absorbed seamlessly. In 2007, Lafley realigned the company again. Partly because it was a more incremental change and mostly because the organization was more accustomed to change, this reorganization was implemented without all the turmoil of the earlier effort.

KEEPING AN ORGANIZATION's change muscles in shape can involve various moves. W.W. Grainger, an industrial supply company, achieved its own rejuvenation by refocusing on its traditional strengths. Founded in 1927, Grainger distributes motors, lighting, fasteners, and hundreds of thousands of other items that all sorts of businesses need to keep their workplaces operating. In the late 1990s, management, led by Dick Keyser, shifted focus to building out the company's Web presence in response to a raft of new dot-com competitors. A significant threat, the Internet-based businesses offered more extensive product selection, Web sites that were easier to use than Grainger's traditional paper catalogs, and lower costs because no investment in local stores was required. In response Grainger learned the Internet and built a credible Web offering, though like many in the era it also lost money and took a charge after investing too heavily in the new medium.

After this bold, expensive move and with its Internet flank protected, Grainger concentrated on its neglected branch infrastructure. Its branch system was its value edge; it was difficult and expensive to build but offered a level of responsiveness with same-day delivery of parts in stock that no centralized Internet competitor could match. When refocusing on the core business, leadership moved more incrementally. Grainger remodeled locations and shrank catalog inventory 17 percent by shedding low-return items. With the whole organization more attuned to competitive pressures and the need for constant change, operating margins improved by 12 percent and the company's 2005 expansion into China proceeded smoothly step by gradual step. The impact was powerful; in the three years after the refocus—from 2002 to 2005—the company grew its revenues by 19 percent and its earnings per share by 70 percent.

Inside Information

- Reexamine your organizational structure as though you were starting from scratch every four to six years. The world and your business environment have probably changed enough during that period that your formerly optimal structure has become suboptimal. Then implement any changes you want to make incrementally.

- Use regular organizational realignments to maintain balance between different priorities (e.g., geographic versus functional) and between different branches of your organization. If your employees understand that power shifts regularly, they will be more responsive to colleagues who are not in their current chain of command.

- Keep your employees adaptable and open to change by implementing limited changes regularly. Remind yourself that people are likely to become overly comfortable in their routines unless change is a constant.

●   ●   ●

Small Steps to Big Changes

Too often, businesses err on the side of too much change too quickly or too little change too slowly. In other words, some organizations are so gung ho on change that they throw the baby out with the bathwater. Others are so rigid that they cannot adapt as their world inevitably changes.

The solution is incrementalism. When change is implemented regularly but in a targeted, moderate manner, employees remain flexible and open to new directions and approaches. But when you attempt to undergo extraordinary, instant transformations, employees' sense of urgency is overwhelmed and they become resistant to critical change initiatives. On the other hand, an incremental approach makes change a regular part of people's routine and makes it easier to achieve success (for both people and capital) because hurdles are lower and fewer resources are utilized for any one initiative.

Leaders who can calibrate the change balance succeed with investors and whomever else they work for. By making small course corrections frequently, you position your business to capitalize on industry and competitive changes. To achieve this incremental ideal for your organization, consider the following questions.

- How do your employees respond to change? If there is a lot of resistance, you need to build up your organization's flexibility. Tell them the business needs to adapt to a faster pace of change, and start making more incremental changes. Ease out those who cannot handle the new pace.

- When was the last time you reorganized yourself? If it's been more than seven years, consider how much the landscape has evolved, how much more global the world has become, how technology usage has shifted, and how upcoming generations see the world differently. Think about how you can re-create your organization to address the new landscape. And never forget that you can't keep change at bay. If your organization has grown comfortable, change will come as a tremendous shock unless you start making incremental changes today.

- How can you break down big changes into smaller pieces? Though lack of change is risky, so are big changes. Find partway solutions to reduce your risk.

- Are you sure you know how trends will play out or how long a given iteration will last before being superseded by the next version? If you want to make major changes because you are behind the curve, do the bare minimum to remain relevant and work to prepare yourself to be ahead of the curve for the next iteration of the trend.

- Do you have the expertise to be successful in the changes you are trying to make? What makes you think you will be better in a new area than others who are already in the space? Though you certainly want to move into higher-return areas, leverage your area of expertise, particularly if you are acquiring your way into a new space.

CHAPTER 11

SHRINK TO GROW AND OTHER

BACKWARD STEPS FORWARD

M Y INVESTING COLLEAGUES AND I EXPECT A LOT: we want continuous growth and ever-improving returns on capital, delivered with no hiccups. However, we also know that this expectation is an unrealistic stretch goal. I've never yet found a leader who has consistently delivered this ideal. There are simply too many ways for things to go awry. But what distinguishes moneymakers is how they handle difficulties and setbacks. Unfortunately, many executives operate under misconceptions that the best way to handle problems is to ignore them and charge ahead. Yet this approach almost never works. Moneymakers overcome difficulties by taking the opposite tack: they step backward to move forward. They know you often paradoxically need to shrink to grow. Let me share how moneymakers not only overcome obstacles but become stronger because of them.

FESS UP

Not infrequently, a company's quarterly earnings will come in a penny shy of what Wall Street expected, and the stock will drop dramatically, say 5 percent or more. These experiences have created a common perception among executives that they should do whatever it takes to deliver the consensus earnings number. But those who believe this forget how often companies announce $1.00 or more in charges and their stocks go up. They also fail to recognize that professional investors are quick to forgive companies with a lot of operating leverage when they fall a bit short of expectations—for instance, we consider any earnings number within ten cents of the expected consensus on target for an airline. What matters is not so much the historical earnings but what they mean for a company's future earnings potential. For a company expected to earn ten cents in a quarter, a one-cent shortfall is a 10 percent miss. Moreover, if this is a high-growth company and that one cent of earnings was expected to grow 20 percent over the next five years, that's 25 percent in lost potential. In this context, a 5 percent price drop suggests that investors see more potential than the company's earnings would suggest.

The key for any manager is not to make a specific number but to possess and communicate a realistic view of your business's prospects. Leaders admit when results haven't lived up to expectations rather than jerry-rig short-term fixes to create the illusion that their businesses are healthier than they are.

Enron's experience best illustrates this lesson. The company had promised the investment community that it was a fast-growing, "new paradigm" company, not a prosaic energy trading company. When results came in below expectations, no one in the company was prepared to bite the bullet and report disappointing numbers, so CFO Andy Fastow manufactured some deals that allowed the company to book gains and continue the pretense that all was well. (As an aside, the investment community is not blameless in this debacle either. There was sufficient information, buried in footnotes, to know that the company's earnings power was not as strong as the net income number suggested. Some particularly diligent and astute investors realized this, and shorted the stock; however, many investors were not so perceptive.) One can only wonder where Enron would be today—certainly alive if not quite as lauded as it was in its heyday—had Ken Lay, Jeffrey Skilling, and Andy Fastow been willing to take their lumps.

Certainly most executives don't resort to creative accounting to make their numbers, but many do adopt tactics that are good for the books but bad for their businesses. For example, cutting marketing or research spending can help meet your budget in the short term, but it's rarely the right move for your business longer term. Pulling money out of reserves helped American International Group (AIG) make its numbers for years, and ultimately led it to take on the risky assets that ultimately torpedoed the company. Massaging numbers creates false expectations of a business's earnings potential among investors, bosses, employees, and potential competitors. It also exacerbates the inevitable future shortfall when numbers can no longer be manufactured, as AIG executives ultimately learned. Moneymakers don't fall into this trap; they recognize a truth I learned from JPMorgan CEO Jamie Dimon:

Problems are not like wine; they don't age well.

Moneymakers know that they need to be forthright about the state of their business, both the good and the bad. Indeed, one of the reasons Stan Rabin, former CEO of Commercial Metals Company, was so highly regarded is that he would bluntly state "We screwed up" when the company made a mistake. Everyone from investors to employees appreciated this level of honesty and knew that the first step in fixing a problem is admitting that you have one.

Inside Information

- Don't massage your numbers. You will only postpone the day of reckoning and make things worse when that day arrives.

- Don't let the short-term pain of admitting to disappointing numbers determine your execution and your spending. Good managers and partners will understand. If you have a good strategy and execution, the earnings will come back and your stock price with it.

FISH OR CUT BAIT

Moneymakers know:

The most successful leaders sometimes fall short of their goals, but they never fail to cut bait when necessary.

Good leaders take smart risks, but sometimes those risks don't pay off. In these situations, the best recognize when they're throwing good money after bad.

The Walt Disney Company's mobile telephony foray in 2006 presented the most challenging "cut bait" scenario a leader can face: a high-potential project that isn't working. The project started with the recognition of a megatrend, the growing penetration and utility of mobile phones. Capitalizing on evolving technology was one of Disney's core goals, so it eagerly sought to establish mobile offerings. In Japan the company has been very successful since 2000 in selling its characters for applications on the NTT DoCoMo system but in the United States the mobile network operators created "walled gardens" that limited how handsets access content and required content companies to share the majority of an offering's economics with the operator. To avoid this obstacle and also leverage the strength of its brands, Disney struck a deal with mobile operator Sprint that allowed Disney to create its own mobile service riding on the Sprint network. With this and an outsourcing deal for the manufacture of handsets, Disney prepared to launch a mobile service under its ESPN brand, creating a phone that offered sports scores and other content. For a separate Disney-branded service, the company developed tracking and security features to appeal to parents and children. The concepts sounded promising, and Disney moved quickly, spending more than $150 million to roll out the phones.

Once the ESPN service was up and running, not enough customers showed up. Mobile phone sales in the United States have historically been driven by three factors: the quality of the network, the availability of the latest handset fashions, and the handset subsidy that operators offer. Disney expected its differentiated features and brand to offset these factors, but they didn't. Motorola's ultra-thin RAZR handsets had become the standard of the day, and they made ESPN's device look clunky. Also, the Sprint network offered spotty coverage, which further limited the appeal of the phones, and Disney had not budgeted to offer subsidies to the same extent as the fully integrated mobile operators.

Given these results and with the millions in spending behind the program, Disney could have rationalized that it was "in for a dime, in for a dollar" or "in for $150 million, in for a billion." Disney's leaders could have told themselves that if they just spent more heavily to increase subsidies or to develop an improved handset, they had a good chance to achieve the sales breakthrough they originally anticipated. Instead, they surveyed the landscape and reevaluated. Disney would never have an advantage in subsidies or handset design relative to specialists. The strength of the Disney and ESPN brands evidently did not warrant enough of a pricing premium in the minds of customers, and on the family-security front, other companies had come out with similar features. Finally, competition between the wireless operators was opening up the walled gardens so that Disney could see a path to using its content without having to operate its own mobile service. Management decided to cut their losses. Though it cost more than $30 million to wind down the two services, Disney's stock did not take a hit. Investors appreciated the company's willingness to experiment as well as cut its losses.

QUEST DIAGNOSTICS AND Cardinal Health are two health care companies that faced similar regulatory difficulties in minor units. Because Quest quickly cut its losses, the problem remained inconsequential, whereas Cardinal's effort to charge ahead turned its minor problem into a major albatross. In 2005, Quest, a $6 billion provider of diagnostic testing services, developed quality problems and Food and Drug Administration (FDA) compliance issues at its Nichols Institute Diagnostics unit, which manufactured test kits. It stopped selling the products and took writedowns on the assets. Then in 2006, it shut down the unit, which represented less than 1 percent of sales. Quest did not have the expertise to take on the litigation risk that went with the quality problems. Shutting down the unit kept CEO Surya Mohapatra and his management team from being distracted and allowed them to continue to build their core diagnostic services business. Quest grew revenues 24 percent and operating profits 28 percent from 2004 prior to the difficulties through 2006, when the unit was shut down. Quest's stock also took the shutdown in stride because management dealt with it so expeditiously, and because their decisive action enabled them to keep the larger Nichols Institute business, which is at the forefront of huge growth in diagnostic testing.

Cardinal Health, a $91 billion distributor of pharmaceuticals, did not deal with its FDA regulatory headaches as effectively. Its problems occurred in a unit that assembled prefilled syringes and other aseptic products. When starting up a new factory in Puerto Rico in 2004, Cardinal experienced substantial difficulties and delays in getting regulators to sign off on the new facility. In September 2004, it acknowledged $5 million in costs from the delays, but committed to fix the problems in the next three months. It didn't, and the regulatory problems continued to plague Cardinal until it shuttered the unit more than a year later. The problems couldn't have come at a worse time, as Cardinal was undergoing a major shift in its core business, as well as a Securities and Exchange Commission investigation into its accounting. With the distraction of the sterilization issues complicating its larger problems, 2005 was a particularly bad year for Cardinal. Overall operating earnings dropped 22 percent, hurt by a 25 percent drop in the segment that included the sterile operations, and a 5 percent drop in its core business. It went from being lauded by *Business Week* as a Best Performer in 2003 to being targeted for the overpayment of its CEO a few years later.

In 2006, undoubtedly influenced by the poor results, the

Cardinal board announced the appointment of a new CEO effective immediately as well as the retirement of the current CEO and the departure of the chief operating officer. New CEO Kerry Clark decided to jettison the entire segment with the troublesome sterile unit in December. Buyout firm Blackstone bought the segment for $3.2 billion, and Cardinal management was finally able to refocus on growing its pharmaceutical distribution business. Investors applauded the divestiture of the segment, since it had long been a drag on results. In one week, its stock price rose 7 percent. However, because Cardinal had stuck with the long-suffering sterile unit so long, it ultimately divested all of the accompanying segment. Blackstone did quite well with its acquisition, renamed Catalent; the division had a hidden gem in its specialized capabilities for manufacturing soft-gel capsules for brands like Advil. Blackstone also understood the advantage of pruning its acquisition down to the best parts; one of the first things the new owners did was put a remaining sterile-manufacturing facility in Arizona up for sale. One can only wonder how much better off Cardinal and its top executives would be today if they had cut bait early on the sterile-manufacturing business; they likely would have solved the problems in the main business sooner and perhaps been able to keep the attractive gel-cap operation and their jobs.

Inside Information

- Don't let hubris, fear of admitting a mistake, or concern about walking away from a prior investment keep you from exiting a problematic business.

- Be realistic about how much management time and attention even a small underperforming business can absorb. Consider the value of your time when considering whether to exit a business.

- Set milestones, based on either time passed or dollars spent, when you'll reassess an endeavor, so incrementalism doesn't lull you into continuing to throw good money after bad.

- Exit underperforming operations even if it means opting out of a potentially lucrative long-term trend. The trend may not yet be "ripe." By getting out of the business now, you will be able to retrench and come back later. Look for alternative ways to participate in the trend rather than stubbornly sticking with a losing proposition.

SHRINK TO GROW

One of the ironies of Cardinal's experience is that by allowing its troubled unit to continue to distract it, it limited its growth in other areas. This points to another paradox that I have uncovered when observing moneymakers:

> **Sometimes the best way to grow your business is to shrink it.**

When a business isn't performing well, executives often look for an acquisition or a new initiative to improve the situation. They believe that if the business has enough scale or an exciting new product, it can become profitable. It may also be that they prefer to think about the potential of a new endeavor rather than deal with the problems at hand.

In most instances, however, to reverse the paradox just stated, addition becomes subtraction. When executives launch a supplemental initiative to solve a problem, they just complicate matters and make it even more difficult to fix their troubled businesses. At The Home Depot, Bob Nardelli ventured into a new business—supplying building materials for contractors—at a time when his core business was struggling. This initiative prompted much of the shareholder ire that led to his ouster. One of the first actions his successor, Frank Blake, took was to sell off the new division, even accepting a lower price than initially expected. Blake understood that just being rid of the operation would be a huge boon for The Home Depot, allowing it to focus on reenergizing its core business. Similarly, John Thain, in one of his first acts as CEO of Merrill Lynch, sold its troubled collateralized debt obligations for 22 cents on the dollar in August 2008; selling these assets at such a steep loss was worth it because it put Merrill's past mistakes behind them and allowed Thain to ultimately sell to Bank of America, thus securing Merrill's future.

WHEN NCR CORPORATION's CEO Lars Nyberg put Mark Hurd in charge of a division that later became known as the Teradata Solutions Group in November 1998, Hurd faced a similar problem. This group created and sold data-warehousing solutions for all nonfinancial and nonretail clients of NCR. With information systems cropping up everywhere and the cost of data storage falling, companies were collecting and analyzing more and more data. Teradata had created innovative central data repositories and the software to access them, so it was poised to benefit immensely from the trend in data usage. Despite the potential, the group was losing money—$113 million in operating losses in 1997. There was considerable pressure on Hurd to expand the group, make acquisitions, and build scale in order to grow into its cost base. Hurd, though, understood that size does not create profit. He knew that he had to achieve profitability to enable growth, not grow to create profitability. So he focused on lowering costs, particularly service costs. He outsourced the manufacture of certain computer products. He reduced his sales force to stem the growth until the cost structure made sense. Knowing that the customer is not always right, he let unprofitable customers leave and cut lower-value product lines. NCR's data-warehousing revenues dropped 5 percent between 1997 and 1999 despite its participation in a growing market. Despite the step backward, the "shrink to grow" strategy worked. With lower costs and an improved mix of business, the Teradata Solutions Group reported $46 million in operating profit in 1999, a $150 million swing in two years despite having a smaller revenue base.

With the value edge established, Hurd and his team set about growing. Data-warehousing efforts in the company's core financial and retail markets were incorporated into the existing data-warehousing segment. With the broader portfolio, the data-warehousing division returned to an operating loss, but applying the same "shrink to grow" discipline, Hurd and his team reduced the loss markedly in 2000 and had the broader-based division earning $112 million in profit by 2002, and double that level by 2004. Mark Hurd's meteoric rise, after delivering these results, also demonstrates the advantages of taking a step backward. In July 2001, Hurd became NCR's president and in 2002, its chief operating officer. In 2003, Lars Nyberg retired and Hurd became NCR's CEO. From this position, he was recruited in 2005 to lead Hewlett-Packard, a company at the time more than thirteen times bigger.

Other corporate histories that I have discussed elsewhere also reinforce the "shrink to grow" paradox. When Cisco's leaders took a huge inventory charge in 2001 and destroyed much of that inventory, they shrank the company's sales prospects in the near term but they were positioning themselves for longer-term growth. They resisted the temptation to conduct a fire sale on products that could cause customers to overbuy because prices were so cheap; such a move might delay for years the normal resumption in demand.

Inside Information

- Shrink troubled operations down to their profitable core; if there is no profitable core, either sell or close the operations.

- Be less incremental when trying to right troubled operations. In the case of divestitures and/or layoffs, the risk-reduction benefit of moving slowly is often offset by the continued drag on morale if people are uncertain when the cutting will be over. Err on the side of cutting too much rather than too little.

- Accept the trade-off of disposing of struggling, non-core businesses to provide people with the time and energy to focus on productive areas.

AMPUTATION OR MINOR SURGERY

All this doesn't mean that you should view cuts as solutions to whatever ails your business. Moneymakers know their response should depend on whether problems are the result of a long-term, secular trend or a cyclical condition. (Before anyone accuses investors of being against religion, let me explain that I'm using the term "secular" in its less common meaning of "lasting from century to century.") This secular or cyclical question is a factor that investors obsess about. If a company is being hurt by a long-term permanent trend, I won't buy until a stock is very cheap, because results will continue to worsen. On the other hand, if a change is cyclical, driven by the natural ebbs and flows of business, I will buy stocks when things look bad and sell them when they look good, because the trend will reverse. Similarly, you should amputate to get back to a healthy core when a long-term change is hurting results and perform only minor surgery when troubles are more cyclical in nature.

To help you determine which situation you are facing, consider the following two checklists:

Indications That Problems Are Caused by Secular Trends

- A significant technological shift threatens to make your product/service/business outmoded.
- A new competitor takes away share due to an improved business model.
- You are in an innovation-driven industry (such as technology or pharmaceuticals) that frequently experiences breakthrough products.
- Your business is not particularly affected by the broader economy or other macroeconomic trends (in other words, you're not sensitive to cyclical conditions).
- Your industry generally does not have that many ups and downs.

Indications That Problems Are Caused by Cyclical Changes

- Inventory shortages or surpluses are the source of your business's troubles.
- Supply disruptions occur regularly in your business or you are several steps removed from the ultimate consumer.
- You operate in a commodity- or resource-based industry.
- Your business is highly sensitive to macroeconomic factors.
- A new competitor is making a significant, negative impact on your revenues but isn't earning sustainable profits.

This checklist may not provide you with the definitive answer to the cause of your business problems. With hindsight, of course, it's easy to figure out why a business downturn took place. In the moment, however, it's sometimes tough to know the causes, but using this checklist will help you discern between secular and cyclical factors. Over time, this perspective will increase the odds that you'll make better decisions, because you'll understand if changes are long-term, where responding too little is the greater risk, or if they are temporary, where overreacting has more downside.

The decision about how aggressively to respond requires some additional considerations. First, if a downturn is caused by cyclical factors, pay attention to how much risk you can absorb—a "stay the course" strategy is certainly riskier—and how long the cycle is likely to last. Every now and then, cyclical industries get "supercycles" where you may not last until things return to more normal levels. How long was the last upswing? The longer the up cycle, the more severe the down cycle, as the late-2000's housing bust has demonstrated.

Second, examine supply and demand, especially supply, to

estimate the length of a cycle. End-user demand tends to be pretty steady; even in recessions, overall consumer spending in the United States has typically grown, albeit at a slower rate. Cycles tend to come from changes in supply and distortions as products move through a supply chain. In 2005, Arjun Murti, an oil analyst at Goldman Sachs, predicted that even though oil remained a cyclical industry, supply constraints meant it was entering a supercycle where the price per barrel would reach $100. Despite skepticism at the time, he was proven right in 2008. Any airline, plastics manufacturer, or other oil purchaser that planned on a rapid return to $20 a barrel faced difficulties. To determine supply and demand in your industry, look at Wall Street and industry research, consider who among your competitors has expanded recently, and use the Internet to dig up information.

Third, analyze where your "stay the course" spending is going. When profits are under stress, keep a sharp eye out for unproductive spending. As long as you are profitable, however, don't eliminate your no-return-expected spending. You can probably pare back some investment dollars, however, if you make the effort to assess this spending. When Procter & Gamble was going through its difficulties early in the 2000s, A. G. Lafley and his team turned a critical eye on their research budget. By jettisoning efforts with less potential, they ended up increasing the number of products that they could take out of development and move into stores. NCR ramped up its marketing spending quickly after shrinking the data-warehousing business to its profitable core. Even Xerox, facing a very real threat of bankruptcy, maintained its research spending at a consistent share of revenue.

SCHLUMBERGER, THE MULTINATIONAL oil-services company, is renowned for staying the course through its industry's regular cycles and for profiting from continued investment when the industry enjoys an upswing. As a supplier of expertise and equipment to the owners of oil fields, Schlumberger works in the most cyclical part of a cyclical industry. Generally the farther away one is from the ultimate consumer, the greater the cyclicality in one's business. Recognizing how often the downturns in its revenues and profits are the result of cyclical factors, Schlumberger's CEO Andrew Gould and his team have worked hard to maintain employees and research budgets during downturns. In 1998–99, when the price of oil collapsed and its clients pared back, Schlumberger's revenues fell by 27 percent and operating profits dropped 82 percent. Yet the company maintained research and engineering expenditures at constant levels. Then-CEO Euan Baird and his team knew that the long-term success of the company relied on the technology and expertise its people could bring to clients, and therefore R&E spending was protected.

Schlumberger did not ignore prevailing market conditions and stay the course out of stubbornness or myopia. In 1998 and 1999, it reduced capacity in its fleet for off-shore, seismic-based exploration and more than ten thousand employees were laid off, a 15 percent reduction. By balancing the need to protect profits during soft periods with the imperative to be ready when the temporary slowdown ended, Schlumberger's profits soared when the industry recovered in 2000.

Similarly, when the industry slowed again with the price of oil in 2002, Schlumberger maintained its R&E spending, excluding some extraordinary costs in 2001. During this downturn, it reduced its WesternGeco division, which specialized in reservoir imaging and other seismic services, an area where industry overcapacity had developed. While bringing capacity and costs down, Schlumberger also invested in aggressively rolling out proprietary technology that it had developed. It invested where high returns existed despite the weak industry fundamentals, and cut in less attractive areas. The leadership team also worked methodically to transition the company toward less cyclical and higher-return businesses, thereby reinforcing its ability to stay the course during weaker times. It developed an Integrated Project Management offering, whereby Schlumberger is hired not solely to drill wells but also to manage reservoirs over multiple years, with bonuses for production above agreed-upon levels. By balancing responsiveness with investment and improving the mix of its business, Schlumberger profited immensely when oil prices and exploration entered the supercycle. Five years after the 2002 slowdown, income from continuing operations had increased more than sevenfold, and the stock price had nearly quintupled.

Inside Information

- Assess whether a slowdown is cyclical or long term, temporary or permanent, and calibrate your response accordingly.

- Even as you make cuts to respond to a slowdown, continue to invest to drive growth when the cyclical slowdown ends. If you completely cut marketing, research, or other investments your company needs to grow, your business may live to fight another day, but it won't be worth it.

- Improve the mix of your business—not only how profitable it is but also how insulated it is from cyclicality.

•   •   •

WHEN BAD THINGS HAPPEN TO GOOD MANAGERS

Every business goes through difficult times, and the mark of moneymakers is how they respond. Exceptional leaders take steps backward in troubled times so they can lay a solid foundation for future growth. To facilitate your effectiveness when it matters most, contemplate the following questions:

- Are the changes that are causing your operations difficulty rooted in long-term trends or cyclical events, or even a combination of both factors? If changes are cyclical, how long can your business last in the current cycle? Have you made preparations to outlast this one? If they're more secular, how can you resize your business today?

- Have you considered a "shrink to grow" strategy? It is often easier to make cuts and reposition your business during down periods than when times are flush—would it be easier for your business?

- How much risk can you bear, since a "stay the course" strategy is frequently riskier than cutting? Are you profitable? If not, unless you are a recent and small start-up, pursue a "shrink to grow" strategy. If you are profitable, particularly highly profitable, you can afford a hit to margins during a downturn; do you feel your company can absorb this hit?

- How are your competitors reacting to the problems? How long can they stay on their current path; how can you respond effectively to their likely responses?

- How long does it take and how costly is it to start up capacity in your industry? If you have short lead times, it makes sense to cut more aggressively in downturns since you can easily ramp back up. Is your business dependent on highly skilled individuals? If so, consider being more cautious. Though in many places labor is a relatively flexible expense, the expertise can be valuable as you go through the downturn. If you gain a reputation as quick to lay off, staff will be harder to attract when you need them.

- When deciding where to invest during a difficult time, what are the goals of the spending? Will it produce a more efficient way to conduct your business? If so, then spend. Does it provide the next leg of growth when the market returns? If yes, then invest—but somewhat more cautiously, since you cannot be sure when the market will return. Does the investment produce better returns but only at volume levels above currently depressed levels? If so, then perhaps tinker around with the idea, but do not devote serious funds to it. Does it create growth but only in a world without the long-term change you are currently seeing? If this is the case, head back to the drawing board.

- Are you still thinking about long-term growth trends and how to improve your mix of business? While these things are easier to do when times are good, there are often more opportunities in tough times, particularly if you are profitable.

- Have you reexamined all aspects to see where you can tweak and tighten? When times are tough, you may find some efficiency opportunities that you'd overlooked. Just make sure to hold the line on no-return-expected spending as much as possible without risking bankruptcy.

WHAT INVESTORS WANT: GOOD
NUMBERS THAT LAST

W HEN I FIRST CONSIDERED WRITING THIS BOOK, I discussed the concept with many friends and business colleagues to test its value edge (and see if anyone had done it before). One friend, an investment banker by trade, chuckled when I told him the idea, remarking, "That's a one-sentence book: 'Make your numbers!'"

There's a lot of truth in what he said—at the most basic level, what investors want is for businesses to generate ever-growing economic profits.

The trick, of course, is making your numbers repeatedly and not just for a quarter. To do so and thus become a money-maker, you need to think like an investor. As the operator of your business, you know better than anyone else how to make the numbers in the short term. But when it comes to long-term profits, tapping into the hard-won wisdom of investors—we who spend our days analyzing companies and their leaders—offers crucial insights into what works for organizations . . . and what doesn't. Based on my experiences and my interviews with other savvy professional investors, here is a checklist of the seven items you need to focus on to make your numbers consistently:

- What three factors most drive the financial results of your business?
- What's your value edge? How do you create value for customers and thereby for your employees and owners? ·
- What feedback mechanisms tell you what is going on throughout your organization?
- What resources are you using to produce results, and what are the costs of those resources, both actual cost and opportunity cost (i.e., could someone else do more with the resources)?
- How much risk you are taking?
- What exogenous factors are impacting your results?
- How long will it all last and what are you doing to prepare for the next phase?

Approaching these fundamental elements of your business with an investor's mind-set leads to success because of one of the bedrock rules of investing: *Follow the money.* Just as investors pay closer attention to what CEOs are doing with their firms' assets than what they say about their businesses, so too can you rely on the business advice of investors because our money is right beside you. When I buy shares in a company, I win only when the company does well. As a result, my fellow investors and I have exhaustively examined what makes business leaders either moneymakers or value destroyers. Throughout this book, I've shown what we've learned and the real-life experiences of businesses and managers that have successfully (or not) mastered these crucial business factors.

The Contrarian Principle

To make a successful stock investment, an investor has to see more value in a business than others do. If a company's potential is well understood, that value is reflected in a company's stock price and there's no opportunity to make profit beyond an overall rise in the stock market. To be successful, therefore, investors need to be contrarians.

The experience of moneymakers shows that business leaders also need to be contrarians to profit, especially in today's era of constant and consequential change. Though most executives naturally follow the conventional wisdom and stick with previously successful practices, this approach increasingly leads to operational pitfalls and earnings shortfalls. With more and more aggressive players in every industry, maintaining your value edge through timeworn product differentiation or pricing power is harder and harder.

In the face of these pressures, success often requires finding a difference: targeting an underserved market segment, focusing on ignored parts of the value chain, or otherwise exploring the white space that competitors are overlooking. Once found, exploiting this difference in an incremental, risk-aware way confers a value edge. Today this contrarian approach more reliably produces the success that once was the preserve of tried-and-true formulas.

Applying contrarianism to managing also requires casting a critical eye on the conventional wisdom that governs everything from leadership to capital deployment. Judgment and knowledge of other businesses' successes and failures are imperative because being contrarian for contrarian's sake can just as easily lead to mistakes and missed opportunities. In many cases the stock market has correctly priced a company's earnings prospects, underserved customers really are unprofitable, and the conventional wisdom is indeed wise. Still, considering a contrary or different position should become a leadership reflex; it can provide you with options for action not otherwise available—options that can give you a sustainable value edge. Throughout this book, I've suggested contrarian strategies appropriate to just about every organization. Here are four that professional investors, from our purely economic perspective, have seen moneymakers repeatedly use to create long-term profitability:

1. *Bad is good.* Be up front and honest about where your challenges, underperformance, and problems lie; the odds are that at least some of your competitors are fooling themselves on these issues. You can improve or fix your operations if you bite the bullet and confront your weaknesses. Build feedback systems to ensure that bad news gets to you, and encourage truth tellers who point to the shortfalls in your organization and whom others want to dismiss as cranks.

2. *Shrink to grow.* Accept the paradox that sometimes you must become smaller to grow larger. If you have a business that is experiencing difficulties, the natural inclination is to diversify away from it by bolting on additional operations to improve the core. Stop. Growth in areas that don't earn their cost of capital is like running on a treadmill—you're working hard but not getting anywhere. You raise your risk profile and have more than ever to worry about. Either get rid of the troubled operation (shut it down or sell it) or shrink it down to a profitable core. Only then should you look to grow, and only in higher-return areas.

3. *Don't let your customers lead you.* The conventional wisdom that espouses listening to customers above all else fails to recognize that your customers have different economic

incentives than you do (e.g., customers like industry capacity growth because it keep prices low), and they can be as short-sighted as anyone else. Of course this doesn't mean you shouldn't talk to them—customers are often the first to tell you where you have a problem, and finding a customer pain point has been the genesis of many of the best businesses. Nonetheless, organizations that are customer fanatics indiscriminately fail to satisfy their own and their shareholders' requirements. Think beyond your customers' needs because you know your operation's capabilities better than they do and you often have as much, or more, insight into the future.

4. *Prepare for but don't project the future.* Look to the horizon, but resist the temptation to map out the future. As a professional investor, I've seen too many companies blindsided by unpredictable events; they were overly confident that they could accurately project the impact of future trends. Hard-coding operations for a specific level of demand or an inevitable development often leads to problems because the future rarely plays out exactly as expected.

However, this doesn't mean you shouldn't prepare for the future. Like hurricanes, long-term trends are generally visible to those who have the tools and are looking, while precisely where they'll make landfall is difficult to predict. Be aware of and prepare for long-term trends without being so convinced of your fortune-telling abilities that you make large, risky commitments to a specific path the future could take.

Horses for Courses

Contrarian advice is neither simple nor easy to follow. In fact, as you may have observed by now, the actions of moneymakers, like business itself, can be paradoxical and ambiguous. Rather than offering hard-and-fast dictates such as "Spend money" or "Don't spend money," I've provided the mind-set that informs moneymakers' decisions. These precepts are designed to be used situationally. You need different horses depending on the courses you are competing on. Not every suggestion from every chapter will apply to your current situation.

What does apply is the general principles behind this investor thinking. Here are a list of questions all prospective moneymakers should ask themselves to determine the best course of action:

- Is your business earning risk-adjusted economic profits (profits over and above the opportunity cost of the resources deployed and risk taken)? If yes, know that competitors will target your business. Spend prudently but not overcautiously to expand the moat that protects your business from competition. Invest more in inefficiency and creative efforts, and look for ways to expand your business.

- If you answered no, shrink your business down to a profitable core. Be willing to shed customers and downsize operations. Maintain as much of your experimentation spending as you can, recognizing that though it's the easiest spending to cut, doing so has the greatest impact on your long-term prospects.

- How differentiated are the offerings in your industry? How new are they, and what's the normal product life cycle in your business? If your products are easily swapped with competitors' or are late in their life cycle, switch to commodity-style management with an intense focus on driving down costs and limiting investment spending (redirect those dollars to more fruitful areas). If you are in an industry of highly differentiated products (e.g., technology), your investment spending will need to be higher and maintained more rigorously.

- Are your employees unhappy? Concentrate on ways to improve their performance and that of the business overall. Everybody likes to be part of a winning organization, so improving performance—and making it easier for employees to perform while still expecting top-tier results—is more important than efforts designed solely to make employees happy.

- What exogenous factors drive your company's profitability, and how important are they? If interest rates, currency exchange rates, commodity prices, or other external influences impact your results, you have a lot of risk, even if things are going well now. Prepare for the day when these factors move against you.

- Are the trends impacting your business secular (long term), cyclical (temporary), or supercycle cyclical (temporary but likely to last for a while)? Look at the history (and chapter 11) to determine which is which. Move aggressively to position your business to capitalize on secular trends. Protect yourself and prepare for reversals in cycles, and manage supercycles gingerly. Don't be lulled into complacency by supercycles; they can and will reverse. Be willing to give up some upside to protect your downside.

- Where do you sit in your industry's value chain? Where are the greatest returns in the value chain in which you operate? Be willing to invest in your business to move it in that direction. Work to reduce your exposure to less valuable pursuits.

- Are you creating value for customers? Over the long run, this is the first requirement for establishing a value edge. In the early days of products and services, worry less about how you split the value creation with customers, partners, and others, and more about creating value. As your products and services become more mature, you need to ensure that you earn an appropriate share of the profits for yourself and your investors.

Tap into the Source: Leveraging Investors' Wisdom for Yourself

This book's advice is a beginning, not an end. In addition to using the principles that professional investors have derived from studying moneymakers to rethink how you manage your business, you can tap directly into the investment community to access specific insights about your particular industry. Make a point of leveraging the investor contacts you have or any introductions that friends can make for you. Set up a meeting or take an investor out to lunch; fundamental investors love to discuss your business as much as you do. At trade shows or conferences you attend, seek out investors; I assure you that there are always at least a few around. Invite investors to speak at your off-site meetings and encourage them to present a contrary view in order to stimulate debate. If you have a brokerage account, get the firm's sell-side analyst's reports on your company, its closest competitors, and your industry. Access as many different analysts' reports as possible, and share them with colleagues. When reading these reports, look not so much at the specific recommendation to buy or sell particular stocks but more at the issues the analysts focus on and where they see risks to your business. In particular, seek out the work of those who are bearish or negative on your business's prospects; it may contain information you are not aware of.

Use online tools to tap into investors' insights. Search for "investor" and your company's stock ticker (or that of the closest publicly traded competitor). While you will need to be discriminating in assessing what you find (there are a lot of shouting matches, especially in amateur-oriented sites), you can unearth nuggets of valuable information and different points of view. Make sure not to dismiss ideas just because they are contrary to your own. Indeed, in all your contacts with the investment community, seek out various opinions and give special attention to those that are most counterintuitive.

Of course, reaching out to professional investors requires courage. There are a million reasons not to: investors will reject your overtures; they'll ask you questions that will make you uncomfortable; your management team will think investors know nothing; you don't have the time. If you hesitate, remember the risk-reward equation. In today's environment, you're not going to gain an edge without taking some risk. In the greater scheme of things, this risk is one that is eminently worth the reward. On the downside, you may suffer some embarrassment or criticism. The upside, though, is significant. Finding these inside-outsiders—professional investors who have been studying your company and your competitors for a sustained period of time—is not as difficult as it may seem, and the reward of our insights will be enormous. You might discover someone who has followed your industry for years and can distill the factors for success over the next three years in the amount of time it takes to have a cup of coffee.

Professional investors are in the habit of keeping our insights about what makes a moneymaker mostly to ourselves. But if you seek us out, you will no doubt find that we are interested in far more than what your quarter's numbers are going to be. Now is your opportunity to take advantage of what we know.

ACKNOWLEDGMENTS

This book draws upon the many experiences, observations, conversations, and interviews that I've taken part in throughout my years as a professional investor. Every interaction contributed in some way to my conviction that investors' wisdom about management was valuable, it was misunderstood, and it offered great value if shared more broadly. I'm grateful to the thousands of people whose experiences informed this book. I won't name them all, but a few deserve special mention.

I most heartily thank Jes Staley and Jamie Dimon at JPMorgan Chase, who provided valuable insights and support on multiple fronts. Within the corporate community, Sumner Redstone of Viacom and CBS; Leslie Moonves, Fred Reynolds, and Marty Shea of CBS; Ken Lowe of Scripps Networks; Tom Staggs of Walt Disney; Sue Decker and Hilary Schneider of Yahoo!; Doug McCorkindale and Gracia Martore of Gannett; Bob Bakish, Carl Folta, and Jim Bombassei of Viacom; Al Gamper of CIT; Jim Young and Mary Jones at Union Pacific; Shari Redstone of National Amusements; Martin Loeffler and Diane Reardon at Amphenol; Randall Weisenberger at Omnicom; Simon Bax at Broadcast Facilities Inc.; Nils Erdmann at Go Fish; Bill Cella; and Lanny Baker contributed support and perspective.

The ideas and examples in this book came from conversations

and debates I've had with fellow members of the investment community over the years. Investors come about their knowledge of management as a by-product of our efforts to identify value and make money in stocks. Rarely do we express those thoughts directly; I'm grateful to the following investors who made a special effort to crystallize their thinking on what makes for good management. I especially appreciate the help of Trevor Harris of Morgan Stanley, Ron Insana and Paul Kim of S.A.C. Capital, Susan Ulick of TIAA-CREF, Michael Cline of Accretive, John Rogers of Ariel Investments, Leon Cooperman of Omega Advisors, Denis Nayden of Oak Hill Capital Partners, Thomas Russo of Gardner Russo & Gardner, Axel Schupf of Neuberger Berman, Roy Smith of New York University's Stern School of Business, Ellen Egeth of CNBC, Matt Carpenter of Citigroup, Lauren Fine, and Tom Wolzien, as well as all my current and former colleagues at J.P. Morgan Asset and Wealth Management.

Had I realized early on what an endeavor writing a book was, I'm not sure I would have started. I owe a debt of gratitude to John Mahaney at Crown Business for his immediate understanding of the project and his skill in shaping prose and distilling meaning, to Ann Marie Kerwin and Bruce Wexler for contributing their professional writer polish to numerous drafts, and to Scott Hoffman, agent extraordinaire.

Last and most especially, I could not have done it without the unflagging support and inspiration of my exceptional husband, Brian, and children, Brianna and Aidan.

Index

About the Author

Anne-Marie Fink has spent more than twelve years studying businesses and investments, as a vice president and analyst at J.P. Morgan Asset and Wealth Management, one of the world's largest investment managers. From discussing business strategy with top CEOs in entertainment, Internet, airlines, and other industries, and evaluating scores of companies, she has learned what works. With prior experience working with smaller businesses, she is passionate about making the wisdom of shareowners accessible to all managers. Anne-Marie has earned the Chartered Financial Analyst designation, an MBA from Columbia Business School, and a bachelor's degree from Yale University. She lives in New York City with her husband and two children.